1. George Catlin at the age of fifty-three.

PURSUIT

OF THE

HORIZON

A LIFE OF GEORGE CATLIN PAINTER &

RECORDER OF THE AMERICAN INDIAN

BY LOYD HABERLY

NEW YORK · THE MACMILLAN COMPANY

1 · 9 · 4 · 8

First Printing

Printed in the United States of America

To Roland and Virginia Klemme
who have made Saint Louis
a lodestar and a happy haven
for admirers of the best

I saw a man pursuing the horizon;
Round and round they sped.
I was disturbed at this;
I accosted the man.
"It is futile," I said,
"You can never—"
"You lie," he cried,
And ran on.

STEPHEN CRANE

CONTENTS

ILLUSTRATIONS

PURSUIT OF THE HORIZON

I

THE KETTLE OF GOLD

IN HIS deaf lonely age, after thirty years abroad, he still signed himself George Catlin of Wilkes-Barre. The poet called Memory had made that fifty-house river town of Pennsylvania's Wyoming Valley his City of the Celestial Frontiers. There the Red Men he had known in their splendor won against the settlers a victory so decisive and terrible that it became the Wyoming Massacre of ballad and legend. There the endless mountains leaned to the west, wolves howled in the forest moonlight, and the Susquehanna was the only road.

George Catlin was born in Wilkes-Barre on the 26th of July, 1796. As the town's reputation for rudeness and litigation kept away all settlers but innocent babies, the birth of a fifth little Catlin was good news. No coast metropolis provided better for small pink newcomers. Granny Sprague—"a dollar a baby, rich or poor"—was a notable midwife. The learned, eccentric William Hooker Smith, M.D., could cure anything but rigor mortis by liberal bleedings. This coming of the annual baby was his great opportunity to tell the busy young lawyer, Putnam Catlin, about his book, published later as *Alchemy Explained and Made Familiar; or A Drop of Honey for the Despairing Alchymist*. Doctor Smith was no Doctor Faustus. As Justice of the Peace, he fined Granny Sprague's divorced husband five shillings for swearing seven profane oaths.

Putnam Catlin had the courage of his old Connecticut ancestry. At the age of twelve he had enlisted in the fifes and drums of his father's regiment, to rub Yankee Doodle into the Redcoats for six years and come out with a Badge of Merit and a commendatory discharge signed by George Washington. He was among the first who ever dared to practice law in Wilkes-Barre. But this yearly battle with death that his gifted wife fought for his love's sake was not to be won by fifes and drums, or by reasoned equity pleadings. Of course she had spirit and faith, and perhaps a leafy angel too. The bloodied hands of the Indians did not harm her when they captured her—seven-year-old Polly Sutton—after the Massacre. When she moaned through the murk of pain that shrouds birth's mysteries, it was surely with memoried dread of war whoops and paint-streaked warriors.

Though "a Methodist and a devout Christian," Polly Catlin could not give her babe a church baptism. Wilkes-Barre had no church, and only occasional visits of the black-coated circuit riders. Jemima Wilkinson, The Universal Friend, had looked the town over but despaired of it as a site for her Community of Saints. Well she might, with the local moonshiners raising a Whisky Rebellion that brought out the United States Army.

Wilkes-Barre was a river-front town, the stopover of boatmen poling barges up the Susquehanna, and of loggers steering timber rafts down on the spring freshets. It was a John Barleycorn town, and the Capitol of Quarreling. Putnam Catlin had worn his health thin in thankless attempts to untangle its feudant titles. It was too near Asylum, the log Paris built by local workmen for lords and ladies of the French Court who whiled away their empty waiting for Marie Antoinette in devilments of fancy dancing and dinners contrived by famous Parisian chefs.

In 1797, the Catlins moved over the New York State border to Broome County, where Putnam had acquired a plantation of a few cultivated fields and many acres of wooded promise. Though his Wilkes-Barre legal connections were not severed for some years, he was henceforth Squire Catlin the gentleman farmer, a sportsman, a philosopher, a fine conservative citizen, and ultimately a father of fourteen children: Charles, Henry, Clara, Juliette, George, Eliza, James, Mary, Julius, Lynde, Sally, Richard, John, and Francis.

With her yearling George in her arms, Polly Catlin happily rode forty-odd miles of forest trackways to the Broome County plantation. This remote new home in a community of a dozen small scattered farms was the green setting that her bright-eyed jewels deserved. It was a roughly wrought setting of rugged craggy mountains, and dark defiles that the Oneidas and fierce Mohawks had barricaded and sternly defended in their retreat from Wyoming's avengers. The wider valley of the settlement bore the Indian name, Oc-qua-go.

There by the Susquehanna the rainbow that was to lead George Catlin up to fame and down to shadowed failure began in a kettle of gold. Though he was only nine or ten years old at the time, that experience was still vivid in 1861 when he wrote for other boys the account of it which his own son died too young and small to hear.

With his little single-barreled shotgun he was already a mighty hunter of pheasants, ducks, quail and squirrels. But his ambition was to kill a deer, and that required a grown-up weapon. His two elder brothers were away at school and their long rifles hung in covers on the wall. He had never fired a rifle and was not yet strong enough to aim one except over a rest. Besides, his father had strictly forbidden him to touch his brothers' guns.

In the dark and still of night the tempted boy took one of the rifles from its cover, put his fowling piece in its place, and lugging the rifle into the fields, hid it for the next evening's deer shoot.

After an endless morning and an uneasy dinner hour he managed to elude the family and the hired men, and got the loaded rifle from the bushes unseen. With his heart rattling away like a whole drum corps, the little Daniel Boone crept down an overgrown abandoned road to the ruins of a sawmill where a salt spring trickled through the rocks and fern.

In earlier times this salt lick had been a famous place for deer. On the ledge above it, the boy found what he called a "snug and sly little box," rigged as a blind by the old hunters. Stretching out in it with his rifle laid over the rock breastwork to command the salt lick, he waited and waited while the light and his courage waned together. The forest rustlings that had at first been spine-tingling footfalls of the delicate-stepping deer grew ominous and dangerous now. In terror he realized that this was the very spot where the panther had leapt like a stroke of lightning upon John Darrow, the greatest hunter in the neighborhood, and thrown him ten feet with the blow. Though the herculean Darrow had killed the beast, a small boy might not fare as well.

This is George Catlin's account of the climax of that adventure:

"The woodlark was at that moment taking its favorite limb in the lofty and evergreen hemlocks for its nightly rest, and making the wooded temple of solitude ring and echo with its liquid notes, whilst all else was still as death, and I was on the eve of descending from my elevated nook and wending my way home.

"Just then I heard the evident distant sounds of footsteps in the leaves, and shortly after discovered in the distance a deer—a huge buck!—timidly and cautiously descending the hill and approaching the lick; stopping often to gaze, and sometimes looking at me, apparently, full in the face, when I was afraid even to wink, lest he should discover me.

"Here my young blood was too boilable, and my nerves decidedly too excitable for my business. Successive chills seemed to rise, I don't recollect where from, but they shook me, each one of them, until they seemed, after actually shaking it, to go out at the top of my head.

"The deer kept advancing, and my shakes increasing—it at length entered the pool and commenced licking; and the resolve that the moment had arrived for my great achievement, set my teeth chattering. My rifle, cocked, was rested before me on the surface of the rock, and all things, save myself, perfectly ready; and after several useless attempts I got my aim, but before I could pull the trigger, from another chill and a shake, I lost it again. I tried again—and again—but in vain, and then more prudently resolved to lie still a few moments until I could get my nerves more steady, and at all events, until I could see more clearly the forward sight of my barrel, which as yet, seemed to be enveloped in a sort of a mist.

"Just at this moment also popped into my head another idea that gave me another or two renewed shivers. I had fired my little fowling piece hundreds of times without harm, but I never had fired a rifle.—'It may be overloaded, or so long loaded as to kick, or to explode!—but never mind, I must run those risks.' And after checking my latter apprehensions for a few moments, and feeling again more calmed, I was getting my aim with tolerable accuracy, when away went another of those frightful chills, like a snake running through me from my feet to the top of my head! because I was just about to pull the trigger.

"The deer at this time seemed to have got enough of licking, and stepping out of the lick, disappeared in the thicket! 'Oh, what a loss—what a misfortune! What a chance is gone! What a coward, and what a poor fool am I! But if he had stopped, though, one minute longer, I am sure I could have killed him, for I don't tremble now.'

"Just at this cool moment the deer came gliding through the bushes and into the lick again, much nearer than before. One little chill began; but by gritting my teeth tight together, I succeeded in getting a more steady aim, when—bang! went the crack and flash of a rifle, a little to the left of me! and the deer, bounding a few rods from the pool to an elevated bank, and tumbling upon the ground quite dead, showed me that I was too late!

"My head and the breech of my rifle were instantly lowered a little more behind my stone breastwork, and then, oh, horrid! what I had never seen before, nor ever dreamed of seeing in that place—the tall

5

and graceful form, but half bent forward, as he pushed his red and naked shoulders and drew himself slowly over the logs and through the bushes, of a huge Indian! trailing his rifle in his left hand, and drawing a large knife, with the other, from its sheath in the hollow of his back, as he advanced to the carcass of the deer, which had fallen much nearer to me than it was when it was shot.

"His rifle he leaned against a tree, and the blade of his bloody knife, which he had drawn across the neck of the deer, he clenched between his teeth, while he suspended the animal by the hind legs from a tree to let it bleed. . . . 'What a fate is mine! What am I to do?'

"No length of life could ever erase from my recollection the impression which this singular and unexpected scene made upon my infant mind, or the ease, and composure, and grace, with which this phantom seated himself upon the trunk of a large and fallen tree, wiping his huge knife upon the moss and laying it by his side, and drawing from his pouch his flint and steel, and spunk, with which he lit his pipe, and from which it seemed, in a few moments, as if he was sending up thanks to the Great Spirit, in the blue clouds of smoke that were curling around him.

"Who will ever imagine the thoughts that were passing through my youthful brain in those exciting moments! for here was before me, for the first time in my life, the living figure of a Red Indian! 'If he sees me, I'm lost; he will scalp me and devour me, and my dear mother will never know what became of me!'

"From the crack of that rifle, however, I had not another chill, nor a shiver; my feeling now was no longer the ebullition of childish anxiety, but the awfully flat and stupid one of dread and fear; and every muscle was quiet. Here was 'perhaps death in a moment' before me. My eyeballs, which seemed elongated as if they were reaching halfway to him, were too tightly strained to tremble, and I could then have aimed at the devil himself without a tremor. An instant thought came to me, when his naked back and shoulders were turned toward

6

me; 'My rifle is levelled and I am perfectly cool; a bullet would put an end to all my fears.' And a better one followed when he turned gently around and moving his piercing eyes over and about the ledge where I was sitting, and the blue streams were curling upwards from his mouth and his nostrils, for I saw then—though a child,—in the momentary glance of that face, what infant human nature could not fail to see, and none but human nature could express. I saw humanity.

"His pipe burned out; the deer, with its fore and hind legs tied together, was slung upon his back, and taking his rifle in his hand, he silently and quietly disappeared in the dusky forest, which at this time was taking the gloom of approaching night.

"My position and reflections were still like lead that could not be removed until a doubly reasonable time had elapsed for this strange apparition to be entirely out of my way; and having seemingly, at last view, to have taken the direction of the 'old road' by which I had expected to return, my attention was now turned to a different, but more difficult route, by climbing the huge precipice still above me, which I commenced as soon as perfect safety seemed to authorize it; and by a run of more than a mile through the woods, scarcely daring to look back, I was safely lodged in my father's back fields, but without hat or rifle, and without the least knowledge of the whereabouts in which either of them had been deposited or dropped. The last of these was recovered on the following day, but the other never came to light."

The pale and breathless boy ran up to the plantation house, shouting, "I've seen an Indian! I've seen an Indian!" As all the local redskins had been killed or driven away years before, nobody believed him, and he went to bed discredited and crying. But his wise mother, who knew her imaginative child, came up at last, knelt by him and said, "My dear George, I do believe your story. You have seen an Indian."

When the sorry little fellow came down, after a restless night, Johny

O'Neil, the Irish hired man, was excitedly announcing that "Jist in the toother eend of the bag whatefield, where ye sae thit lattle smohk areesin, has kimmed thae gapsies."

"There are no Gypsies in this country," said Squire Catlin. "I'll be bound those are George's Indians." Putting on his hat and taking his son's hand, the Squire followed O'Neil out to the wheatfield.

"We found my Indian warrior seated on a bearskin spread upon the ground," George Catlin recalled almost half a century later. "His legs were crossed—his elbows resting on his knees, and his pipe at his lips; with his wife, and his little daughter of ten years old, with blankets wrapped around them, and their necks covered with beads, reclining by the side of him; and over them all, to screen them from the sun, a blanket, suspended by the corners from four crotches fastened into the ground, and a small fire in front of the group, with a steak of venison cooking for their breakfast.

" 'There's the gapsies!' said Johny O'Neil. 'There is the Indian, father!' said I; and my father, who had been familiar with Indians, and had learned to sing their songs, and speak somewhat of their language, in his early life, said to me, 'George, my boy, you were right,—these are Indians.' 'Yes,' said I, 'and that's the very man I saw!'

"He was smoking away, and looking us steadily in the face as we approached; and though I began to feel something of the alarm I had felt the day before, my father's stepping up to him and taking him by the hand with a mutual 'How—how—how,' and the friendly grip of his soft and delicate hand which was extended to me also, soon dissipated all my fears, and turned my alarm to perfect admiration.

"Understanding and speaking a little English, he easily explained to my father that he was an Oneida, living near Cayuga Lake, some one hundred and fifty miles distant, that his name was On-o-gong-way (a great warrior). He asked us to sit down by him, when he cleaned out his pipe, and charging it afresh with tobacco, lighted, and gave it to my father to smoke, and then handed it to me, which my father explained was a pledge of his friendship.

"My father then explained to him the story of my adventure the day before, at the 'Old Saw-mill Lick,' to every sentence of which I was nodding 'yes,' and trembling, as the Indian was smoking his pipe, and almost, but not quite, commencing a smile, as he was earnestly looking me in the face.

"The story finished, he took me by both hands, and repeated the words, 'Good—good—good hunter.' He laid his pipe down, and very deliberately climbing over the fence, stepped into the shade of the forest, where he had suspended it, and brought a small saddle of venison, and laying it by my side, exclaiming, as he laid his hand on my head, 'Dat you, you half—very good;' meaning that I was a good hunter and that half of the venison belonged to me.

"His father, he said, had been one of the warriors in the battle of Wyoming, and afterwards, amongst them, was driven by the white soldiers, with many battles and great slaughter, up the shores of the Susquehanna to the country where the remnant of his tribe now lived, between the Oneida and Cayuga Lakes.

"During this disastrous retreat he was a boy, about my size, and his father made him assist in carrying many heavy things which they had plundered from the white people, where they fought a great battle, at the mouth of the Tunkhannock, and amongst which, and one of the most valuable, as well as one of the most difficult to carry, was a kettle of gold. 'What!' said my father, 'a kettle of gold?' 'Yes, father,' said he,—'now listen.'

" 'The white soldiers came through the narrows you see yonder— (pointing to a narrow gorge in the mountains, through which the river passes)—; and on those very fields, which then were covered with trees (pointing to my father's fields, lying beneath and in front of us), was a great battle, and many were the warriors that fell on both sides; but at that time another army of white men came from the north and were entering the valley on that side, and the poor Indians had no way but to leave the river and all their canoes, and to cross these high mountains behind us. . . .

" 'On the banks of that creek (pointing to the creek on which the "Old Saw-mill" was built) many things were buried by the Indians, who were unable to carry them over the mountains, and amongst them, somewhere near that bridge where the road crosses, on the further bank, I saw my father and my mother bury the kettle of gold, with other things, in the ground.

" 'When my father was old and infirm, I was obliged to hunt for him, and I could not come; but since he has gone to the land of his fathers, I have made the journey a great way, to dig up the kettle of gold. But I see this day, from where I now sit, there is no use in looking for it, and my heart is very sad.

" 'We buried the kettle of gold at the foot of a large pine tree that stood on the bank; but I see the trees are all gone, and all now is covered with green grass, and where shall I go to look? This . . . I kept a secret for many years, but I see there is no use in keeping it a secret any longer, and this makes my heart sad. I have come a great way, and my road in going back I know is beset with many enemies.

" 'These green fields . . . which are now so beautiful to look upon, were once covered with large and beautiful trees, and they were then the hunting grounds of my fathers, and they were many and strong, but we are now but a very few—we live a great way off, and we are your children.' "

In answer to Squire Catlin's questions about the size of the kettle of gold, the Indian made a circle of the full reach of his arms with the fingers' ends barely touching. "There," said he, "it was about this large, and just as much as I could lift; and must be of great value."

After a few minutes of musing, the Squire sent George to the house to ask his mother for the little brass kettle that Buel Rowley, one of the hired men, had turned up on that very spot when the land was first ploughed a few years before. Running as he had run only once before, the boy brought the kettle to the Indian. Silently the warrior turned it over and over in his hands and gazed at it while the Squire explained to him that it was not valuable gold, but useful and cheap brass. Then the Indian spoke. "After a pause of a few minutes, and without the change of a muscle, but drawing a deep sigh, as if he recognized the long hidden treasure, and trying his knife two or three times on the upper rim of it, he laid it down, and drawing a deep breath or two through his pipe, said . . . that he had no doubt but it was the same kettle, but that two things troubled his mind very much—the first was, that the kettle should be so small, and the other, that he found it was not a kettle of gold. . . .

"Poor ignorant child of the forest! he had learned from his teachers something of the value of gold before he knew what it was; and he had risked his life; and those of his wife and his little daughter, in wending his way for hundreds of miles through the forests infested with hunters whose rifles were levelled upon any Indian they could meet. His long journey had cost him no gold, for he had none to spend; his rifle had supplied him and his family with food, and he had thus far escaped his enemies, and in this wise accomplished his object; but his dangerous steps, which were to be retraced, were rendered tenfold more dangerous from the vague reports which had accidentally and unfortunately got into circulation amongst the hunters and brigands of the forests through which he had to pass, that he had dug up, and was returning with, a kettle of gold."

The Indian family immediately became great favorites in the neighborhood. Squire Catlin and other farmers often visited their camp, and little George raided his mother's pantry for them, and clung to the tawny warrior like a shadow. He already had a cabinet of Indian implements he had picked up, or that the men had brought in for him. Among them was a rusty iron pipe-tomahawk. The Indian replaced its rotted handle with a new one of young hickory, bored through to make a pipestem, and demonstrated to his young friend the mysterious art of so throwing it that from any distance, and after any number of revolutions, it would invariably sink its blade deep into the bark of the target tree. Deftly, though with evident sadness, he shafted and feathered the boy's flint arrowheads, made him a hickory bow plumed with woodpecker feathers, and lastly, from the skin of the deer, a quiver to hold his arrows.

Greatly concerned for the safety of his dusky guests, good Squire Catlin was arranging to send them home by a more secure route at his own cost. But the Indian would not be a burden. In the night he and his little family stole away, leaving on a hook of the plantation woodhouse a saddle of venison with one of the eagle quills of his head-dress set in it as a brave farewell.

"I'll be shot if thot mon's not a gintleman," exclaimed Johny O'Neil when they found the venison.

A few days later the dead body of On-o-gong-way, the gentleman savage, was found, pierced by two rifle bullets, in a dark reach of forest eight or ten miles from the Catlin plantation. No one ever learned what became of his wife and little daughter, or of the tragic kettle of gold that he so sadly carried away.

But the boy who acted a part in this pathetic tragedy was to remember it when failure and slander made him doubt whether Destiny had really elected him to make known the truth about the American Indians. And he was to carry a reminder of it with him to the grave.

The neighboring boys tried to master the art of throwing the iron tomahawk, ground now to gleaming brightness. A bad throw glanced from the tree it was aimed at, and the keen blade cut deep into George Catlin's cheekbone, scarring the left side of his face for life.

THREE CHOSEN SCHOOLS

DESTINY makes very good bricks with very short straw. Our educators would hardly accredit George Catlin's wildwood childhood as a school, yet it was the best primary in the world for the work he was to do. To thread the wilderness safely from Labrador to Patagonia, from Florida to the Aleutians, he needed woodcraft, horsemanship, accurate aim, and mastery of the paddle. All these he acquired at Oc-qua-go and on the later Catlin plantation at Hop Bottom, Pennsylvania, where the family moved in 1808. John Darrow, a ne'er-do-well in all occupations but Man's oldest, taught him woodcraft so well that he was never in real danger from either wild beasts or wild men. Brought up with horses, he thought little of riding alone over five hundred miles of trackless prairies. Even in his late fifties, an unbroken and unsaddled stallion of the Pampas could not throw him. When he exchanged the accurate long rifle of his boyhood for a short repeating carbine, he could still hit the hearts of six running buffalos with six shots, or drill a leaping puma squarely between the eyes. Susquehanna settlers were by necessity amphibians, with boats for buggies and market wagons. From them he learned such river lore that the French-Canadian voyageurs whose only book was the brown Missouri set him to steer where the snags were thickest, or when the canoe swept into the dangerous millings of thousands of swimming buffalos.

The communal ways of painted tribesmen, and the dignities of their chiefs and elders were never to be strange or outlandish to him. His people also pastured their cattle together on the common ranges that were yet unfenced. His father's plantation household was a community, populous as the smaller Indian villages. It had its division of duties and its subtle hierarchy of distinction between family and even the most faithful hired girls and hired men. Its elder brothers were war sachems and sages in their younger brothers' eyes. Indoors it had matriarchy, with Polly Catlin presiding over house and dairy, spindle and loom, sick-bed, schoolroom, and prayers. Outdoors, Squire Catlin was a frontier combination of Roman paterfamilias and English feudal lord.

The company the Squire kept was the cream of any boy's desire. There was Grandfather Sutton, who had escaped the Massacre by swimming away under water in a shower of arrows. There were lawyers and judges and Revolutionary Colonels and officers of the militia in which Squire Catlin had been Captain and Brigade Inspector. There were trappers and hunters and Indian fighters and politicians and itinerant preachers whose tongues mixed brimstone and honey. In the long winter candlelight Talk was king, and a king richly robed in wit and circumstance. From these men George Catlin learned to spin a story as a spider spins a web, weaving upon the few threads of supporting fact a fabric perfect and inevitable as a demonstration of Euclidian geometry. A story is true only when the teller creates in his hearers, by emphasis and embroidery, an excitement approximating the incident itself. That is what our frontier storytellers could do.

Ethnologists and anthropologists have probed and wheedled in vain for the mysteries and dusky secrets of Indian religion that priests and medicine men freely divulged to George Catlin. Somehow they sensed that the seal of their own Great Spirit was set upon his Susquehanna childhood. They were not mistaken. The strong river, the overpowering mountains, the forests roaring in storm, humbled all the intellectual conceit of the eighteenth century out of him. Death in the ineffably sorrowful eyes of the broken-shouldered buck, life wiggling to the wet tip of the new lamb's tail, and the awe that tensed his hold on the plough-handles as his share opened to the sun the eternally hidden secrets of virgin ground, made him a near neighbor of the ancient realities.

The boy's alert senses, and his imagination—that highest art of mind—had plenty of blue and brown texts and tall green teachers there.

I have it from his grandson that his second school was the academy set up in 1807 in the courtroom and jail of Wilkes-Barre's old log courthouse, decently clapboarded for its new purpose. The trustees of this school resolved that: "In the 1st branch shall be taught the application of the rules of English Grammar, Geography and the use of the Globes, History, Composition, the Latter as far as the four first Aeneids, and the Greek language as far as the Four Evangelists, to be at $5 per Quarter; . . . pursuing the same languages further, Rhetoric, Logic, Matthematics, including Natural Philosophy and Astronomy, $6 per Quarter."

Garrick Mallery, the headmaster, was a Yale man of sound learning and eloquent expression who communicated both to his gifted pupil. George Catlin learned there to write a good and fluent, though ornate style, that makes his books easy, pleasant reading, and he picked up enough of history and logic to hold his own at law school with graduates of Yale and Princeton. The Homer and Virgil, and the classical mythology he read at Wilkes-Barre Academy were to mean much to him among the Indians.

When Benjamin West, our original expatriate artist, first saw the Apollo Belvedere, he exclaimed, "My God! how like a young Mohawk Indian." Again and again, Catlin compared red warriors and Homeric heroes. But what blind Homer created from imagination and the melody and magic of a rich language, he saw in the round and warm fulness of living reality. The lares and the legends, the oracles and the omen-readers of the ancient Mediterranean world opened for him a door of understanding upon Indian ritual and priest-craft. Broad-minded Virgil taught him a tolerance unknown to his narrow and complacently Protestant time.

The town taught him too. Wilkes-Barre was a lively, grotesque miniature of the new westering America, a boiling kettle bubbling over with big and quickly bursting projects. It built a seagoing ship of such size that the vessel foundered and broke up in the river rapids on the way to the ocean. Its Godly lottery which was to build a cathedral of a church offered prizes so much larger than the ticket sales that the project ended in a loss of eight thousand dollars. Its crack militia company, the Wyoming Blues, "particularly desirable young men," wore "a dark blue short coat or sailor's jacket, faced and trimmed with scarlet, white waistcoat and blue pantaloons edged with scarlet, black stock and high crowned hat, with bear skin on same." Yet they melted away like a blue mist when the War of 1812 broke out.

A Wilkes-Barre visitor wrote in his diary this account of a short stay:

"March 20, 1810. . . . Came down into the town—found it regularly laid out—handsome place, although too many small houses for beauty. Streets terribly muddy—almost impossible to get along. Wonder the inhabitants don't have a sidewalk, at least, so that foot people may not have their legs pulled out by the roots. . . .

"Walked up to the centre of the place—saw a meetinghouse—a good sign, though seldom seen in this country—court-house, an academy, I guess, with one end of it fenced in—a jail, probably, by the high yard fence—four public buildings, religion, justice, knowledge, and iniquity—curious compound. . . . Went a little further —stopped at I cannot tell whose house—found six great, robust men playing cards without any concealment. Inquired if they had any laws in this state, or, perhaps their magistrates are blind, like Justice of old. . . . Saw a man drunk—he had business on both sides of the way. Saw another man moving with great obliquity—made inquiry afterwards—found he was candidate for sheriff. Do all sheriffs in Pennsylvania step quick two or three times, and then with a long side-way stride? . . .

"Two men rode up from the river—one horse kicked up and threw the rider head and heels in the mud—the people flocked around just as they do to see dogs fight—made inquiry, and found the man was a Methodist minister. Well, if I remember right, this sect of Christians hold to *falling*. . . .

"March 21. Rose at 6—walked out upon the bank—saw only one man up, and he, from his looks, will be down before night. At 7, went to the store opposite the ferry—found all closed and silent— perhaps this may be holy time with them—inquired if they be Jews and this be the Passover. . . . Returned to the tavern—found a good many men come in to get their morning charge. . . . After breakfast walked round town—at 11 o'clock went by the academy— steeple as big as an eel basket—saw a number of great tall boys gaping, and leaning against the side of the house, and stretching as if for victory. Heard a man talk very loud within.

> " 'With what a braying noise he muttered,
>   And thought, no doubt, hell trembled as he uttered.'

Went on—saw many things which I shall never forget, but which I must not at present mention. Returned to my lodgings sick—evening pleasant—many people came in, and as they poured down the whiskey, they drowned out the politics. Went up street—going by the court-house heard a stamping, like a livery stable in fly-time— made inquiry afterwards and found there was a dancing school kept there. Mem.—

> " 'He that will not work, by right should not eat,
>   And he that has no head may use his feet.'

"March 22. In the morning—Over! Over! Over! Halloo, ferryman! P.S. I shall return this way."

Schooled in such a setting, Catlin could never keep a certain Hogarthian quality from creeping into his paintings of even the most solemn Indian ceremonies. Nor could he avoid contrasting that raw and rowdy way of life with Indian grace and decorum.

"Agin the guvment" at all times, the Wilkes-Barre conservatives opposed the new Democratic Party with the fierce fervor that only anti-New-Dealers know. So far as I can learn, none of the Catlin boys enlisted in the unpopular War of 1812. The Blues and other young men of the town flatly refused to fight anybody except the recruiting officers. Their stand was somewhat justified by the Prussian practices of these intruders. "Mr. Dixon, a civil, inoffensive, but feeble man," with a wife and four children, weakened and enlisted—to be beaten to death by a sergeant because he tired and dropped out of ranks.

Convinced that things had come to a pass where the only course for an honest man was "to butter his own bread and lament the fate of his country," the natives sold their wheat at $2.50 a bushel and grumbled at the shortages in the shops. Young latin-choppers from the academy hung dead dogs and cats on the butcher's empty meat-hooks. The *Susquehanna Democrat* justly complained that "the conduct of Wilkesbarre, with some few exceptions, is a disgrace to the American name; every pains has been taken to discourage the men, urge them to mutiny and prevail upon them to return home. The Lawyers particularly have set such an infamous example as in any other country would richly entitle them all to the benefits of a halter."

Here was an unusual lesson for a young American: his countrymen might be wrong! It was a lesson that heartened and strengthened Catlin in his lifelong and losing fight to save the Indians and their immemorial pious culture from the shouting western progress of the ruthless new god-on-wheels.

His third and last school was unique in history. Perhaps it could be fitted in somewhere between Plato's leafy lecture room and the little Academe of *Love's Labour's Lost*. It was America's original law school kept under the elms and maples of South Street, in Litchfield, Connecticut, by Judge Tapping Reeve and his grave young partner, James Gould.

When George Catlin entered the school in 1817, the venerable and eccentric Judge was a living legend who "descanted with glowing eloquence upon the sacredness and majesty of law." One of the Beechers recalled that "He had a pair of soft dark eyes of rare beauty, a beaming expression of intelligence and benevolence, while his soft gray hair fell in silver tresses on his shoulders in a style peculiar to himself. His figure was large and portly, and his manners gentle and dignified. His voice was singular, having failed from some unknown cause, so that he always spoke in a whisper, and yet so distinctly that a hundred students at once could take notes as he delivered his law lectures."

James Gould, a former Yale tutor, was less colorful but more precise. He was "of fine personal appearance, polished manners, extensive acquaintance with the English Classics, and in all matters of rhetorical or verbal criticism his word was law."

These men were even more influential than Chief Justice Marshall in the shaping of our liberal legal system and philosophy. Between 1774 and 1833 they trained two Vice Presidents, six Cabinet members, thirty-seven Federal and State Supreme Court Judges, a hundred and twenty-nine Senators and Congressmen, twenty-four Governors and Lieutenant Governors, and hundreds of successful lawyers, teachers and financiers.

Neither was skilled, or even interested, in the tricks and traps of courtroom controversy. Like the masters of the ideal school in Xenophon's *Cyropaedia* they taught justice, and upheld with well-worded logic the equality of all men, and women too, before the law. For his long and lonely advocacy of the Indian cause, Catlin could not have found better teachers.

Old Judge Reeve was distinguished "by that appreciation of the gentler sex which never fails to mark the true man." He once said that "he never saw a little girl but he wished to kiss her, for if she was not good she would be." Such sentiments made him a gallant and effective champion of women's rights. With his aid, Miss Sarah Pierce had set up on North Street her famous Female Academy. Miss Pierce's academy taught style as well as history, elegant composition, and sketching in water colors. The highest compliment the early nineteenth century could pay a young lady was, "She would pass on Litchfield Hill."

At Lyman Beecher's church the "sparkling, modest and blushing girls" from Pierce's sat on one side of the singers' gallery and the "fiery, forward and confident young men" from Reeve's on the other, but the students of both schools roomed in select private houses where they mingled at meals and prayers. Though the athletic, elderly Miss Pierce led her lovely flock on long afternoon walks enlivened by the tootling of flute and flageolet, they were not too exhausted for evenings of chaperoned romance. The lawyers took them boating on Bantam Lake, and sleigh-riding to outlying inns where they danced and ate turkey and oysters. They entertained the lawyers with teas and amateur theatricals and catechized them in poetry and painting.

These bankers' daughters in flowered crinolines and these planters' sons in pink gingham frock-coats were men and women of the world, of which Litchfield was then a thriving and populous part. Its many mills and factories turned out lumber, flour, sea anchors, nails, paper, carriages, cloth, combs, leather and felt hats. One of its sixteen "mercantile stores" was about to install "a fountain of soda water." It had printers and publishers and booksellers whose lists of latest titles took up columns of newsprint. Through Litchfield with horns braying and whips cracking, lumbered red four-horse coaches posting between

Hartford and West Point, or up and down the great inland route from New York to Boston and Albany.

Judge Reeve, who was not without worldly wisdom, also said that "he never saw a little boy but he wished to whip him, for if he was not bad he would be." Though his young gentlemen came from the wealthiest and most aristocratic families of both North and South he set them hard lessons and harder benches in a small unheated building at the back of his handsome and ample house. There they took his long dictations with their feet on hot bricks and their bodies bundled in greatcoats and mufflers.

But the school's austerity was more than matched by the richness and grace of Litchfield life, lived in mansions that still make broad tree-lined North and South streets memorable.

Through his kinsmen, Dr. Abel Catlin, and old Grove Catlin who kept the tavern on the Litchfield Green, the shy handsome youth from Wilkes-Barre had easy access to that life and to the many distinguished Litchfielders who lived it. Over them all towered seven-foot Governor Oliver Wolcott who had served in Washington's Cabinet. The army was represented by Colonel Talmage of the Light Dragoons, another giant, often mistaken for General Washington. Uriah Tracy still cracked the whip of wit he once wielded as a Senator from Connecticut. Standing on the Capitol steps when a drove of mules passed, Senator Randolph of Virginia said to him, "There, Tracy, are some of your constituents." "Yes, sir," said Tracy, "they are going to Virginia to keep school." These old gentlemen and one or two retired Judges still wore powdered queues, silk stockings, and knee breeches with buckles.

All their wit and sophisticated wisdom met its match in Miss Pierce and the enormous Mrs. Reeve, who had once been her husband's housekeeper. For heavier fare they turned to the Reverend Lyman Beecher, or to Miss Pierce's nephew and right-hand assistant, Mr. Brace, pedagogue, poet and geologist. Beecher, on five hundred dollars a year, was preaching the best sermons in America and starting our first Temperance Movement among his own tolerant vestry and wardens. His only fault was the fiddling of lively tunes a little too soon after funerals.

Listening to the best of talk in rooms furnished in the best of taste and hung with Anson Dickinson miniatures and the magnificent portraits painted by Ralph Earle during his 1796 visit, young Catlin sometimes saw another listener, Lyman Beecher's daughter, the little bright-eyed girl whose *Uncle Tom's Cabin* was to set the sons of his classmates at each other's throats. She had just acquired a stepmother to whom she said: "Because you have come and married my pa, when I am big enough I mean to go and marry your pa."

Grove Catlin also had a gifted daughter Flora, "the Belle of Litchfield," and Dr. Catlin had adopted one named Mary Peck. Both these girls became drawing-mistresses in Miss Pierce's school. Their country kinsman was quick to learn how they handled crayons and brushes, and before long he produced a portrait of Judge Reeve sitting cross-legged in the school library with spectacles in hand and lecture manuscripts on his knee. In it the young Catlin caught both the wise preceptor and the absent-minded eccentric who led an empty bridle up the street and tied its reins securely around a hitching post.

Catlin passed his finals and his bar examinations as successfully as his classmates who had come up from Yale and Princeton, or the best Southern colleges. Polished in manners now, and at ease in conversation, he would never be at a disadvantage in any company, either of eagle-fathered chiefs or of Europe's kings.

III

APPRENTICED TO DESTINY

THE law, as practiced in Lucerne County, Pennsylvania, displayed little of the dignity and majesty on which Judge Reeve had descanted. In Catlin's only recorded case, the eloquent young "nimrodical lawyer" defended and cleared an Irishman who declared he was guilty of the charge of stealing a broadaxe. The verdict enraged the Irishman. He was willing to have the jury declare him a thief, but not a liar.

Idling the good days away in office and courtroom, Catlin employed his pencil on culprits, counsel and jurors. It moved swiftly and surely. Gradually he became aware that these whimsicalities of line were catching hints of character that his eyes were not conscious of seeing. To learn how these impressions—as he later called them— were conveyed to an artist's inner mind he spent night after night before his mirror, studying and sketching his own features as he simulated in turn rage, joy, wonder, scorn, ecstasy. The Neville Museum at Green Bay, Wisconsin, has twenty-three of these sketches, in charcoal and white chalk on brown paper. Through Theodore Burr Catlin, the artist's nephew, they came into the possession of Clark's Marine Saloon, in that city. For decades they adorned its bar, and were the confusion and deep trouble of its heavier drinkers.

As he stalked browsing deer on the Susquehanna's moon-enchanted banks, or whipped its ripples with his alert fly-rod, Catlin mused on the employment of his newly discovered talent, which he knew was no common one.

In great houses he had seen the huge individual and group portraits of the static and settled past. But this new age of movement needed miniatures, portable portraits, that could be carried in pocket or locket down the western rivers and over the stagecoach roads. At Litchfield parties, little likenesses had often been handed round for criticism as well as admiration. Litchfielders knew good miniatures, for Anson Dickinson, who did some of the best of them, was their fellow townsman. And Catlin knew that Dickinson had taught himself to paint his tiny masterpieces.

Late in 1820, other young Lucerne County lawyers whose lack of briefs left them leisure for reading were buying the Catlin law library at bargain prices. It fetched enough to carry its handsome and venturesome owner to Philadelphia and set him up there in a little studio on quiet Walnut Street, with an optimistic shingle inscribed "George Catlin, Miniature Painter."

Philadelphia was no longer the American Rome, but it was still our Florence, and the May exhibitions of its Pennsylvania Academy of Art were the great goal of young painters. While the exhibition committee deliberated on Catlin's miniature entries in those early months of 1821, he divided his time between the antique rooms of the Academy and Peale's amazing Philadelphia Museum.

Its elderly but lively proprietor, Charles Wilson Peale, whose gifted children had already justified his naming them Raphael, Rembrandt, and Titian, will one day have his place in our Pantheon. As a young captain under Washington he painted the outstanding commanders and events of the Revolution. When peace came, he painted the statesmen and distinguished citizens of the new republic. With his gallery of Founding Fathers completed, he founded in Philadelphia the father of the innumerable private museums that did more than all our colleges to advance science and the arts during the first half of the nineteenth century.

In Peale's Museum, ingenious mechanics had their inventiveness stirred by models of the latest looms, steam engines and sewing machines. Emigrants to the opening West visited it to learn the look of the ores and crystals and rare minerals they might well find on their new lands. Its cases contained mounted specimens of every obtainable insect, fish, bird, and beast of America, and many examples of Indian handiwork, including a good part of the collection gathered by Lewis and Clark on their famous trip to the Pacific. And to show that we, too, have an ancient history, it housed the complete skeleton of a mastodon that Peale had unearthed in the earliest recorded scientific excavation. On special occasions he set a dinner table for thirteen within the barred chamber of the extinct beast's ribs. For old Peale had learned that success in art demands showmanship. Tens of thousands knew his portraits of great Americans because they were hung in long, long rows over cases containing a white blackbird and the gizzard of a Muscovy duck that had swallowed too many pins.

Bred among the awing and mysterious Wilkes-Barre outcrops of ancient jungle floors beaten and blackened into stone-coal, Catlin eagerly studied Peale's mineral specimens as well as the pictures ranged above them. Gems and crystals had the exquisitely tiny, clean-cut perfection he so desperately and despairingly strove to attain in his painting.

Others saw greatness in his first small portraits on ivory. The Pennsylvania Academy Exhibition showed four of them that year, and six in 1822. They brought him commissions, a local reputation, and invitations to the famous studios of Thomas Sully, John Neagle, and the several Peales.

Late in life Catlin recalled that during those first studio years his mind was continually reaching for some high enterprise of art worthy of a whole enthusiastic lifetime. Often, at the Museum, he unconsciously paused before Peale's portraits of tribal Indians, comparing them with his own vivid recollections of the warrior who had returned for the kettle of gold. One day, in the winter of 1822–23, he found

Peale's portraits walking the huge hall in the round and feathered fullness of life. Startled, he stared in awed admiration at the delegation of prairie chiefs who were being shown these wonder-rooms on their way back from Washington to the western wilds. They were "noble and dignified," he wrote, "arrayed and equipped in all their classic beauty, with shield and helmet, with tunic and manteau, tinted and tasseled off exactly for the painter's palette."

Instantly he knew that destiny had picked him out to portray these magnificent red heroes of a more tragic Ilium before they and their tented towns became only a memory. Where Peale had painted the triumphant beginning of one nation, he would record on canvas the gallant ending of all the tawny nations left between the Alleghenies and the Pacific shore.

And he would have a museum—a traveling museum of everything Indian and everything animal, vegetable, or mineral that had shaped and colored Indian culture. His brother Julius, still a cadet at West Point, would collect specimens at frontier military posts. Then, with hundreds of Indian paintings and thousands of examples of Indian handiwork and Western birds, animals, plants, ores and fossils, the two would tour the world in a new American triumph.

Cadet Julius, as adventurous as his brother, and already a good amateur naturalist and artist, was delighted with the project, and set himself to prepare for the scientist's part in it.

Catlin also disclosed his high and difficult purpose to a few artist intimates who wondered why he submitted only one miniature for the 1823 Academy Exhibition. Painting on ivory now only for the few dollars a week necessary for his austere living, he set himself to master a skilled and rapid style of painting in oils the life-sized portraits and large subject pictures that the Catlin Indian museum would require.

He had heard his father and Colonel Timothy Pickering talk of their expedition to treat with Red Jacket, "the perfect Indian," whose eloquence ruled the remnant of the Seneca tribe. No Sachem was better known on the frontier or better suited for the first canvas of an Indian gallery. In April of that year, Catlin wrote to his father and the Colonel that he was planning an historic painting of the reception Red Jacket gave them, and that he would welcome detailed accounts of it.

His father replied: "The Indians came marching in straggling order and made a halt on discovering the Colonel, who then made a short address welcoming their arrival, etc., saying he had brought some spirits to wash the dust down their throats, etc. The place was a pitch-pine plain. Their orator (Red Jacket) advanced and made a reply to Colonel Pickering's address in very handsome style. The position of the orator was most interesting. As he commenced his speech, he stepped on a log to gain a little elevation, and perfect silence was observed, except that the infant lashed to his back, with its face out-wards, began to cry. At that instant, his wife standing near him ad-vanced on the log, as he stepped on the ground, and gracefully gave her breast to the child so as to prevent the least interruption of the oration."

Colonel Pickering wrote that he could recall nothing in the meeting that would be "of any interest in an historic painting. In a word, I think the entire scene of too little moment to be the subject of one."

After a year of tireless practice and thoughtful study of the Dutch, English and American paintings in Philadelphia collections, Catlin completed his first attempt on canvas, a remarkable self portrait.

His miniatures had already established his reputation for unusual skill and sincerity in portraying individual character. This new work, a daring departure from both stiff formalism and what contemporary artists advertised as "photographic likeness," showed his freshness and power. By the judgment of such competent painters as Sully and Rembrandt Peale he was the first to be named a Pennsylvania Acade-mician when that coveted title was revived in 1824. Unaided, in three years he had become one of the outstanding painters of his day.

Though the Philadelphia Directory listed Catlin at the Walnut

Street address in 1824 and 1825, those lodgings seldom saw him. He was in New York, Hartford, Litchfield, West Point. But his best address was "c/o the Erie Canal."

By luck he had found another Red Jacket enthusiast—Colonel William Stone, who later wrote a biography of that great Indian orator. Stone was then publishing the New York *Commercial Advertiser* and setting the pattern of modern city journalism by spicing the accepted dullness of political, foreign, and shipping despatches with sensational human interest stories of murders, robberies, ravishments, rich eccentrics in attics and forlorn lovers leaping over cliffs. Discovering that Catlin was, like himself, backwoods born, with gifts and spirit and fantastic ambitions, he delightedly set to work to make the young man known, and to get for him the profitable public commissions needed to finance expeditions on the Western prairies where Catlin would have to go to paint tribal Indians.

As De Witt Clinton was deeply indebted to Stone for the *Commercial Advertiser's* vigorous backing of his political policies and his beloved Erie Canal, the great man readily gave Catlin sittings that winter for the first of his series of Clinton portraits.

Clinton was highly pleased by it, and by the company of this romantic yet resolute young lawyer-artist-naturalist who shared his scientific interest in geology and the classification of American fish and birds. During the next three years Catlin shared too in the fruits of Clinton's return to prestige and power. The Governor's introductions got him commissions in Albany and the raw new towns rising along the route of the Big Ditch. And early in 1825 he was naturally drawn into the preparation of America's first great Hollywood show, the opening of the Erie Canal.

Colonel William Stone, its publicity agent, employed him to make half a dozen drawings of construction work on the canal, and of its locks and harbors, to be lithographed by Antoine Imbert for illustration of an official souvenir book entitled *Narrative of the Festivities observed in honor of the Completion of the Erie Canal.* In one of these Catlin caught the dramatic pictorial possibilities of big machinery—a long line of towering cranes and derricks grappling up blastings of rock. But his most dramatic canal pictures were the huge pair that he painted secretly in Buffalo and smuggled by night on to the *Seneca Chief,* a beflagged barge that was to lead the procession of canal boats down to New York City. When Clinton entered the *Seneca Chief's* cabin on the October morning of the opening, Catlin's two paintings were unveiled to his understandable astonishment. One was an elaborate view of Buffalo harbor with the pageant of boats ready to enter the canal. The other, Colonel Stone's *Narrative* terms "a classic emblematical production of the pencil. This piece, on the extreme left, exhibited a figure of Hercules in a sitting posture, leaning on his favourite club, and resting from the severe labour just completed. The centre shows a section of the canal, with a lock, and in the foreground is a full length figure of Governor Clinton, in Roman costume; he is supposed to have just thrown open a lock gate, and with the right hand extended (the arm being bare) seems in the act of inviting Neptune, who appears upon the water, to pass through and take possession of the watery regions which the canal has attached to his former domains; the God of the Sea is upon the right of the piece, and stands erect in his chariot of shell, which is drawn by sea horses, holding his trident, and in the act of recoiling with his body, as if confounded by the fact of the opening of the lock; Naiads are sporting around the sea horses in the water. . . ."

An imagination fertile and lively enough to fit a Governor of New York into such a scene is a dangerous asset.

Catlin's part in this spectacular show brought him a medal, election to the New York National Academy, and more portrait work on ivory and canvas than he could possibly do. Though he still received only forty or fifty dollars for such fine private work as his portrait of General Winfield Scott, the New York Common Council now paid him six hundred for an immense, and pompous canvas of De Witt Clinton.

But he was not born to paint for money. With commissions waiting, he took time off for a pair of charming colored lithographs of West Point and a masterly miniature of his mother—a frontier woman whose stern and utterly honest little likeness almost speaks the edged Wilkes-Barre accent. And he kept faith with his first Indian dream by painting an oil portrait of Red Jacket, signed and dated "Buffalo, 1826." Painted with strong free strokes and superb draughtsmanship, it set the pattern for the best he was to do. Its pallid greens and grays are movingly symbolic of the evening of the Senecas and the last hopes of this old orator, who drowsed out his despair in drunken sleep in the fence corners of one of the concentration camps that we still call reservations. But for this picture he is posed erect, with plumed head high, and arms folded in pride. His corded neck is strong, and his torn left ear is turned toward the spectator. His loose orator's mouth is tightened to a hard line, and over his eyes of undying, age-dimmed hate one lid droops heavily. Yet under these features of proud defiance and power, a second glance discovers the pallor of dissipation and the shrunken skin of the old.

Such selective, stressed realism seemed brutal and ugly to that generation of eastern Americans. Having wiped out or driven out the native tribes, they were now picturing the Indian as a romantic hybrid mixture of Hector and Hiawatha.

Distressed, and for a time deterred in his Indian plans by harsh criticism of his Red Jacket picture, Catlin went on with more conventional society and public painting. He had to work out a way to get at prairie Indians, as well as a way to paint them. His brother Julius, now a Lieutenant stationed on the Southwest frontier, wrote discouragingly. The Indians were becoming hostile and difficult to approach. A painting expedition among them would have to be expensively outfitted and guarded. "Put money in your purse," he said. "Then after a year or two we can come out here together, properly equipped and collect our specimens for both the museum and the Indian gallery."

Making money was growing easier, but keeping it was increasingly difficult. A gentleman's tastes eat heavily into an artist's income, especially when he is in love. And Catlin was in love, up to the buckles of his expensive new patent suspenders. With his Indians unpainted and his old bills for brushes and ivory unpaid, he spent precious hours drawing and coloring plump cupids and writing verses under them in a handsome copperplate hand.

How could a man of dreams, so bent on a solitary enterprise, persuade himself to take a flesh-and-blood partner? Catlin liked Albany —the oldest of our cities—and Clara Gregory lived there. He liked a fine house kept in fine old-fashioned style, and her father, Benjamin Gregory, a rich accountant, kept such an establishment on Orange Street. He liked fine names, and Miss Gregory had been christened Clarissa. He liked to talk, and she was a devoted quiet listener, happy to hear him devise plans evening after evening while she bent her pretty aquiline face and black ringlets over the thrice-worn silk gown she was remodeling for the poor gallant Greeks. And besides he had fallen in love.

Her father, who had bought up a good part of Albany cheap at sheriff's sales, did not object to having a well-bred and well-connected son-in-law, whom the local papers referred to as "the celebrated Mr. Catlin." Clara was not happy with her new stepmother. And there might be money in this museum business, he thought, with the great governor so interested in it, and Benjamin Gregory's money and shrewdness behind it.

But Governor Clinton died in mid-February of 1828. None of the hundreds of orators and editors who extolled the dead man's virtues and achievements mourned him more sincerely than did Catlin, who had built high hopes on the Governor's ability to provide him with public commissions and introductions to important men on the edge of the Indian country.

Despite this loss of an influential friend whose like he might never find again, and the emptiness of his small honors, Clara was willing to make his hopes her home, his dreams her certainties.

By desperate dunning of slow-paying clients he raised money enough to buy a brown frock-coat suit with fancy waistcoat, and an unostentatious ring. He and Clara were married in Albany on the 28th of that May, by the Rev. M. Lacey.

That was one of Catlin's happiest summers. Julius, who had resigned his army commission, came to Albany with all sorts of museum plans and all sorts of Southwestern curios. The two brothers and the lovely new bride went on river parties in the first steamboat with a piano, and rattled off in the "splendid red coaches" of Erastus Young and the "superior yellow coaches" of Rice and Baker to look at near-by reservation Indians. They rambled through pig-patrolled streets, "more Dutch than decent," to admire ancient brick houses with crow-step gables and eyelids of upper windows under the eaves. They spent hours in the Albany museum which now showed nearly one hundred thousand exhibits.

Sometimes on these tours, or in the evenings at the ample Orange Street mansion when Catlin worked at a large scale model of Niagara Falls, they had the shy company of Joseph Henry, whose name should be as well known as Bell's or Edison's. This able young instructor at the Albany Academy was then developing an "intensity magnet" for his successful 1829 demonstration that the mysterious power called electricity could ring a bell at the end of a mile of wire. He told them too of the new steam locomotive and the company which was being formed in Albany to build one of the first American railroads, from that city to Schenectady.

Even during this honeymoon time Catlin worked much at his easel, painting a copy of one of his Clinton portraits for the Franklin Institute of Rochester. In September his brother Julius delivered the finished picture. He was something of an artist as well as a scientific inquirer, and having free time in Rochester he went to sketch the near-by

2. *Red Jacket, the Seneca orator. See p. 30.*

3. Bread, the half-blood chief of the Oneidas. See p. 33.

Genesee Falls. To get a view of the cataract from below, he stripped and swam out into the tail of its whirlpool. A lounger on the bank heard him cry: "Help! for God's sake, help me!" as the chill water sucked his cramped young body down. So at least the lounger swore before a coronor's jury. When Julius went down to the water's edge he had on his chain a valuable new pocket time-piece, then called "a watch establishment." It was missing when his clothes were searched for identity marks. Suspecting foul play, but lacking evidence to support that suspicion, the coroner entered a verdict of accidental drowning.

Catlin loved this brother above all his kindred. For years they had played together, hunted together, worked and dreamed as one. The thought that he had sent his dearest friend on this errand of death haunted his days, and that last terrible cry, "For God's sake, help me!" startled his fitful sleep. He paled and thinned until the doctors feared consumption. Hoping that the out-of-doors and his Indian enthusiasms would help him to lay hold on life again, Clara took him to the Oneida and Tuscarora reservations. The misery and poverty of these dying tribes depressed him even more as he painted the unromantic Chief Bread who spoke good English and was "a gentlemanly man in his deportment," and Chief Cusick, a Baptist minister in a black frock coat.

To save him from the bitter upstate winter she went with him to Richmond, Virginia, late in 1829. There he was commissioned to paint the 115 delegates assembled for the framing of a new state constitution.

The delightful hilltop capital city was crowded with celebrities that winter, and gay with parties and balls. Catlin had friends there and old Litchfield schoolmates. But as he was in no mood for society, Clara was content to take lodgings with him in a country inn, some miles out, among the healthful pines and the high pillared plantation homes.

Here was his great chance to rival Peale as a painter of the Founding

Fathers. In that long-drawn-out Constitutional Convention he saw Madison, Monroe, Marshall, and John Randolph together for the last time. They were pathetic old men now, out of another age. Little Mr. Madison's queer eyes were dim under a dome of forehead and he spoke in a husky whisper. Monroe had grown dull of speech and his weathered face was a map of wrinkles. A breath would have blown John Randolph down; he was so withered, wan and frail. Only Marshall, grim and gaunt in his antique blue surtout, still showed the vigor of mind and the fire that had forged a new nation.

In a small oil sketch for a grand-style painting, that he never even began, Catlin made that august convention a crowded parliament of gnomes with huge heads and warped dwarf bodies. For while he sketched he worried. Clara was trying hard to hide the illness that drained the freshness from her young cheeks and the brightness from her vivacious eyes, but he was not deceived. Chills shook her sleep and her small hand was hot to his perceptive touch. The doctor confirmed his worst fears. She had contracted the dreaded "intermittent fever" that had cursed those rich fair tidelands from the time of Jamestown's founding.

Dolly Madison, who lived near, heard that a young northern woman was ill at the inn. Unasked she came to see her, and insisted on nursing and tending her until the crisis passed, so that Catlin could get his sketch done before the convention adjourned. Stirred by deep gratitude he painted the great lady in miniature—lovably lively and droll in her quaint turban.

But he was far from well, in body as well as mind. Racked by coughing as he paced the bleak tobacco lands in search of flint implements he roused his dull mind to desperate and cruel resolution. He dared not delay another year. Legislation was shaping in Congress to move all the Eastern Indians across the Mississippi, where they would corrupt and alter the prairie tribes. Swiftly the steamboats and the coming railroads would carry emigrant hordes even into that last refuge of ancient American culture.

As soon as Clara was safely and comfortably settled in his father's house for the long, slow convalescence, Catlin sternly announced that he was going west at once to devote the rest of his life to painting Indians. "I tried fairly and faithfully," he wrote later, "but it was in vain to reason with those whose anxieties were ready to fabricate every difficulty and danger that could be imagined, without being able to understand the extent and importance of my designs, and I broke from them all,—from my wife and my aged parents,—myself my only adviser and protector."

That announcement before his departure for Saint Louis was, perhaps, over-dramatic. Solid Saint Louis shopkeepers would have been astonished to learn that they lived in a hazardous testing-ground of heroes. And Catlin's idea of recording the looks and ways of the prairie tribes was not wholly original. Our Government had already begun a collection of portraits of those tribes; and our writers, among them Washington Irving, were planning trips to the prairies. So too were such distinguished foreigners as the Prince Maximilian of Neuweid, and the Honourable Charles Murray, later Master of the Household at Queen Victoria's Court. Prairie Indians were in the air.

IV

SAINT LOUIS

No MAN now living remembers the Saint Louis that Catlin entered through its water gate in the spring of 1830. New life coursed the arteries of the ancient West, up-current and down current, with steam power stolen from riparian forests of ash and cedar and oak. *The Neptune, The Phoenix, The Red Rover*—swift and powerful packet boats such as Catlin rode—were the great white owls with the great white eyes preying on that sleeping Indian land.

Travel had never been so cheap, and never would be again. One day's work at his easel had more than paid his passage on that open deck which served as diner, dance hall and dormitory for a medley of immigrants, pedlars, trappers, and intriguingly silent Indians returning from the bewilderments of Washington.

Catlin could not waste that last river night in sleep. Erect as a prairie chief he walked the empty upper deck while black sons of Vulcan stoked cordwood under the row of boilers in the bows and made African melodies on an Indian name:

"Ohio, Ohio, Oh—i—o"

In the river-scented dawn, his deep blue eyes measured ancient burial mounds like immature mountains as the steamboat leaned and swung shoreward. Saint Louis, lustiest child of the Father of Waters, neared in a clustered brightness of whitewashed stone walls and tin roofs. Its long level waterfront was toothed with the white three-deck towers of tall cabin boats and their taller black smokestacks. Above and below the cobbled levee, wood smoke drifted over undulating islands of acres of lesser flat-craft moored in whole villages, pennanted with flapping washing and loud with lowing and crowing.

The other deck passengers disembarked, bearded and noisy, calling each other and the crewmen by the nicknames of easy familiarity. Many went breakfast-hunting with the friends they had made en route. But Catlin carried his bag and his big portfolio off alone. He was a trifle deaf on one side or he would have heard the comments. "Don't drink, don't smoke, don't gamble, don't swear. Must be a preacher."

Here, as on the steamboat, he was more an aloof observer than a natural part of the confusion of traders, drays, and slaves straining their black brawn against whisky barrels and bales of beaver. Anxious, but unbent by his heavy baggage, he followed a troop of blanketed Indians up into the region of new brick streets that was rising behind the limestone warehouses.

High, galleried houses of the old French fur princes scowled forbiddingly over gardens walled from sight. Sharp-faced loungers, already settled for their day's whittling and chewing on the stoops of disreputable inns, appraised him with shifty eyes. There would be poor pickings in the breast pocket of his threadbare but well-cut coat.

At a hotel decent enough to let him have a bed of his own and only one room-mate, everyone in the shabby lobby was ready and eager to direct him to General Clark's Indian Office. The old Governor might be in, but again he mightn't. "If you want to sell him anything, talk Injun," they said.

That phrase at least was a good and sustaining omen for him as he sat with his portfolio on his knees, in the waiting-room of the superintendency from which General William Clark ruled the vast West, from Canada to Mexico, from the Mississippi to the Pacific. No white man could travel, trap, or trade in all that region without his permit.

Unconsciously Catlin's slim fingers stroked the tomahawk scar on his cheek. The talk he heard paled his tight lips and brought anger to his eyes and the thrust of his determined chin. These men who had come to claim damages from the local tribes or to wheedle licenses to swindle and debauch them were not Indian-lovers. But the great hearty laugh that rang through the closed office door was human enough and kind.

Pale under his travel tan, Catlin at last followed his letters of introduction into a room walled with maps and littered with official papers. The General, "a tall robust, grey-headed old man, with beetle brows and uncouth aspect," was signing a report to the Secretary of War, his trigger finger crooked awkwardly across the goose quill.

His was a dull, almost stupid face, such as sometimes conceals a low kind of cunning. Rumor had whispered that crossing the Rockies was his only recommendation. Yes, and that he used his office to forward his private ventures, and made the Indian agencies sinecures for his relatives and friends.

His bluff greeting as he looked up from Catlin's introductions disarmed and quieted such troubling thoughts. "Mr. Catlin, some of my good friends in the East seem to think highly of your talents and your project. Sit down, son, and tell me what I can do for you. Are these samples of your work?"

Catlin untied the tapes of his ingenious portfolio and opened it out like a diptych to display a pair of his oil portraits of Indians—an Oneida and a Seneca. Over and over on the boat he had rehearsed this moment and memorized eloquent phrases to win this old frontiersman's interest and aid. But Clark's sudden change of expression kept him silent. As if dull age were a mask to be doffed at will, the General's heavily thatched eyes alerted and brightened. Leaning forward, he studied Catlin's superb broad-line draughtsmanship, his strongly emphasized characterization, his symbolic use of color. Then he looked up from the painted faces to the even darker anxious face of the young artist and smiled, happily, yet a little wistfully too, as if the lost wilderness days haunted him.

"Mr. Catlin, I both congratulate and envy you. These have the strange reality of truth. Which of our tribesmen do you wish to paint?"

"All of them, sir. I want to give my life to it while their lives last." Catlin's precise, level voice trembled and his scar reddened, shamed by this unintended display of deep feeling.

"Yes," said the General, slowly, "the red sands are running out." His eyes saddened like the last stars of a mountain morning as he gazed long and thoughtfully at a great map he had drawn of Indian wilds that he and Meriwether Lewis laid open to the white tide. Then, shrewdly narrowed, they appraised his young visitor's determined face and trim small body.

Laying his huge age-specked paw on the fine sensitive hands clasped over Catlin's knee, he asked, "Are these your means?"

"Yes, sir."

Pleased by the note of pride, the General rose and with a battered scabbard for a pointer circled a small area northwest of Saint Louis on his map. "Here I and my agents can help you to a few real Western tribes and a good many Eastern remnants," he said. "They will be around the agencies in late summer fitting out for the fall hunts. Meanwhile you had best stay in Saint Louis and paint the Indian delegations that are coming almost every day to see me. Make yourself at home in here until I clear off my morning appointments."

Shuffling a little now, but still with the long, in-toeing prairie stride, he ushered Catlin through painted deerskin curtains into his fine private museum of Indian costumes, handiwork and weapons. Around its walls, portraits of chiefs and warriors hung between horned frontlets of gigantic elk and buffalo festooned with medicine bags, papoose cradles and the curious painted heraldry of bull-hide shields.

Clark frowned at the paintings. "Too smooth—too academic—too alike. Indians are as different as we; as rough-featured; as subtle. Your brush, young man, is the first to paint them as they are." Though Catlin never bragged or belittled the work of other artists, he nodded thoughtfully with a forefinger laid along his scar.

That was the beginning of one of the most fruitful friendships in the history of American painting. Catlin had his stool and his easel beside Clark and the General's secretary in the parley room, where daubed and bedecked Indian delegations sat along the opposite wall—their chief on their right—all very solemn and grave with their darkening future.

Before conferences began, the General introduced Catlin and had him show the tribesmen some Indian portraits, which they greeted with a wondering "Ahah."

Spread-eagle oratory—a native American product infinitely older than the Fourth of July—was the great Indian art, an art that often made the lonely prairies loud with practice speeches repeated over and over with only the howling wolves to applaud. Holding their long and richly beaded calumet pipes in the left hand, the Indian orators in Clark's parley room employed all the orator's dramatic devices of expression and gesticulation, with subtleties and sudden changes of guttural tone.

The resident agents and halfbreeds who interpreted the utterly different languages that had grown up behind the perpetual iron curtain of war, which cut every tribe completely off from its neighbors, translated this eloquence into dull commonplaces.

"Here where the Father of Waters bends an arm of love around his red children and his white children alike, the embers of our hearts glow again with the honest warmth of your welcome," declared the orator.

"By zee revoir he sweat to meet you," said the interpreter.

But Catlin knew red poetry when he saw its rhythms sway the speaker like great winds, and light the troubled brown-black eyes in the rows of masklike faces. At the end of a conference he closely searched the secrecies behind those masks as each delegate shook his hand and looked steadfastly for a moment into his intent, pondering eyes.

Day after day he sketched painted Indians in the Superintendency or at the waterfront warehouse where their delegations lodged. Night after night he talked Indians with the General, who knew more of their ways and customs than any other white man.

Catlin needed a hero to humanize his strict impersonal purpose, and here he had one, of the old heroic mold. Clark was more than a soldier, an explorer and an administrator. First, last and always he was a gentleman of the eighteenth century breed that Catlin most admired. He combined courage with courtesy, competence with indolence, and simple tastes with a high style of hospitality befitting his position but beyond his meager government salary.

Neglected always, and now past hoping for any due recognition by his country of his part in extending its frontiers, he needed this cultivated young hero worshiper who could appreciate his museum, his excellent pen drawings, his just dealing with the Indians; and who could match him, story for story, until mockingbirds sang the small hours in. Talking endlessly of painting, they agreed that it depends, like a good story, on emphasis—amounting even to exaggeration— that will re-create in others something of the particular effect of an event or scene upon him who saw it.

Struck by the narrowness of Indian shoulders—never broadened by the heavy tools white laborers use—Catlin had from the first instinctively narrowed them further on his canvases. Rationalizing on that instinct now, he sloped them to effeminacy. Deliberately too he neglected warrior hands or drew them with almost childish strokes. He sharpened sharp faces, lengthened the long bear-claws of necklaces, brightened colors in beadwork and feathering.

Generous with money as with his praise of these works, the old General tried to buy them all for his museum. But Catlin was readier to give them than to sell them to a friend. Foiled in this attempt to keep the young man's hotel bills paid, Clark urged him to paint some Saint Louisans, and introduced him to everybody who was anybody in the City of the Sainted King.

The Saint Louis population of six or seven thousand was still cleanly divided by a line of language along the crest of the waterfront slope. Along the river drowsed old France with its cafés, its conservatism, its harpsichord music and vivacious speech. Back into the oak and walnut country bustled new America, building shops, factories, and fancy houses and making fortunes in real estate.

There was wealth enough in both sections to keep such a competent portrait painter as Catlin well supplied with commissions when he could spare time from his Indians. Apparently his only local competitor in the portrait field was a Miss Honeywell who cut profile likenesses in a few seconds for a fifty-cent fee, with children at half price. The Saint Louis *Republican* announced that this interesting lady, born without arms, had such skill with a pair of scissors held in her mouth that she could cut out of paper "even the Lord's Prayer, perfectly legible."

The society portrait painting that came from Clark's enthusiastic introductions was only bread-and-butter work to be hurried through here on the edge of Indianland. Catlin kept no journal in those days, but his Indian pictures show how he took every opportunity Clark could provide for him to get among the tribesmen in their prairie camps.

He was up the Mississippi at Prairie du Chien and its Fort Crawford in July when General Clark made treaties there with the Ioways, Missouris, Sioux, Omahas, and the Sacs and Foxes.

He was up the Missouri at Cantonment Leavenworth that fall, painting the near-by calico tribes—Delawares, Ioways, Kickapoos, Potowatomies, Weahs, Peorias, Shewanos, and Kaskaskias, who had been moved to that region to farm and to loiter around the white Cantonment with the ague-shaken garrison. Another Leavenworth guest found them an amusing nuisance. "Here and there," he wrote in his journal, "some curious fellows might be seen, peering through the windows of the dwelling houses or stealing through some open door into the interior. Their step is so hushed and noiseless, that there is nothing to warn you of their approach. I have frequently been surprised, upon looking round in my chamber, to find a dozen of these fellows quietly seated upon chairs, others upon the floor, and all apparently as much at their ease as if they had made it their resting place for the last half century. . . . They would sit for hours, in the same attitude, making no remarks, holding no conversation, and were it not for their glistening snaky eyes, which were ever fastened on your face, creating a feeling of restless uneasiness, there was little in their company to annoy you."

Plentiful and willing as these sitters were, their begging, their brass-buttoned frock coats, and their pride in wearing government-issue derby hats still done up in brown wrapping paper and green string made Catlin long for wilder game.

Then Clark came up-river and took him out to the Konzas country. In Indian file the two riders followed their half-breed guide through forests of ancient silence and over endless undulations of browning prairie where grouse whirred from the tall tindery grass and wolves stalked through it like sinuous gray snakes.

Here and there they caught sight of solitary Indians sunning themselves on hilltops well out of earshot of annoying squaws and offspring. At nearer view these solitaries were less romantic; lean little dried herrings of men in horn-rimmed spectacles and round chubby men whose shaven vermilioned heads looked like enormous red potatoes. But the Konzas were authentic storybook Indians, hung with scalps and bear-claws and crested in homeric style with tufts of dyed deer's hair and colored feathers.

Dozens of yelping cur-dogs ushered the travelers into Konzas towns of noise, mess and primitive disorder. The gaunt, erect old General in his stained buckskins and mangy coonskin cap awed even the goblin children and the most voluble and wrinkled grandmothers, for he was the giver of bacon and ribbons and the chief of white warriors. But Catlin in his new leather jacket and visored hunting cap also had their respect. No rudely curious young braves pawed his canvas roll and paint box or tried to pull his rifle away. Naked little brown boys did not mob him nor pepper him with their toy arrows. Handsome as he was, he met none of the ogled invitations of matrons who had learned what white men expected in exchange for a flask of corn liquor.

When he began to paint one of the warriors, the searching intensity of his look, and his stern silence kept the circle of tawny watchers orderly and awed. Under heavy brows the General saw all this and approved. He had warned his young friend never to let Indians have the upper hand, and never to treat them as intimates.

Catlin worked swiftly at his folding easel in the brown trodden lanes between the brown dusty lodges. Surrounded by their native strangeness, he could not paint these prairie men familiarly. Aloof from the world he knew, they stared out of their stone age at sights hidden from him. Along with that dark distrustful aloofness, he caught something of the incalculable threat of savage power, tempered by the pathos and puzzlement that lurks in the eyes of wild things that hunt and are hunted.

Among the Konzas, Catlin painted a tribal dandy, Wi-hon-ga-shee. "The beau or dandy," he wrote, "is familiarly known and countenanced in every tribe. . . . They plume themselves with swan's-down and the quills of ducks, with braids and plaits of sweet-scented grass and other harmless and unmeaning ornaments, which have no other merit than they themselves have, that of looking pretty and ornamental.

"These gay and tinselled bucks may be seen on a pleasant day in all their plumes, astride their pied or dappled ponies, with a fan in the right hand, made of a turkey's tail, with whip and a fly brush attached to the wrist of the same hand, and underneath them a white, beautiful and soft pleasure saddle, ornamented with porcupine quills and ermine, parading through and lounging about the village for an hour or so, when they will cautiously bend their course to the suburbs of the town, where they will sit or recline upon their horses for an hour or two, watching the beautiful games where the braves and the young aspirants are contending in manly and athletic amusements; when they are fatigued by this severe effort, they wend their way back again, lift off their fine saddle of doeskin, which is wadded with buffalo hair, turn out their pony, take a little refreshment, smoke a pipe, fan themselves to sleep and doze away the rest of the day."

Just before ice locked the great rivers, Catlin went East to show his anxious lady and his friends what great things he had done. It was good to be loved and sought after again, but cultivated society could not keep him contented. Before long he was filling orders for charming small water colors of Indians made from his field sketches. That winter he drew on lithographic stone and hand-tinted a little book of views of Niagara Falls for publication in Baltimore. In Washington, he painted an entire delegation of Menominies, with their wives and children. They are almost his only happy looking Indians—made so by his own happiness in the success of his first expedition to the West.

Soon he was off alone on a second expedition. At Saint Louis he gathered the gear he had left in the house of Clark's nephew, Major Benjamin O'Fallon. Community of Indian interests had brought Catlin into close friendship with this cultivated frontiersman and tribal agent, who was about the best judge in Saint Louis of a good horse, a good bourbon, a good duelist, and a good picture. The Major had married well and could afford to buy many Catlin pictures as well as house the whole collection attractively in his suburban mansion which had become Catlin's western home.

The talk of the river town in those days was the sturdy steamboat *Yellowstone* which Pierre Chouteau, western manager of Astor's American Fur Company, was testing on the Missouri in preparation for a run the next year up to the Company's far northeastern posts in the Crow and Mandan country. Passage on that first run up-river was now Catlin's eager ambition.

At the Prairie du Chien treaty-making, he had made friends with Major John Dougherty, agent for the Ottoes, Omahas and Pawnees. All Indian agents were courtesy majors, but Dougherty had the earned title of "Honest John." No fur trader could corrupt him to let whisky in, and he was one of the few agents who did not pad the census of their tribes to draw extra government supplies for their own profit.

From Dougherty's agency at Bellevue, above Leavenworth, Catlin rode out with him in that spring of 1831 into the wild tribal country of the Platte. Through a green land flowered with blossoms and bright parakeets they went warily, watching every distant ridge by day, and staking their horses close by night. They had crossed the crusted salt marshes of the Saline when Catlin's keen eyes caught their first glimpse of a naked wild rider of the prairies, an outguard of the Ottoes' earth-built town. As they neared that settlement, down on them from the bluffs poured a terrifying flood of hundreds of similar horsemen, vermilioned until they looked like men newly skinned. Yelling and brandishing tomahawks and feathered spears, they circled the travelers in a swirling devil's dance of welcome.

Wilder still was the reception at the four Pawnee towns further up the Platte. There the horsemen charged by shrill thousands. Bright plumage of cardinals and orioles crested the scalp tufts on their shaven heads, and black buffalo horns and masks were painted on their vermilion faces and chests. Their thick-necked horses with bearded fetlocks were as fantastically streaked and splotched and banded with bright colors as the acrobats who rode them. In the Pawnee towns, under the eyes of hundreds of squaws and naked children crowding the enormous domed rooftops, Catlin painted some of his most striking Indian portraits.

Historians have denied his simple statement that he rode on from the Pawnee country up the Platte and through the Rocky Mountain passes to Great Salt Lake. I see no reason to doubt his word. At Leavenworth he had heard much of the Western wilds from Major Dodge and his mounted rangers who patrolled the Santa Fe and Utah trails. Saint Louis trappers knew the Salt Lake region well. It is likely that he fell in with an expedition of them that went west up the Platte in August to divide in trapping-parties at the mouth of the Laramie River. He must have met with disasters or bitter disappointments, for he brought no pictures back and wrote nothing in all his books of this mysterious expedition. Perhaps he referred to it in a later letter, which said his life would not be safe in the Far West if he told all he knew.

When first snow drifted the prairie and ice threatened the Missouri, he was again in Saint Louis painting a party of Knisteneux and Assiniboins who were en route from the Missouri's headwaters to Washington with their able and personable agent, John F. A. Sandford, another of the well-bred young men whom Clark had drawn into the Indian service.

Sandford had already begun what was to be a successful wooing of wealthy Pierre Chouteau's daughter. To make the best use of his few evenings in the Chouteau parlor, he took Catlin along to entertain father Pierre and to show the young lady that his connections were not all with the "lard-eaters" of backwoods trading posts. Chouteau was as amused by Catlin's French as by his romantic ideas of Indians. But he liked the young artist, and invited him to go up the Missouri the following spring as the fur company's guest on the steamer *Yellowstone*.

V

UP THE MISSOURI

ON THE 29th of January, 1832, Catlin was back in Saint Louis, writing to the Secretary of War a successful application for guest privileges at up-river Indian agencies. Days before the 26th of March, when the steamboat *Yellowstone* began her epoch-making voyage, he was aboard with his rolls of canvas, his easel and his little case of bladders bulging with oil-colors.

The *Yellowstone* was no common river boat. One hundred and thirty feet long, broad in beam, and too shallow of draft for much of a below-deck hold, she was heavily timbered and powered with mighty engines to meet the Missouri's torrents. She had carpenter shops and smithies for the repairs that would be needed when sharp rocks and hidden snags tore her planking and splintered her huge side-paddles.

Her voyage was no common casual trip of a little trading boat. Both Washington and London were anxiously awaiting its outcome. If a steamboat could run up to the mouth of the Yellowstone River, American traders would soon drive the British Hudson's Bay Company from the Crow and Blackfoot country and dominate the Northwest.

On a sharp spring morning she steamed upstream from the crowded levee, with a great shouting and blazing away of muskets and small deck cannon. Hers was an odd cargo: guns, beads, blankets, Indian delegations returning from Washington, and Indian-looking French *engagés* of the fur company returning to their trading posts or to their traps and keelboats in the far northern wilds. By special permit from

4. *Kee-món-saw, the Little Chief, a civilized Kaskaskia.*

5. *Om-pa-ton-ga, the Big Elk, a famous Omaha warrior.*

General Clark she carried the last barreled alcohol that was legally to enter that Indian country.

For the temperance movement launched in Litchfield by the Reverend Lyman Beecher was now a nation-wide enthusiasm that forced our government to at least try to end the scandalous debauching of Indians by the fur companies. This was not easy. Without alcohol, the traders said, they would have to go out of business, beaten by the whisky-selling Hudson's Bay men. As the prairie Indians were well fed, well clothed, and contented with tepee life, they would not barter their furs for ordinary civilized wares. But judicious gifts of a few gallons of whisky gave whole villages such a desire for more that they would sell their very bed robes to get it.

Our plains Indians had no intoxicants and no hereditary immunity against their subtle power. As alcohol gave them an exaltation akin to the religious experience produced by their devotional fastings and dervish-like ritual dances, its hold on them was mystical as well as physical, and almost beyond resistance. Saint Louis traders had a trick said to quicken and double that exaltation. By soaking a shredded plug of tobacco in a keg of corn liquor, they supercharged it with more potency than pure alcohol.

The imps of irony must have smiled to see little Catlin and his host, the magnificent Chouteau, pacing the Captain's bridge together as the boat swung westward into the swift Missouri. For Chouteau, whose shrewdness and guile were to make him rich and feared in Wall Street finance, was making this trip to perfect with his up-river agents a plan that would further corrupt and undermine the Indians with whisky in spite of Federal laws.

At Saint Charles—Spanish San Carlos del Missouri—where Aaron Burr had plotted for a private Empire of the West and where the prairie-schooner armies would soon have their bridgehead into Indian-land, the ladies and the notable guests disembarked and drove back to Saint Louis. Half-breed Dufond, "a tall slender brown man" and the best keelboat pilot on the Missouri, took over the bridge and the long, long battle of pulsing steam-power with silent treacherous river-power began in earnest.

Day after day rose for Catlin as out of old wonderful dreams. The wooded banks greened, and were lit with redbud and dogwood. Cranes and geese snowed the colored dawns, and curious parakeets circled the *Yellowstone's* upper deck to peep into its coops of hens. Often he and the other passengers lightened the boat by taking short cuts across some green peninsula that the winding river almost encircled. More often they landed to man the cordell ropes and haul their craft off sand bars.

At nightfall, and during the wild wet gales, the *Yellowstone* moored in the shelter of inlets or islands, where Chouteau's men, warned of her coming by fleet Indian runners, had cut ricks of ash and red mulberry firewood. Then by the light of a ship's lantern or beach bonfire Catlin talked long and late with the traders and young Sandford who was bringing the Assiniboins home. Intermittently too he took notes for the upper-Missouri letters which Colonel Stone had urged him to contribute to the *Commercial Advertiser*.

At occasional fur company posts, all hands hurried to unload trade goods. Stops had to be short, for the shallows ahead could only be navigated on the brief and uncertain floodwaters from melting snow. During the hustle and hubbub of these unloadings Catlin sketched local tribesmen who had gathered to wonder at "the Great Medicine Canoe with eyes."

His Indian technique was established now for all conditions. If he had an hour or two, he used brush and canvas, painting faces, and particularly expression and eyes with precise care, but merely drafting figure outlines and dress with long continuous strokes of sepia brown. Then, quickly, he drew the subject at full length in pencil, with all important details of costume and ornament. Comparison of a surviving costume with his portrait of the Indian who wore it shows that he recorded these details with fair accuracy. If he had only a few moments, he penciled lightning sketches for his amazing visual memory to fill out with form and color when he turned to them in the leisure of his winter painting room.

Landing at an abandoned camp site of the Puncas, he saw one of the few recorded exposures of an old Indian who had begged his tribe to leave him behind to die. The sticks of firewood and the half-picked buffalo bones beside the self-doomed veteran were not needed, for night would bring wolves and the mangling mercy of their fangs. Catlin was too moved to paint this heart-rending omen of the fate soon to fall on all prairie tribes. He could only shake the old man's hand.

Far behind now were the flowered forest fringes of fairy pear and plum. Behind too were the great grass levels that he painted on his deck easel by halving a canvas with a horizontal line and coloring the upper half louring gray and the lower vivid green. He had livened the dullness of that passage by weighing gigantic catfish, netting up specimens of floating pumice, and testing the turbid river's opacity to find that a silver coin could not be seen through an eighth of an inch of Missouri water.

This was not the mud floods carry. Here among towers of rainbow rock and the ashes of coal strata burnt out by prairie fires, the river ran so low that the shallow steamboat grounded in mid-channel. Catlin and seventeen of his fellow passengers landed and went across country to the Company's Fort Tecumseh, at the junction of the Teton and the Missouri. They reached the fort on the 23rd of May, and William Laidlaw, its uniformed captain or Burgois, quartered them within his 325 by 340 foot palisaded enclosure.

Hot-tempered Laidlaw, like most of the canny, fearless fur trade executives, was Scotch by birth, though only mildly Presbyterian. "He occupies spacious and comfortable apartments," Catlin noted, "which are well supplied with the comforts and luxuries of life and neatly and respectably conducted by a fine looking, modest, and dignified Sioux woman, the kind and affectionate mother of his little flock of pretty and interesting children."

Great plans were already afoot for the *Yellowstone's* arrival, with the distinguished and imperious Pierre Chouteau. In his honor the post was to be renamed Fort Pierre. Kenneth McKenzie, "King of the Upper Missouri," who outranked even Laidlaw in the company's hierarchy, had come down from Fort Union at the mouth of the Yellowstone, and the surrounding country was now a ranked city of the rain-soaked tepees of Sioux Indians gathered to see and to take part in the celebrations.

Catlin set up his easel in the painting room Laidlaw provided, and went to work on these warriors. His first sitter was their handsome high-chief, Ha-wan-je-tah, the One Horn. This self-made monarch told Catlin that he took his name from the single, horn-shaped shell he wore on a necklace. Because it had belonged to his father, it meant more to him than any of the trophies he had won in famous hunts and battles. Although he had taken many scalps and could outrun a buffalo and drive an arrow through its heart as he ran, the One Horn was an epicure in clothes. His white elkskin tunic, Catlin noted, "is fringed with a profusion of porcupine quills and scalp-locks; and his hair, which is very long and profuse, is divided into two parts, and lifted up and crossed, over the top of his head, with a simple tie, giving it somewhat the appearance of a Turkish turban."

Chouteau arrived on the Yellowstone on the 31st of May, heralded by cannon and excited Indian whoops. The tribesmen entertained him with games and horse races. He and McKenzie, Sandford, and Catlin were their guests of honor at a feast of dog meat held in a huge semi-circular tent formed by combining two tepees. Before the guests began their polite but gingerly sampling of that very special fare, the One Horn rose and addressed Major Sandford, the Government agent:

"My father—We offer you today, not the best we have—for we

have a plenty of good buffalo hump and marrow—but we give you our hearts in this feast—we have killed our faithful dogs to feed you —and the Great Spirit will seal our friendship. I have no more to say."

Though there was much smoking of peace pipes, Catlin's experiences in his painting room were far from serene. In spite of declarations by the medicine men "that those who were painted would soon die in consequence, and that these pictures which had life to a considerable degree in them, would live in the hands of white men after they were dead, and make them sleepless and endless trouble," all the Indians of note wanted their portraits taken, and taken before those of their rivals.

To expedite his portraying, the artist unwisely began to paint Mah-to-tchee-ga, Little Bear, in profile or half face. This gave Shon-ka, the Dog, a surly fellow of another band, an opening for a sneering insult:

"Mah-to-tchee-ga gets only half a face because he is but half a man."

"Who says that?"

"Shon-ka says it."

"When the Dog says it, let him prove it."

A few minutes after the sitting ended, two guns blazed at once; Little Bear fell, mortally wounded; the Dog fled; and the peaceful prairie was suddenly loud with war whoops and musketry.

Perhaps the clerk who kept the diary and logbook of Fort Pierre considered the murder of an Indian or two as routine. He merely recorded the day of that desperate encounter as a rainy 4th of June, on which the Indians "lifted their lodges and went off."

Their departure and the returning rain left Catlin with a free day to ply his pen on this account of Indian decamping:

"The chief sends his runners or criers through the village, a few hours before they are to start;—at the time announced, the lodge of the chief is seen flapping in the wind, a part of the poles having been taken out from under it; this is the signal, and in one minute, six hundred of them, which before had been strained tight and fixed, are seen waving and flapping in the wind, and in one minute more all are flat upon the ground. Their horses and dogs, of which they have a vast number, have all been secured upon the spot in readiness; and each one is speedily loaded with the burthen allotted to it, and ready to fall into the grand procession.

"For this strange cavalcade, preparation is made in the following manner: the poles of a lodge are divided into two bunches, and the little ends of each bunch fastened upon the shoulders or withers of a horse, a brace or pole is tied across, which keeps the poles in their respective places; and then upon that and the poles behind the horse, is placed the lodge or tent, which is rolled up and also numerous other articles of household and domestic furniture, and on top of all, two, three, and even (sometimes) four women and children! Each one of these horses has a conductress, who sometimes walks before and leads him, with a tremendous pack upon her own back; and at others she sits astride of his back, with a child, perhaps, at her breast, and another astride of the horse's back behind her; clinging to her waist with one arm, while it affectionately embraces a sneaking dog-pup in the other.

"In this way five or six hundred wigwams, with all their furniture may be seen drawn out for miles, creeping over the grass-covered plains of this country; and three times that number of men, on good horses, strolling along in front or in the flank . . . ; at least five times that number of dogs, which fall into the rank, and follow in the train and company of the women; and every cur of them, who is large enough, and not too cunning to be enslaved, is encumbered with a car or sled, on which he patiently drags his load—a part of the household goods and furniture of the lodge to which he belongs."

Catlin painted the fantastic procession, and the next day embarked again.

Above Fort Pierre the *Yellowstone* steamed past headlands and promontories that reminded his lively imagination of "some ancient and boundless city in ruins—ramparts, terraces, domes, towers, citadels and castles,—cupolas and magnificent porticoes, and here and there a solitary column and crumbling pedestal."

He gazed in ecstasy, and put his marvelings into floridly lyrical phrases, but when he reared his easel and began to ply his brush he disciplined his rapture and painted landscapes stern and strong, primitive as the backgrounds of early Flemish miniatures. Here he was indeed his only adviser, of no school known to his day. Reflecting upon canvas the meditations of his strange mind, he made massed naked hills a symbol of aloof inhuman majesty; and with greens that never grew from earthly roots he turned the quiet prairie grass into a carpet of warning and danger.

Grizzlies, antelope, wild sheep, and wilder men watched the *Yellowstone* warp its way unerringly among the spears of snags. Whenever the steamer neared a tepee town, her crew fired cannon and swivel guns and blew off terrifying clouds of shrieking steam. Then Catlin saw the Children of Nature turned to children of folly and fear, who tumbled over each other in flight, grasped the ground in terror, or desperately shot down their horses and dogs to appease the offended Great Spirit.

The flash of that gunpowder did not blind him to the Grecian beauty of Indian bodies shaped to lithe hardihood by hunting and war. But it revealed to him the pathetic, the grotesque, and the absurd in even the finest savagery. His Indians were human too, and he must always paint them so.

VI

FORT UNION

BY JULY 16th, when the *Yellowstone* moored at the mouth of her namesake river, Catlin had learned all the known lore of the Northwest's mounted tribes from Chouteau and Sandford, and from Kenneth McKenzie who captained Fort Union on the water's edge at the junction of the Missouri and Yellowstone rivers.

McKenzie had reason to be proud of the stronghold into which he led his three guests. Its palisades and stone bastions were strong, and its ample court contained some eight or ten log cabins, storehouses, and fur-baling sheds. Here he was master of fifty men, a hundred and fifty horses, and a vast wild empire. He had in his trading stocks blue, green, and scarlet Mackinack blankets, Scotch bonnets, frock coats, red flannel shirts, fancy calicoes, flints, fishhooks, files, scalping knives, tomahawks, kegs of plug tobacco, tons of powder and ball, hundreds of hawk bells, bushels of bright beads, 21,600 finger rings, and enough vermilion and verdigris to decorate a nation. He had little whisky or rum, but forty barrels of pure alcohol, the cheapest liquor to transport. He was too astute to have diluted stuff poled and hauled in keelboats two thousand miles upstream from Saint Louis.

As Pierre Chouteau was to return home on the *Yellowstone* as soon as the boat could be loaded with furs and re-stocked, he and McKenzie were in constant conference over inventories, far-Western extensions, and their top secret project. To beat the new Government ban against shipping intoxicants into the Indian country, the American Fur Company was about to buy and secretly ship to Fort Union

56

a complete distillery. Chouteau had come to plan with McKenzie for the installation of vats, boilers, etc., and for the local growing and grinding of corn and rye suitable for conversion into whisky.

As these matters were not for Catlin's ears, he was generously provided with private quarters and a painting room in one of the two towering bastions that stood out, foursquare, beyond opposite corners of the fort, so that their cannon ports and musketry embrasures flanked all its outer doors.

The sentry walk bracketed out all around his bastion at its upper floor level gave him a lofty view of green distances dark-flecked with buffalo, and of the strange colorful tepee life of half a dozen mounted tribes who had pitched their camps near the fort for their summer trading. Even at midnight those camps were aglow with lodge fires and loud with voices. Having no schedule of business, the Indians went to bed if and when they chose. As they never slapped or spanked their little offspring, every brown brat who woke and wailed for a bite of fat buffalo hump was orally dissuaded, but went on screaming until he got his titbit and set a hundred dogs howling.

When dawn turned shadows to shapes and hues, squaws and children stirred among the towering painted tepees of creamy white buffalo hide smoked to dry soft after rain. Of these, every family had two or three, as much as twenty-five feet high and big enough to seat forty men. Alike in their conic shape, smoke flaps and curtained entrances, these comfortable habitations were decorated from pegging to peak with bold symbolic designs of a heraldry ancient and obscure as anything that decked the pavilions of the Field of the Cloth of Gold.

Catlin had to wait and scribble away at his journal a long time before the warriors came out to display themselves. All Indian men used make-up, and it was the vermilion on their faces and bodies that got them the name of Redskins. In war their streaking and splotching of varied bright hues was a camouflage so effective that their unseen chiefs had to direct unseen followers by signals shrilled on whistles of turkey bone. Even an ordinary peacetime Indian, without a scalp to fringe his leggings, spent hours spitting on dry colors and, with his finger for a brush and his imagination for a mirror, patterned and re-patterned his person with circles, squares and chevrons of an aesthetic no white man could ever comprehend.

The sturdy, black-moccasined Blackfeet and tall Crows who finally emerged and mounted under Catlin's eye were not ordinary Indians, but a red élite, the Knighthood of the Western World. Little over a hundred years before, they had learned to lasso and tame the herds of wild horses that worked northward from Mexican ranges. In a century on horseback they had developed a mounted civilization of striking beauty, and unmatched ease. Horses put at their mercy im-mense wandering herds of buffalo that amply fed them, clothed them, robed them, and housed them in snug, lined tents of skin. Leisure from all labor but the chase left them free to make war like an Arthurian chivalry and to live in perpetual pageantry. No knight-at-arms could match the graceful beauty of a mounted Crow warrior six and a half feet tall galloping against the wind with his lance pennon and the fringes of his white leather jerkin and leggings fluttering, and his gayly-feathered hair streaming out ten feet behind.

The weapons, the garments, and the most humble implements of these tribes were adorned and garnished with paint and beads and dyed porcupine quills and feathers. Their fire-hardened shields of bull-hide were emblazoned with armorial charges. The helmets of their heroes were of ermine, surmounted by a pair of polished buffalo horns.

Heroes of such startling stamp were not, at first, eager to have even a thin layer of themselves transferred to canvas. But the persuasions of McKenzie, and a display of portraits that Catlin now carried with him as decoys, finally enticed them to the bastion studio.

Perched there on the breech of a twelve-pounder, he drew and painted, at incredible speed, everything and everybody; camps, implements, prairie vistas, warriors, squaws, and a little Indian boy too young to have a name. During the first few days he portrayed in oils Stu-mick-o-sucks, or the Buffalo's Back Fat; Pe-toh-pee-kiss, or the Eagle Ribs; Mix-ke-mote-skin-na, or the Iron Horn; Tcha-aes-sa-ko-mah-oee, or the Bear's Child; Princess Eeh-nis-kim, or the Crystal Stone; and half a dozen others.

Though a number of these oils are full length, and show details of ornate costume, his eagerness to hurry on to more sitters made him return to the half-length portraits that are his typical work. Quick intelligence had long since warned him against the temptation to generalize or type his subjects, or to romanticize on canvas. Every Indian was an individual, and Catlin's skill in defining and recording that individuality was his true genius.

To save the precious paints that he had carried so far, and must carry so much further in frail bladders, he spread his pigments smooth in the thinnest possible film. This method also hastened drying, and enabled him the sooner to take the finished canvas from its stretcher and pack it away.

Probably because he was losing track of who was who in his rapidly growing gallery of Indian pictures, Catlin had with him now a pack of printed certificate forms to affix to the back of each new canvas. When filled out, a typical certificate read:

No. 131. Pe-toh-pee-kiss (the Eagle Ribs). I hereby certify that this portrait was painted from the life, at Fort Union, mouth of Yellowstone, in the year 1832, by George Catlin, and that the Indian sat in the costume in which it is painted.

> John F. A. Sandford,
> United States Indian Agent.

Though Catlin believed that these certificates "signed by Indian Agents, officers of the Army or other persons who were present when the picture was painted," would remain inseparably attached to his works, they have all been removed, and only one unattached sample has survived. Some others that were photographed in 1885 indicate that they never were consistently filled out, and either lacked numbers entirely, or were numbered out of turn. A picture painted at Fort Union, only a few days after No. 131, was numbered 189.

After his day's work in the bastion or in the tepee towns outside, Catlin joined the select little dinner party in McKenzie's private quarters. Like Laidlaw at Fort Pierre, Kenneth McKenzie wore a uniform, and lived, ruled and entertained in the style of a feudal Highland laird. His chief assistant and companion was a mysterious Mr. Hamilton, an English gentleman "of the most pleasing and entertaining conversation, whose mind seems to be a complete store-house of ancient and modern literature and art." Reputed to be a nobleman in exile for his romantic wrongdoings, Hamilton, whose real name was Archibald Palmer, dressed in the latest London fashions, insisted on his morning bath, imported good Madeira and Port, called the Indians beasts, and once threw into the fire his best colored silk handkerchief because a Redskin had touched it.

McKenzie, a master hunter and incomparable horseman, took his guest on a buffalo chase, as the meat houses in the post had been emptied to provision the *Yellowstone's* homeward voyage. Mounted, and coatless, with bandanas tied round their heads and waists, powder cartridges in their waistcoat pockets, and half a dozen bullets in their mouths, the hunting party stalked up close to the grazing buffalo herd. When the huge beasts detected them and ran, the hunters charged into the thundering dust cloud that hid their quarry. Horses, bulls, and cows were soon mingled in a flying mass. In a headlong run of one mile McKenzie recharged his rifle four times, selected five fat young cows, and shot each of them through the heart.

Catlin's one shot broke the shoulder of a tremendous old bull. From the saddle he sketched the helpless monster's defiance: "swelling with rage;—his mouth open, and his horrid rage hissing in streams of smoke and blood from his mouth and through his nostrils." Catlin turned the sketches made on this hunt into primitively crude but powerful oils, the first authentic buffalos in art.

All this high pitched activity left him little time for journalizing. In what he had meant to make a full day-by-day diary, he wrote: "Impressions . . . of the most vivid kind are rapidly and indelibly made by the fleeting incidents of savage life, and for the mind that can ruminate upon them with pleasure there are abundant materials clinging to it for its endless entertainment in driving the quill. . . . The mind susceptible of such impressions catches volumes of incidents which are easy to write; it is but to unfold a web which the fascinations of this shorn country and its allurements have spun over the soul."

"Impressions . . . impressions . . ." Not the mere thing, but the meaning and significance of the thing to the susceptible working mind. In writing, as in painting, he honestly reared a mountain to show the importance of a hill. If his work sometimes outruns fact, it is to keep abreast of truth. The candid camera and the exact court stenographer are poor historians of those vast moments on the peaks or in the abyss of life. Catlin was just such a secretary as the Recording Angel employs.

From his bastion he watched another feud flare into a pitched battle between Knisteneaux and Blackfoot warriors.

"And then," he wrote, "I saw what I never before saw in my life —I saw a 'medicine man' performing his mysteries over a dying man."

Through a huge crowd that had hushed, drawn back, and opened for him, the fantastic healer approached the dying Blackfoot warrior "with his body in a crouching position, with a slow and tilting step— his body and head were entirely covered with the skin of a yellow bear, the head of which (his own head being inside it) served as a mask; the huge claws of which also were dangling on his wrists and ankles; in one hand he shook a frightful rattle, and in the other brandished his medicine spear or magic wand; to the rattling din and discord of all of which, he added the wild and startling jumps and

61

yelps of the Indian, and the horrid and appalling grunts, and snarls, and growls of the grizzly bear, in ejaculatory and guttural incantations to the Good and Bad Spirits, in behalf of his patient, who was rolling and groaning in the agonies of death, whilst he was dancing around him, jumping over him, and pawing him about, and rolling him in every direction." This went on for half an hour before the Blackfoot died.

Catlin later obtained the medicine-man's outfit for his collection, and described it in detail: "It is the strangest medley and mixture, perhaps, of the mysteries of the animal and vegetable kingdoms that was ever seen. Besides the skin of the yellow bear (which being almost an anomaly in that country, is out of the regular order of nature . . .), there are attached to it the skins of many animals, which are also anomalies or deformities, . . . and there are also the skins of snakes, and frogs, and bats,—beaks, and toes and tails of birds,—hoofs of deer, goats and antelopes. . . ."

The Indian name for such a combined priest and healer was translated into "médecin" by the French fur traders. In its English form "medicine" came to mean any mysterious or unaccountable practice, rite or taboo of the tribesmen. Catlin's art soon made him aware of the universality of the mysterious among these ancient and profoundly religious peoples. Its ever-present symbol was the medicine bag carried at all times by adult males.

The significance of this strange equivalent of Oriental talismans, or our Christian medals was, Catlin observed, "the key of Indian life and Indian character. These bags are constructed of the skins of animals, of birds, or of reptiles, and ornamented and preserved in a thousand different ways, as suits the taste or freak of the person who constructs them. These skins are generally attached to some part of the clothing of the Indian, or carried in his hand—they are oftentimes decorated in such a manner as to be exceedingly ornamental to his person, and generally are stuffed with grass or moss, or something of the kind; and generally without drugs or medicines in them, as they are religiously closed and sealed, and seldom, if ever, to be opened. I find that every Indian in his primitive state carries his medicine-bag in some form or other, to which he pays the greatest homage, and to which he looks for safety and protection through life—and, in fact, it might almost be called a species of idolatry; for it would seem in some instances as if he actually worshipped it. Feasts are often made, and dogs and horses sacrificed, to a man's medicine; and days, and even weeks of fasting and penance of various kinds are often suffered, to appease his medicine, which he imagines he has in some way offended. . . .

"The manner in which this curious and important article is instituted is this: a boy, at the age of fourteen or fifteen years . . . wanders away from his father's lodge, and absents himself for the space of two or three, and sometimes even four or five days; lying on the ground in some remote or secluded spot, crying to the Great Spirit, and fasting the whole time. During this period of peril and abstinence, when he falls asleep, the first animal, bird, or reptile, of which he dreams (or pretends to have dreamed, perhaps), he considers the Great Spirit has designated for his mysterious protector through life. He then returns home to his father's lodge, and relates his success; and after allaying his thirst, and satiating his appetite, he sallies forth with weapons or traps, until he can procure the animal or bird, the skin of which he preserves entire, and ornaments it according to his own fancy, and carries it with him through life, for 'good luck,' as his strength in battle—and in death his guardian Spirit; that is buried with him . . . to conduct him safe to the beautiful hunting grounds. . . .

"The value of the medicine-bag to the Indian is beyond all price; for to sell it, or give it away, would subject him to such signal disgrace in his tribe, that he could never rise above it; and again his superstition would stand in the way of any such disposition of it, for he considers it a gift of the Great Spirit. An Indian carries his medicine-bag into battle, and trusts to it for his protection; and if he loses it thus, when fighting ever so bravely for his country, he suffers a disgrace scarcely less than that which occurs when he sells it or gives it away; his enemy carries it off and displays it to his own people as a trophy; whilst the loser is cut off of the respect that is due to other young men of his tribe, and forever subjected to the degrading epithet of 'a man without medicine,' or 'he who has lost his medicine;' until he can replace it again, which can only be done, by rushing into battle and plundering one from an enemy whom he slays by his own hand. This done, his medicine is restored, and he is reinstated again in the estimation of his tribe; and even higher than before, for such is called the best of medicine, or 'Medicine Honourable.'"

Before his wholly materialistic frontier associates, and even in his own conventional asides, Catlin treated such mysteries lightly, even flippantly; but when he wrote seriously of them, the rush and flow of his subconscious words drowned out all smug and intellectually conceited questioning. Then he realized that he was dealing with a devout civilization immeasurably older than his own, and in many ways wiser; a civilization that was, except for its warrior cult, almost Utopian. These Indians were pious without priests; just and honest without laws or jails; wise and eloquent without schools. They had no rich or poor; but shared, and shared alike, in good times and bad. They could control their tongues, and the appetites of their bodies. Their children did not die in childhood, nor grow up sickly, feeble-minded, hunchbacked, or in any wise deformed. Above all, they were a happy people.

It was hard for an educated American of Catlin's time to admit that science and progress and education were not the only roads to happiness. But now he began to muse on the matter, and to make comparisons between white men and Indians:

"What degree of happiness these sons of Nature may attain to in the world, in their own way; or in what proportion they may relish the pleasures of life, compared to the sum of happiness belonging to civilized society . . . I cannot undertake to decide at this time. I would say this much, however, that if the thirst for knowledge has entailed everlasting miseries on mankind from the beginning of the world; if refined and intellectual pains increase in proportion to our intellectual pleasures, I do not see that we gain much advantage over them on that score; and judging from the full-toned enjoyment that beams from their happy faces, I would give it as my opinion, that their lives were much more happy than ours. . . ."

Pacing the high parapet, in morning mists that omened a fine day for his departure, Catlin almost envied the Scottish lord of this cotton-wood castle and these green realms greater than many a European kingdom. McKenzie's new heraldry, a gun and six scalps, was blazoned over the barred and cannon-guarded gateway. Catlin himself was no more romantic than the Scotsman now streaking in, like a buck-skin centaur, on the finest buffalo horse the prairies could breed.

Here was another man after his own heart, competent, daring, aristocratic, with scientific interests and a taste for good pictures. Of course Catlin had painted him, and refused payment for the portrait.

Together the two friends entered a log-built warehouse converted into a museum for McKenzie's mineral collection and Indian curios. Catlin's recent paintings were to hang there until the next company keelboat took them to Saint Louis. Two of the best had been purchased by his liberal host, for more than the price of the skiff and supplies required for the down-river journey.

Pointing to racks of rich Indian costumes, McKenzie said in his precise burred accent, "Pick what you like from these. I will send it on with the outfits of those fellows you painted. They will sell them for a dram or two when their throats get dry enough."

Coming out among the bunkhouses and fur presses, Catlin was surprised to see the clerk Bogard, and Ba'tiste, a French Canadian free-trapper, sitting on their leather packs in the trading shed by the gatehouse wall. "Company for your voyage to Saint Louis," McKenzie explained. "They were going down anyway. You may be grateful for a couple of good marksmen when those damned Riccarees see you. Keep in midstream through their country."

For weeks Catlin had planned to paddle down through all the Indian country alone, but he accepted these lively and amusing companions with good grace. Their eagerness to get back to waterfront bars and civilized wantoning sent the laden skiff flying downstream. Its owner-captain, pistoled and whiskered like a pirate, steered, sketched, and jotted down such stories as only a Ba'tiste, in Indian garb and gewgaws, could tell. From his absurdly mixed French-English Catlin learned a good deal about Indian ladies which he delicately abstained from writing home. Ba'tiste had played their favorite party game of kissing under the buffalo robe while all the assembled company applauded and urged something more. He had heard them, in mixed company, comment frankly on his personal parts and tell stories that would bring blushes to a cavalry messroom. Indians, he said, were really as excitable and pleasure-loving as his own race; noisy, bragging, amatory, practical jokers who talked all day and danced, sang, and whooped half the night. Their braves showed no chivalry even to their own sisters, and no squaw who was not very old and very ugly ever ventured out alone. To rob a neighbor tribe, to carry off its women and knock its men on the head, was, he believed, the one Indian ambition.

Catlin did not record such comments. They were already well known, in gross exaggerations. Remembering the shadow of death in the dark eyes of Clark's Indian delegations, he kept the Roman maxim, "De mortuis nil nisi bonum."

VII

MANDANS

AFTER several pleasant days and a most unpleasant night when a family of grizzly bears raided their camp and chewed Catlin's precious paints, the three travelers sighted the palisades and round rooftops of the People of the Pheasants, whom traders called Mandans. Some five or six hundred of their dogs, who could and did mix unnoticed with the native wolves, rushed to the riverside and howled themselves hoarse at the strange skiff. So Catlin, Ba'tiste, and Bogard paddled on to Fort Clark, the Fur Company's Mandan post.

Its Captain, James Kipp, a giant, a superb horseman, and the first white man to master the elusive Mandan language, took Catlin in as his guest. Like Laidlaw and McKenzie he had "married" into the tribe he traded with. Like them too, he collected Indian relics and curios. During those midsummer days of 1832, his introductions and explanations enabled Catlin to paint and record some of the strangest scenes and incidents in American history.

Some of the Mandans were of fair complexion, with soft hair and blue, gray, or hazel eyes. Many others had, from childhood, hair of bright silver gray. Though small in stature, they were a fine-looking people, erect, supple and graceful. The men combed their long-haired plumage straight back and let it hang behind them in two flat plaits, painted with bands of vermilion and permanently stuck together with glue. The women too wore their hair long, but kept it smooth and shining by oiling it and dressing it with rough combs made by fitting a trimmed porcupine's tail over a kind of wooden or bone dibble.

67

Like the Crow and Blackfoot women, they parted their hair in the middle and painted the crease with a vivid vermilion line.

Every morning during the summer, they and their young daughters swam in the river above the village, while armed warriors guarded their nude privacy on the encircling plateau. The men and boys also swam daily, and afterwards oiled their bodies with bear's fat and rubbed them to a bronze gloss with soft wash-leather pads. All the tribe were amphibious, and masters of what we now term the crawl stroke, which Catlin was the first to describe. For winter, and for sickness, they had hot vapor baths or sudatories on the bank of the river, into whose chill current they plunged after their aromatic, herbscented steaming.

Instead of the usual birch-bark canoes, capricious and graceful, they used wicker-built boats covered with buffalo hide, and round as the seagoing bowl of the Wise Men of Gotham. These they propelled by reaching the paddle out ahead and pulling it through the water toward them.

They made earthenware bowls too—though without the potter's wheel—and fired them in kilns dug in the hillside. They ground trade glassware to powder, and from it made blue beads which they valued above those the traders sold.

Mandans dressed richly, but neatly; the women in fringed smocks of embroidered doeskin, trimmed with ermine; and the men in deerskin tunics and tight leggings, fringed with scalp locks and gay with porcupine-quill embroidery. Over one shoulder and under the other, the warriors draped short robes cut from the woolly hides of young buffalo, painted on the skin-side with pictorial records of the wearer's great hunts and battles. Their heads were decked with lofty plumage of ravens and war eagles. "There is occasionally," Catlin noted, "a chief or warrior of so extraordinary renown that he is allowed to wear horns on his head-dress, which give to his aspect a strange and majestic effect. These are made of about a third part of the horns of a buffalo bull; the horn having been split from end to end, . . . shaved thin and light, and highly polished. These are attached to the top of the head-dress on each side; . . . rising out of a mat of ermine skins and tails . . . and by an ingenious motion of the head, which is so slight as to be almost imperceptible—they are made to balance to and fro, and sometimes, one backward and the other forward like a horse's ears. . . ."

As the Mandans were a small tribe, beset by powerful foes, they trained from childhood to defend their riverside fortress. Catlin saw little boys shooting straws in sham battles; and he painted archery trials where eight arrows were in the air at once from a single swiftly drawn bow. Such machine-gun shooting was needed when the tribal hunters raced their mounts among flying buffalos.

They were not wholly a hunting tribe like the Blackfeet. The squaws cultivated fields of a dwarf corn that eared no longer than a man's thumb. They stored their grain underground in jug-shaped cellars, along with dried squash and fruits and a kind of wild turnip.

Their life was essentially urban, in their weird palisaded town of earthen houses that looked like overturned bowls. Crowded together higgledy-piggledy in the trodden brown enclosures, with barely room for a rider to squeeze between their steep clay walls, these habitations were bigger and better engineered than anything America knew until the Pennsylvania Dutch began building barns. They were round houses of a single lofty room, forty to sixty feet in diameter. Their inner walls were of upright logs, set close together in the ground and cut off at head-height to support a tight raftering of long poles sloping upward to a central opening that served both as chimney and skylight. A square frame of timbers borne by four stout posts carried the small upper ends of this raftering and the great weight of the domed roof of waterproof clay.

On fine days these domed roofs were the perch of the whole tribe, and their countless dogs. On them too were skins spread to dry, sleds, pottery, round boats, and buffalo skulls. From tall poles reared by the vestibuled doorways hung scalps, and shields, and sacrificial strips of colored trade-cloth.

Catlin found the floors of these lodges "so hardened by use, and swept so clean, that they have almost a polish and would scarcely soil the whitest linen." In the center of each floor, under the smoke hole, was a round sunken hearth, curbed with stone. On its embers always simmered a pot of buffalo stew. The surrounding level was spread with rush mats and skin rugs on which the family and their guests reclined. Ranged round the outer wall were curtained beds like pullman berths, with space between for chests and lockers and a peg-studded pole used as a hanger for garments, quivers, headdresses, etc. The combined spring and mattress of the beds was a buffalo robe, stretched while green over a pole frame, and drawn taut by drying. The hair-side, turned uppermost, made a soft warm lower blanket. Another buffalo robe served as coverlet, and a third was folded into a pillow. The bed curtains were fringed, beaded, and embroidered, or painted with hieroglyphic designs. By the bed of every man in the tribe hung the horned head of a buffalo, made into a mask for him to wear in the buffalo dances.

Though the women and the medicine men made a great outcry against Catlin's art, which apparently divided one man into two, he painted many Mandan portraits. "All married up" as he was, he must have been tempted to take little Mint, the lovely gray-haired maiden, in exchange for his picture of her. His favorite sitter was Chief Mah-to-toh-pa, the Four Bears. He dined with this striking Mandan in one of the largest lodges.

"I was," he wrote, "seated on a very handsome robe, most ingeniously painted and garnished with hieroglyphics; and he seated himself gracefully on another one at a little distance from me; with the feast prepared in several dishes, resting on a beautiful rush mat, which was placed between us."

After the chief had lighted his pipe and shared a few whiffs of it with his guest, he cut a slice from the rib-roast and threw it into the fire as a sacrifice. He signaled Catlin to begin, and silently watched him eat; for a western chief never ate with his guests, but sat by and waited on them. Then he filled his pipe with k'nick-k'neck, or bark of red willow mixed with shavings of castor, dusted it with powdered buffalo dung that served as tinder for easy lighting, and the two friends settled themselves to smoke and converse by pantomime and gestures of sign language.

After his daily labors, Catlin wandered out to the oddest of graveyards. The Mandans laid their robe-wrapped dead aloft on platforms of poles and sticks, out of reach of dogs and wolves. When these scaffolds rotted away, relatives of the dead buried the fallen bones, but not the bleached and naked skulls. These they added to immense family circles of older skulls, all facing inward, on the open prairie.

"There are several of these 'Golgothas' or circles, of twenty or thirty feet in diameter," Catlin noted; "and in the centre of each ring or circle is a little mound three feet high, on which uniformly rests two buffalo skulls (a male and a female); and in the centre of the little mound is erected a 'medicine pole,' about twenty feet high, supporting many curious articles of mystery and superstition. . . .

"Every one of these skulls is placed upon a bunch of wild sage, which has been pulled and placed under it. The wife knows the skull of her husband or her child; . . . and there seldom passes a day that she does not visit it, with a dish of the best cooked food . . . which she sets before the skull. . . .

"There is scarcely an hour in a pleasant day, but more or less of these women may be seen sitting or lying by the skull of their child or husband, talking to it in the most pleasant and endearing language . . . and seemingly getting an answer back. It is not infrequently the case, that the woman brings her needle-work with her, spending the greater part of the day."

On the advice of Sandford, sub-agent for the Mandans, Catlin had come in time for annual rites, ferocious and obscene. Through Kipp's influence, and because of his own mysterious calling, he was allowed to enter the most sacred circle and the dark temple of tortures.

Mandan religion envisioned an eternally frozen Hell and a warm and luxurious Heaven. But even in Heaven where the Good Spirit dwells, there were devils continually tricking the souls of the blest into transgressions which sent them back for another term in Hell. To please the Good Spirit, and to appease the Bad One, the tribe annually went through four days of ceremonial dances and cruel tortures. There were, Catlin learned from Kipp and his Mandan lady, three purposes in these rituals: celebration of the subsiding of the Flood; invocation of fertility in the buffalo herds; proof of the manhood and endurance of young warriors. As no Indians kept calendar days, the date of this triple ceremonial was determined by the first full growth of the willow leaves. For it was their tradition that their sacred bird, the turtle dove, brought a green willow bough back over a world of waters to the Big Canoe. Noah's Ark had become for them a huge hooped wooden barrel that stood on end in a large level open space in the middle of their town. By it was the temple, or mystery lodge.

The ceremonies opened with the arrival from the prairie of a naked man, painted white, robed in white wolfskins, helmeted with a bonnet of ravens' skins, and bearing a large pipe. Announced as Nu-mohk-muck-a-nah, the first and only man, he opened the mystery lodge and then visited every house in the village, relating the story of the flood that he, and he alone, had survived by landing his big canoe on a mountain peak. Every household gave him presents, which were thrown over the cliff into deep water at the end of the rituals.

"During the first night," Catlin recorded, "no one could tell where he slept; and every person, both old and young, and dogs, and all living things were kept within doors, and dead silence reigned every-where. On the next morning at sunrise, however, he made his appearance again, and entered the *medicine-lodge* and at his heels all the young men who were candidates for the self-tortures. . . . About fifty young men entered the lists, and as they went into the sacred lodge, each one's body was chiefly naked, and covered with clay of different colours; some were red, others were yellow, and some were covered with white clay, giving them the appearance of white men. Each one of them carried in his right hand his *medicine-bag*—on his left arm, his shield of bull's hide—in his left hand, his bow and arrows, with the quiver slung on his back."

During that and the two following days these young men fasted and prayed in the medicine lodge, while their brothers danced the fantastic Bull Dance at regular intervals around the Big Canoe outside, to time kept by four old red-painted fellows drumming on leather water bags. There was continuous shrill chanting, and chatter of rattles, and thunderous applause from the whole gathered tribe.

The Bull Dancers "were eight men, with the entire skins of buffalos thrown over their backs, and with the horns and hoofs and tails remaining on; their bodies in a horizontal position, enabling them to imitate the actions of the buffalo, while they were looking out of its eyes as through a mask."

These eight were painted all over with similar designs in either red, black or yellow. Each held a rattle and a long white wand, and carried on his back a sheaf of green willow boughs. With them danced four wardens of the Big Canoe, two painted charcoal-black, and two vermilion-red. These wore kilts and headdresses of eagle's quills and ermine.

"The supernumeraries or other characters who play their parts in this grand spectacle are numerous," Catlin noted. "By the side of the big canoe are seen two men with the skins of grizzly bears thrown over them, using the skins as a mask over their heads. These ravenous animals are continually growling and threatening to devour everything before them, and interfering with the forms of the religious ceremony. To appease them, the women are continually bringing and placing before them dishes of meat, which are as often snatched up and carried to the prairie by two men, whose bodies are painted black and their heads white, whom they call bald eagles. . . . These are again chased upon the plain by a hundred or more small boys, who are naked, with their bodies painted yellow and their heads white, whom they call *Clabris* or antelopes; who at length get the food away from them and devour it."

During the last of these dances, a yelling devil-man, painted black, and dappled with small white circles, zigzagged down the prairie "like a boy in pursuit of a butterfly" and dashed into the screaming crowd of squaws around the dance floor, sliding on the ground ahead of him a sinister eight-foot wand, tipped by a red ball, with which he threatened the innocent ladies. Though anthropological detail was in those days usually printed in Latin, Catlin employed an Indian vocabulary to add that the devil-man also had "Ung gee ah waheea notch taheks tcha, ung gee an ung hutch tow a tow ah ches menny," and "Ung gee ah to to wun nee, ahkst to wan ee eigh's taw." With all this formidable equipment, unfit for representation on a Victorian canvas, the black devil was, however, stopped in his tracks by a wave of the medicine man's pipe, amidst loud general applause of "matrons, and even of their tender-aged and timid daughters, whose education had taught them to receive the *moral* of these scenes without the shock of impropriety."

Turning now to the Bull Dancers, the black monster followed four of the eight in turn, "placing himself in the attitude of a buffalo—hi ung ee a wahkstia," etc., "to deafening shouts which pealed from every mouth in the multitude, who were all praying to the Great Spirit to send them buffalos to supply them with food during the season."

Exhausted by these simulated exertions, the devil was set upon by the women with such rudeness that he began to cry. One of the tawny maenads snatched away his wand and broke it over her knee. Others broke it into smaller bits and threw them at him as he bolted across the prairie, pursued by a female mob who cuffed and kicked him and pelted him with clods.

The tortures followed. To eerie music, in a setting of grave solemnity and feathered finery, the fifty young men who had been fasting were hauled aloft in the medicine lodge by cords attached to wooden skewers thrust through cuts made with a saw-edged knife under the skin of their breasts, shoulders, and thighs. Their quivers and shields, and horned buffalo skulls were then hung on the bloody skewers. So soon as a victim fainted dead away and dropped the medicine bag in his hand, he was lowered by the men on the roof and left on the ground to revive. Recovering a little strength, he crawled over to a hatchet-man, who chopped off the little finger of his left hand on a buffalo-skull block.

When six or eight were thus mutilated, they were led out to the open space around the Big Canoe. There thongs were tied round their wrists. Two young men seized each victim by these thongs and raced him between them, round the circle, with the skulls and quiver attached to the remaining skewers clattering behind. If he fell, he was dragged on until these weights pulled the skewers through his flesh and skin and dropped off. This "last race" ended with the circle strewn with apparently lifeless bodies.

Under the skylight of a vast empty lodge there between the cloudy river of treacheries and the wolf-haunted prairie, Catlin painted four terrible scenes from these diabolic performances. Fevered by excitement and oncoming illness, he made them hectic with splashes of queer discordant color that startle the prevailing somber brown. Putting aside anatomy and just proportion, he crowded them with caricatured monsters and maniac grotesques of men. Like colored stills from a movie of Hell's frolicking, they create an impression of savage wildness and action that is unforgettable.

The traditionally prescribed forms of the ceremonies he had witnessed, and of other customs for which he could discover no reasonable explanation, led Catlin to believe that the Mandan culture was the remnant of an ancient declining civilization, rather than a middle stage in the development of a new one. The prevalence of fair hair and blue and gray eyes among the Mandans, and their biblical legend of the Flood, indicated to him a European source of both their customs and their blood. They paddled round boats very like Welsh coracles, and some of their words sounded like the words he had heard among Welsh-speaking miners in the Pennsylvania coal country. On these evidences, he decided to suggest to the learned world that these strange Indians were descendants of a Prince Madoc and his followers who sailed from Wales in the Middle Ages into the West and were never heard of again. Unfortunately for ethnology, as well as for the Mandans, smallpox was brought to the upper Missouri by crewmen of the steamboat *St. Peter's* in the summer of 1837. The few Mandans who survived it scattered among surrounding tribes, and their strange culture and customs perished.

In a neighboring and somewhat similar village of the Minatarees, the "People of the Willows" were holding their annual feast and dance of the Green Corn. Catlin got a picture of it, and another spirited one of a great mounted hunt or "surround" of buffalos.

"In this grand turmoil," he wrote, "a cloud of dust was soon raised, which in parts obscured the throng where the hunters were galloping their horses around and driving the whizzing arrows or their long lances into the hearts of these noble animals; which in many instances, becoming infuriated with deadly wounds in their sides, erected their shaggy manes over their blood-shot eyes and furiously plunged forward at the sides of their assailants' horses, sometimes goring them to death at a lunge, and putting their dismounted riders to flight for their lives; sometimes their dense crowd was opened, and the blinded horsemen, too intent on their prey amidst the cloud of dust, were hemmed and wedged in amongst the crowding beasts, over whose backs they were obliged to leap for security, leaving their horses to the fate that might await them in the results of this mighty war."

When all the hundreds of animals in the herd were down, the hunters went among them afoot, reclaiming the arrows which bore their private marks. Out then streamed the women, children, and dogs, to skin and dismember this prodigious prey, and to carry and drag it, like a procession of ants, back to the village.

Catlin's painting of that savage, milling "surround," with mounted spearman and bowman wildly riding the right flank of their flying prey, became the pattern for all later pictures of Indian buffalo hunts. In movement, and in crude power, it was never surpassed.

Many Minataree warriors had died in their losing wars, and their village was peopled largely by man-hungry squaws, "beautiful and voluptuous looking." Catlin's Bogard and Ba'tiste were not notable resisters of these temptations which he, in his letters home, ignored. But a swarm of lively and mischievous naked girls, swimming around his boat and whirling and rocking it, pleased his artistic eye.

An attack of the pleurisy and cough which had sent him to Virginia in 1829 returned, and for several days he lay deathly sick in a lower Mandan settlement, with the greasy body of a visiting Riccaree as a pillow. Then, at his insistence, Bogard and Ba'tiste helped him into the skiff and headed it again downstream. Ba'tiste's boat-songs and the lap of the water lulled him into healing sleep. He was able to aim a steady rifle when the Riccarees threatened, and to examine pitted sites of earlier Mandan towns. The Fort Pierre diarist recorded his arrival there on August 14th, and his departure for Saint Louis two days later.

VIII

THE ORIGINAL WILD WEST SHOW

THAT was the Cholera Year. Though most of the thousands of agony-twisted dead were buried now, and burning tar barrels were no longer pouring out their vain smudges in the streets of Western towns, travel on crowded steamboats was still unwise. So Catlin stayed on, in and around Saint Louis, signing Indian treaties along with General Clark, and painting Black Hawk and his chief warriors, then prisoners at Jefferson Barracks.

Lieutenant Jefferson Davis, who had fought against them alongside High-Private Abraham Lincoln, watched and admired as Catlin painted these proud men—riveted to chains and cannon balls which they held up and said, "Make us so, and show us to the White Father."

"Black Hawk is an Indian," their old leader cried. "He has done nothing of which an Indian ought to be ashamed. He has fought the battles of his country against the white man, who came year after year to cheat his people and take away their lands. You know the cause of our making war. It is known to all white men. They ought to be ashamed of it. The white men despise the Indians and drive them from their homes. But the Indians are not deceitful. Indians do not steal. Black Hawk is satisfied. He will go to the world of spirits contented. He has done his duty. His father will meet and reward him. The white men do not scalp the heads, but they do worse, they poison the heart. It is not pure with them. . . ."

Indian summer, most serene of Midwest seasons, was now

sharpening silver knives of frost. The Indian burial hills above Saint Louis levee stood stark under leafless persimmon trees. The furs of the year were in, and the trappers out again for their frost-ripened harvest. It was time to go; for the big steamboats were going, to ply the lower river until spring. Leaving his upper Missouri collection with Benjamin O'Fallon, Catlin embarked for the East.

He had worked and traveled too strenuously, and sustained excitements beyond his strength. Arriving with the New Year in Pittsburgh, his lungs inflamed again, and for a month he lay desperately ill. But he was cheered that his Indian letters published in the *Commercial Advertiser* were so well received and so widely read.

Clara had made the sickroom bright with extravagant potted flowers, and hung its walls with his colorful Indian curios from Fort Union. Even more pleasant than her quiet company were his plans for returning with the spring to McKenzie's verdant realm. This time he would paddle up the Yellowstone with the trappers, far up to the country of the Rocky Mountain tribes.

In the midst of this dream-devising, he realized the implications of a hint from a Western friend that what he had published in the *Commercial Advertiser* about the upper Missouri fur trade was not likely to please Pierre Chouteau.

Instantly Catlin sent Chouteau a wise and discreet explanation and followed it to Saint Louis as soon as his anxious lady would let him travel. The great Pierre was delighted, as always, to see him, and laughed off the *Commercial Advertiser* letters. But when Catlin turned their talk to the steamer *Yellowstone's* approaching trip up to Union, with her new sister ship, the *Assiniboin,* the master trader grew grave. "There ees bad news from Laidlaw," he said in his smooth accented English. "Thet affair of ze Dawg. Much bad blood toward you, Catalaine. Relateeves of ze daid man you painted sideways say you made his death. Zay wait to keel you.

My Company cannot take ze reesk to let you go up-reevair again."

With all his courtesy, Chouteau was absolute in his refusal, as he had good reason to be. The steamer *Assiniboin,* this trip, would be loaded with a complete distillery. The last thing the Company wished was to display her cargo to an Indian enthusiast who was already the correspondent of a liberal New York paper.

Hoping against hope, Catlin lingered in Saint Louis, retouching Indian portraits and painting copies for Clark and Benjamin O'Fallon, until he learned that the only guests the Company's boats were likely to carry up-river were safe German-speaking foreigners, the Prince Maximilian of Neuweid, and a Swiss artist, Karl Bodmer.

Deep in despondency, he went to General Clark for advice. "Cat," said the old man sternly, "this will be the worst year in Indian history. Cholera and smallpox together! Go back to that neglected lady of yours and get well. Frame those pictures at Ben's and show the East what Indians really are. Speak out for them. You can. I need your help—in a losing fight."

The *Pittsburgh Gazette* for April 23rd that year printed the following report:

Mr. Catlin.—This Gentleman has, during the past week, frequently exhibited a portion of his extensive collection of Indian portraits, landscapes, and other paintings. . . . The total number which he commenced during his expedition is very large; most of them are yet in an unfinished state, he only having had sufficient leisure to secure correct likenesses of the various living subjects of his pencil and the general features of the scenery which he had selected, the back grounds and details being reserved for the labours of a future time. Those which he has publicly exhibited here exceed one hundred.

Still pallid and frail, and no longer at ease in frock coat and cravat, Catlin had watched the first-nighters of his first show there in Pittsburgh enter from a street gloomed by smoke of foundries and forges. He had seen them smile at his strange paintings and nod knowingly to their companions. His good ear had picked up their comments—

6. *Shon-ka-ki-he-ga, the Horse Chief, head chief of the Grand Pawnees.* See p. 46.

7. *Wuk-mi-ser, Corn, a Sioux warrior.*

"uncouth" . . . "crude" . . . "absurd." In the front row his father had angrily thumped the floor with the stick he leaned on, and Clara had bitten her trembling lip. But her unfaltering eyes of love had been full of Clark's assurance: "Speak out for them. You can."

So he had spoken, as he always spoke to her, kindly, sincerely, simply, trustingly. He had called from the flat canvases living Indians who laughed at little jokes and practiced little vanities and wept when their little brown sons lied. He had conjured up green dangers of prairie days and blue dangers of prairie nights, lovely, but loud with wolves and the thousand answering watchdogs that guarded the tepees of an assembled tribe. He had pleaded with incidents, and argued with whimsical anecdotes when the chastened faces before him grew too sad. He had shown them what Indians really are. And the reporter had written: "His modest and unassuming deportment—the simple and unostentatious manner of his explanations and narrations, were perfectly satisfactory guarantees of every assertion which he made."

But his pictures should speak for themselves, as they assuredly would when completed. Packing them on an Ohio boat, he and Clara slipped away without leaving an address. Her brother Walter, now a Cincinnati publisher, had engaged rooms for them at the Pearl Street House in that thriving river town. There they lodged until fall in such retired seclusion that even Catlin's Cincinnati friends thought he was again on the prairies. In spirit he was, and Clara with him. While she sewed her fine seams in chiffon and taffeta, or merely admired and listened, he described to her the costume details and the backgrounds his tireless brush was coloring in. Though he had wholly recovered now she had to call often to bring him from his candle and foolscap to her bed that had been lonely so long. For he had begun to expand his *Commercial Advertiser* letters into what would become the most influential and enduring book ever written about Indians.

Cyrus Kimball, the Cincinnati frame-maker and gilder, was

astounded by the orders Catlin gave him that summer. A hundred frames! Fifty! Fifty more! And when every frame had an Indian in it, or a wild landscape, Walter Gregory had his best printer pull more posters and notices and invitations and admission cards than the Queen City of the Ohio had ever heard of. Young Walter wanted to put Cincinnati on the map of the arts, and here was his opportunity. The Indian Gallery which his brother-in-law had ready for exhibition would be about the biggest one-man show in history. And his sister Clara assured him that it would be the best.

His own eyes told him that it was something entirely new, which was what the up-and-coming citizens of the western metropolis were alert for. Though a dowdy sort of envy, and the flop of her fantastic bazaar, had made Mrs. Trollope say nasty things about their domestic manners, they were the soul and seed of the New America. They thought Shakespeare shady in morals, but they poured money and excess energy into colleges, libraries, hospitals, and museums. And by eager reading, and listening, and traveling, they created the true culture of our Middle West, a culture ever seeking and ever finding the fine enriching things.

When Catlin, looking very urbane and civilized in his new fifty-one dollar suit, talked to them of the pictures that walled his exhibition hall, they were all ears for explanations of this new kind of art. He never forgot the faces of that intelligent audience. His drawing teacher, now Mary Peck Mansfield, was there with her husband, Cincinnati's foremost newspaper man. Beside them sat Lyman Beecher and his daughter Harriet. Judge James Hall, editor of the *Western Monthly Magazine,* and editor-to-be of the famous McKenna and Hall Indian portfolios, was there taking copious notes for the following appraisal, which appeared in the October issue of his magazine:

There is now in this city a collection of paintings, which we consider the most extraordinary and interesting that we have ever witnessed; and one which constitutes a most valuable addition to the history of our continent, as well as to the arts of our country. Mr. Catlin engaged some time since in the very arduous and novel enterprise, of visiting the distant tribes of our western frontiers, for the purpose of painting from nature a series of portraits and landscapes illustrative of the country and its inhabitants, and has succeeded thus far beyond his most sanguine hopes. . . . His gallery now contains about one hundred and forty pictures; and we are informed that he has in his possession an equal number in an unfinished state. . . .

There is also a series of landscapes, embracing views of the scenery of the Missouri River. To us, who have traversed the prairie in its length and breadth, . . . these graphic delineations served to awaken agreeable images of past pleasure. To others they will communicate valuable information—to all who have never had the good fortune to see a prairie, they will convey some idea of the appearance of those vast meadows, so boundless, so beautiful, so rich in scenic attraction. The shores of the Missouri have a peculiar and strongly marked character. They are like nothing else in nature but themselves. . . . We are glad that we have a native artist, who . . . has had the good sense to train his taste in the school of nature, and the patriotism to employ his genius on subjects connected with his own country. We are proud of such men as Audubon and Catlin. . . .

The names of these two great outdoor painters had been linked together a few days earlier in a newspaper article, now lost, which led to the following comment and correspondence, printed in the Cincinnati *Daily Gazette* on the 15th of that triumphant November:

FROM THE LOUISVILLE HERALD
Mr. Catlin's Gallery.

We take pleasure in laying before the public the following communication from Mr. George Catlin, at present of Cincinnati in reply to an article copied into the Louisville Herald from a Philadelphia paper, concerning principally himself and Mr. Audubon, the naturalist. We assure Mr. Catlin, that in republishing the article alluded to, our only object was to do justice to another, and that it was no part of our wish to injure or detract from the high reputation he has acquired as an accomplished native artist. We dislike this exaltation of one man at the expense of another: and certainly there was no public purpose, much less was there any good private end, to be gained, by instituting a comparison between two gentlemen whose objects are different, yet equally to be lauded and commended. But if prudent and impartial friends must make such comparison, we are sure Mr. Catlin will bear us out in saying, that few individuals have less to fear from them than his great co-laborer, whose "works and beautiful designs" are likely to become yet more familiar to the public.

We understand that Mr. Catlin intends favoring the citizens of Louisville with a sight of his "Indian Portrait Gallery" in the course of a few days.

FOR THE LOUISVILLE HERALD

Mr. Editor:—In explanation of an article copied in your paper a few weeks since from the Philadelphia Commercial Herald, calculated to prejudice the public mind against my gallery of Indian portraits, I would briefly state, that the portrait of Black Hawk therein spoken of, was not my original portrait of that man, but a very small sketch in water colors, the head not an inch in diameter, which was procured from me in St. Louis and painted within the diminished limits which were carefully prescribed for it. This sketch might not have been a faithful likeness of Black Hawk. The original portrait, the size of life, will continue to stand in my gallery and speak for itself. I intend in a few days to lay the original before you, when you and the public who have seen Black Hawk, can be your own judges. All I desire is, that the public may withhold their decision until they can see for themselves, and not condemn the whole result of my hard labors, as the writer would have them, upon the above mentioned sketch.

With the writer's opinion of Mr. Audubon's talents I exactly agree. I know him not, but his works and his beautiful designs are familiar to me, and in our rambling lives, I should hail the day with pleasure that would bring me in contact with the man whose works would seem to hold a rank between living nature and art.

Geo. Catlin.

Under such meteor showers as no man had seen, the Catlins shipped to Louisville. There, as that good year went out, they closed another successful exhibition with a champagne dinner and embarked for New Orleans and for Pensacola, where Catlin's brother James managed a bank.

Though a bitter Northwester winged with sleet was roaring through the darkness as they entered the Mississippi, Catlin asked Clara to come out with him on the starboard deck. "That is where I want to take you," he shouted against the storm, as he pointed up the great river.

Wrapped in one of his painted robes, she watched him grip the icy rail and look long to the forbidden Indian North, where she knew that more than half his heart was.

Realizing at last that he was very cold, and not alone, he turned to Clara and found her crying.

IX

A TOUR IN TEXAS

ON THEIR way up-river in the early spring of 1834, Catlin gayly assured his wife that his expedition into Texas with Colonel Dodge's new Dragoon Regiment would be a continual picnic. Even so, Clara was very loath to leave him at Natchez on her way up to Alton, Illinois, where she would await his return in the home of friends. And Catlin was not wholly at ease in mind there under the Hill, as he waited for the steamer *Arkansas* to take on caissons and stout field-guns, and burlap bales marked "U.S. Army, Fort Gibson." In the cozy ship's bar, the talk of two lively-looking young fellows— one of them in regimentals—let him guess that all was not right with the Dragoons.

In fact, everything was wrong with them. They had recruited slowly, despite advertisements of three years' service "beyond the frontiers," and eight dollars a month for mere privates. The first five companies, yet without uniforms, had received riding orders at Jefferson Barracks at the end of November, and straggled into Fort Gibson in mid-December with the mercury at eight degrees below. Thawed now, but as spiritless and lean as their wretched horses, they were still waiting for the other five companies to form and fit out and join them.

Recognizing Catlin, one of the young fellows warmly welcomed him. "I'm Joe Chadwick from Saint Louis," he said. "You don't remember, but I was at the big party the O'Fallons gave when you came back from Union. Meet Lieutenant Seaton."

86

Catlin did remember, and was delighted to have the companionship of the young man whose good manners and gaiety had so pleased him. The Lieutenant was a madcap gentleman too, and a merry one. In their company, the great artist and grave crusader became "good old Cat," a kind of senior boy, full of droll stories and ready for any adventure. For he was essentially a man's man, more at home with them there on that wheezing sidewheeler than he would ever be in drawing rooms crowded with crinolines.

Their trip to Fort Gibson, far up the Arkansas River, might well have been tedious, with the pilot taking his time, and the shallow water stranding their craft for days. But it certainly was not. When hunting and fishing staled, they caught centipedes or tarantulas, and had hilarious evenings matching these little monsters in quick and deadly battles.

Arriving at the God-forsaken Fort, they had to wait two months for the laggard companies to arrive and train. Fortunately for Catlin, all the Indians within a hundred miles had come to see this novelty of an army on horseback, and he had good hunting with his brush. He painted Osages seven feet tall, with an extra foot of vermilioned topknot. Riding out to the Choctaw camps, he painted spirited action pictures of an incredibly crowded, noisy and confused lacrosse game between whole tribes of breech-clouted players wearing tails and manes of dyed horsehair and wielding in either hand a stick with a little webbed hoop on its end. Between these hoops they had to catch, hold, and throw the ball.

At sundown the playing field was ceremonially measured, and the goal posts set up. "Each party had their goal made with two upright posts, about 25 feet high and six feet apart, set firm in the ground, with a pole across the top. These goals were about forty or fifty rods apart; and at a point just half way between, was another small stake, driven down, where the ball was to be thrown up at the firing of a gun, to be struggled for by the players. All this preparation was made by some old men; who were, it seems, selected to be the judges of the play."

These elders then drew a straight "betting line" from one goal to the other. Up to it, from the woods on each side, came an immense crowd, bringing horses, blankets, guns, knives, and pottery to bet across this line. Stake-holders took over these wagers and watched them until dawn.

Soon after dark, a torchlight procession escorted the players out from the rival camps; drums struck up; and to the monotonous chanting of choruses of squaws, the two teams danced, sang and rattled their playing-sticks round and round their respective goals. They repeated this performance at half-hour intervals until nine o'clock in the morning when the game commenced.

"An instant struggle ensued between the players, who were some six or seven hundred in numbers, and were mutually endeavouring to catch the ball in their sticks, and throw it home and between their respective stakes; which, whenever successfully done, counts for one game. . . . In these desperate struggles for the ball . . . where hundreds are running together and leaping, actually over each other's heads, and darting between their adversaries' legs, tripping and throwing, and foiling each other in every possible manner, and every voice raised to the highest key, in shrill yelps and barks, there are rapid successions of feats. . . . Every mode is used that can be devised, to oppose the progress of the foremost, who is likely to get the ball; and these obstructions often meet desperate individual resistance, which terminates in a violent scuffle and sometimes in fisticuffs; when their sticks are dropped, and the parties are unmolested, whilst they are settling it between themselves; unless it be by a general *stampedo,* to which they are subject who are down, if the ball happens to pass in their direction. . . .

"There are times, when the ball gets to the ground, and such a confused mass rushing around it, and knocking their sticks together, without the possibility of anyone getting or seeing it, for the dust that they raise, that the spectator loses his strength, and everything else but his senses; when the condensed mass of ball-sticks, and shins, and bloody noses, is carried around the different parts of the ground, for a quarter of an hour at a time, without any one of the mass being able to see the ball; and which they are often thus scuffling for, several minutes after it has been thrown off, and played over another part of the ground."

With halts of about a minute after the scoring of each goal, the game went on until an hour before sunset, when the winning side attained the necessary one hundred points.

On the 19th of June, with the thermometer reading 108 degrees in the scanty shade, the ill-prepared and ill-starred expedition set out for Texas. General Henry Leavenworth was in command, with Catlin's old friend, Colonel Henry Dodge, leading the Dragoons. Among their officers were Lieutenant Jefferson Davis and Captain Nathan Boone, a son of the famous frontiersman. Though this new mounted regiment could muster barely two-thirds of its authorized strength of 715 troopers, it made a handsome show on the prairies with its troop of grays; its troop of bays, its blacks, its whites, and its palominos. Catlin, now an aide on the General's staff, rode in rank and style on a prairie stallion named Charley. To shade his sketchbook from the blinding sun, he carried a big cotton umbrella.

At first the way was all vineyard and orchard—miles of wild grapes and plums and currants and gooseberries—that opened on prairies brown with buffalos. Galloping after them with the staff officers Catlin was swept from the saddle by a low branch. Recovering his horse he rode up a little hill and saw General Leavenworth's flying charger stumble and fling his rider almost under the hooves of the calf he was closely pursuing. The General made light of his fall, but fainted when Catlin helped him up.

While the two rode together the next day, Leavenworth said, "It was a very lucky thing, Catlin, that you painted the portrait of me before we started." Coughing violently, he spat blood from the internal injury that would soon lay him low, along with half his command.

In spite of many other omens of disaster, the troops jogged on. Inseparable now, Catlin and young Chadwick ranged at will, talking, exploring, gathering mineral specimens from gullies and outcrops, popping away at eagles and equally swift antelopes.

That Theocritan idyll ended at the mouth of the False Washita, now the Red River. Oven heat, contaminated food, and foul water from shrunken ponds so thick with oil scum that frogs could hop across them, had brought on the expedition an epidemic of "bilious fever" which struck down horses and men alike. General Leavenworth, deathly sick, ordered Dodge to go on with the two hundred troopers still able to ride.

Catlin and Chadwick accompanied this puny host into the country of the fierce Comanches. Congress had authorized the Dragoons especially to awe and intimidate these tribesmen. But now it was the white horsemen who rode and camped in fear, spied on by encircling bands of armed red riders, always within sight and never within carbine range.

On the fourth day out Colonel Dodge managed to meet a Comanche band who answered his flag of truce with one cut from the skin of a white buffalo. This friendly band guided the troopers to a large tepee village of their tribe, where Catlin got many portraits and sketches of Indian horsemanship at its daredevil best.

Here too he saw wild horses taken and instantly tamed. "The Indian," he wrote, "when he starts for a wild horse, mounts one of the fleetest he can get, and coiling his lasso on his arm, starts off, under the 'full whip,' till he can enter the band, when he soon gets it over the neck of one of the number; when he instantly dismounts, leaving his own horse, and runs as fast as he can, letting the lasso pass out gradually and carefully through his hands, until the horse falls for want of breath, and lies helplessly on the ground, at which time the Indian advances slowly toward the horse's head, keeping his lasso tight upon its neck, until he fastens a pair of hobbles on the animal's two fore feet, and also loosens the lasso (giving the horse a chance to breathe) and gives it a noose around the under jaw, by which he gets great power over the affrighted animal. . . . By this means he gradually advances, until he is able to place his hands on the animal's nose, and over its eyes; and at length to breathe in its nostrils, when it soon becomes docile and conquered."

The Indians who watched him paint this performance suddenly realized what a big boon his sun umbrella would be to them when the fall rains came. It would keep their fine feathers from getting bedraggled, and their laborious paint-jobs from streaking and dribbling down their chins. They offered him dogs and horses and wives for it. He could have made a fortune, there and then, by taking orders for a whole caravan of cotton umbrellas.

But he was a very sick man—too sick to ride another mile. He lay weak and fevered in that Comanche village for fifteen days while the wretched remnant of the Dragoons visited the Wicos, the Kioways, and the curious Pawnee Picts, who lived in thatched houses like straw beehives, and whose constant riding made them awkward and ungainly on foot. Joe Chadwick went on with the expedition, and took notes and made sketches for him. As warriors of all three of the tribes visited turned up later at the Comanche village, he had a chance to verify his friend's sketches of them.

The return to Fort Gibson was a nightmare. "After leaving the headwaters of the Canadian," Catlin wrote, "my illness continually increased, and losing strength every day, I soon got so reduced that I was necessarily lifted on to and off from, my horse; and at last, so that I could not ride at all. I was then put into a baggage-wagon which was going back empty, except with several soldiers sick, and in this condition rode eight days, most of the time in a delirious state, lying on the hard planks of the wagon, and made still harder by the jarring and jolting, until the skin from my elbows and knees was literally 'worn out.' "

But for his friend Chadwick, who nursed and tended him with a woman's tenderness, he would have died. General Leavenworth and a third of his officers and men were dead. The surviving troops, in whose ragged train Catlin at last reached Fort Gibson, were living skeletons of men.

Helpless in the post hospital, he heard the muffled drums beat "Roslin Castle" every few hours, as the caissons rumbled another poor trooper's body to the baked burial ground. Lying there he remembered his brother Julius, and what he must still do to justify himself in those dead eyes whose keen sight the Genesee had darkened forever. And he remembered Clark's plea for his help in a losing fight, and Clara's hope and prayers that soon she would bear him a child.

By strength of spirit alone, he dragged himself from that loathsome sick-bay, directed Chadwick to send his pictures by boat to Saint Louis, and called for his prairie stallion.

"So," he wrote, "one fine morning, Charley was brought up and saddled, and a bear-skin and a buffalo robe being spread upon his saddle, and a coffee pot and a tin cup tied to it also—with a few pounds of hard biscuit in my portmanteau—with my fowling-piece in my hand, and my pistols in my belt—with my sketch book slung on my back, and a small compass in my pocket; I took leave of Fort Gibson, even against the advice of my surgeon and all the officers of the garrison, who gathered around me to bid me farewell."

Riding, and resting when too weak to ride, he covered five hundred lonely and dangerous miles of unmapped prairie. He lived by his gun, though fever still unsteadied his aim. He swam streams, and rafted his belongings ahead of him. Unerring in his sense of direction, he reached the Missouri by Booneville, ferried over, and joined Clara at Alton.

X

CATLINITE

THE Great Design was on canvas now, save for a few tawny and green details. To obtain these, Catlin steamed up the Mississippi as far as the Falls of Saint Anthony in the spring of 1835. There, and on the way down, he painted Sioux, Ojibbeways, and Saukies, and river scenes to balance those previously painted along the Missouri. Clara had come with him to Saint Peter's, where he rejoined her for a trip to the Dubuque lead mines and Fort Des Moines.

Riding out to visit old Keokuk, the slyest fox that ever wore feathers, he saw the Foxes engaged in an extraordinary ceremonial of polite larceny which the Western tribes called "smoking horses."

"When General Street and I arrived at Ke-o-kuk's village," he wrote, "we were just in time to see this amusing scene, on the prairie a little back of his village. The Foxes, who were making up a war party to go against the Sioux, and had not suitable horses enough by twenty, had sent word to the Sacs, the day before (according to an ancient custom), that they were coming on that day, at a certain hour, to 'smoke' that number of horses, and they must not fail to have them ready. On that day, and at the hour, the twenty young men who were beggars for horses, were on the spot, and seated themselves on the ground in a circle, where they went to smoking. The villagers flocked around them in a dense crowd, and soon after appeared on the prairie, at half a mile distance, an equal number of young men of the Sac tribe, who had agreed, each to give a horse, and who were then galloping them about at full speed; and gradually, as they went around in a circuit, coming in nearer to the centre, until they were at last close around the ring of young fellows seated on the ground. Whilst dashing about thus, each one, with a heavy whip in his hand, as he came within reach of the group on the ground, selected the one to whom he decided to present his horse, and as he passed him, gave him the most tremendous cut with his lash, over his naked shoulders; and as he darted around again he plied the whip as before, and again and again with a violent 'crack' until the blood could be seen trickling down over his naked shoulders, upon which he instantly dismounted, and placed the bridle and whip in his hands, saying, "Here, you are a beggar—I present you a horse, but you will carry my mark on your back."

There too he saw and sketched the shadowed dance of the Berdashe, wherein a man called the I-coo-coo-a or Berdashe was dressed, because of his classical but questionable habits, in woman's clothes, and circled round by those young men of the tribe who could dance forward and chant their shameless confessions. Puzzled, and not a little pained that his noble Indians took this as a matter of course, Catlin, with a Corporal Allen, paddled down to Saint Louis. Clara had already reached that city by steamer.

For the past three years, Laidlaw and Kipp and McKenzie, and all Clark's agents and sub-agents on the upper reaches of the two great rivers had been collecting Indian costumes, weapons and curios and shipping them to the Fur Company's Saint Louis warehouse in bales marked "To be held for Mr. Catlin's arrival." What with opening these, exulting over their contents, and repacking them and the rest of his wares for shipment to upstate New York, Mr. Catlin was a very busy man.

But he was not too busy to show his Clara's pretty face and pretty old-fashioned graces to the aging General Clark, or to introduce her to Saint Louis society and juleps and iris borders at the Ben O'Fallon's garden party. There his host led him aside, to say: "Cat, the greatest pleasure the General has now is in showing your paintings. Whenever you have more spare copies than spare cash, send them to him and send me the bill. An honest-to-God bill, too."

Catlin accepted few other commissions for that crowded winter. Ice-locked at Utica in a studio overlooking Clinton's canal, he painted and retouched and tidied canvases piled higher than the top of his tall easel. When the brief daylight failed he catalogued curios and listed the subjects of his portraits by their puzzling names.

"No Indian will volunteer his name," he once lamented to Clara. "Only occasions or other Indians will reveal it to you. And most chiefs have a dozen names, which they use according to caprice or circumstance." Indian caprice was impish, and ready to sign solemn treaties with such fantastic inventions as Cho-shin-ga, He that Cooks Little in a Small Kettle; Hon-eh-cook, the Buffalo that Urinates and Smells It; or even Cha-sa-wa-ne-che, the One that Has No Name.

Many Indian names could only be approximately written down in our alien alphabet with its limited tonal range. And when written, many were untranslatable. Yet Romance has no roster of titles comparable to those in the Catalogue of Catlin's Gallery. He painted the Handsome Bird; the Grizzly Bear that Runs Without Regard; No Heart; the Bloody Hand; and the Wolf on the Hill. He painted the Busy Man; He Who Fights with a Feather; the Very Sweet Man; and He Who Drinks the Juice of the Stone. The names of his canvas ladies are a delight to the tongue: the Great Wonder; the Pure Fountain; the Bending Willow; the Red Thing that Touches in Marching.

He was barely in time to catch these fleeting melodies of metaphor. By mid-century the Indian census listed pedestrians only: a Tom Potato, a Pig Mike, a James Tin-Cup, an Adam Mouse, and a Walter Horse-Fly.

After months of preparation, Catlin was ready early in July, 1836, for the first combined showing of his paintings and his thousands of large and small articles of Indian manufacture. For this exhibition he hired an ex-church in Buffalo. Following Peale's example, he displayed his curios attractively on racks and in cases along the walls, and over them hung long lines of his pictures. On the platform where the pulpit had stood he set up a tall, adjustable easel to hold one after another of his chosen paintings high while he lectured on them. To entice the public in, he advertised in the local papers, and employed billposters and boys to distribute hundreds of handbills.

Of all the exhibits in the show, the most popular was a case containing his unique collection of Indian pipes, curiously shaped and richly carved in brick-colored stone. These, at least, the pipe-smoking public could identify. Some of the farmers who came in for the show had plowed up similar pipes of red stone. When question-time came, Catlin was always asked how they were made, and where. As he lectured, he grew more and more aware of the deep significance of pipe-smoking in Indian ceremonies and religious rituals, and of the interest his audiences took in this strange importance of a practice to which most of the gentlemen, and some of the ladies too, were addicted. So, when he closed the show after a successful month, he went by steamer to Green Bay, Wisconsin, to find the secret quarries from which all the red pipestone of the continent came. On the way, of course, he painted lake scenes and aquatic Chippeways, and a portrait of Eleazer Williams, the half-breed who claimed to be the Lost Dauphin of France.

Legend placed the pipestone quarries west of Lake Superior, on a ridge between the Saint Peter's River and the upper Mississippi. So, from Green Bay, Catlin set off again in a huge bark boat paddled by singing French voyageurs and enlivened by the company of an Army Lieutenant, a New York hotel manager, and two gifted young adventurers, Robert Serrel Wood of England, and John Treat Irving, a nephew of Washington Irving, and himself the author of a brilliant, witty account of a visit to the Pawnees.

airie bluffs of the Upper Missouri, 1,050 miles above Saint Louis. *See p. 55.*

9. *Wah-pe-kee-suck, White Cloud, a Sac captured with Black Hawk. See p. 78.*

Catlin and Wood bought a canoe at Fort Winnebago, paddled it down the Ouisconsin to Prairie du Chien, and then up the Mississippi and the Saint Peter's to the rising hill country called "Couteau des Prairies."

Robert Serrell Wood reminded Catlin of Joseph Chadwick. He was as companionable, and as irrepressible in spirits. He had a guitar, a good singing voice, and a great stock of sentimental ditties mingled with hairy-chested songs. He had dabbled in science, and later would write on electricity and the chemistry of soils. Knowing the galleries of Europe well, he knew that Catlin's work was masterly, and constantly urged him to show it abroad.

Their talk one day turned to another gifted English traveler, the Honorable Charles Murray, who had got to know the Catlins in the lead mine country in 1835, after his daring visit to the Pawnees. As handsome and gracious and reckless as men are made, that young aristocrat combined an All Souls Fellowship at Oxford, and an affection for Indians, with the strength to bend a rifle barrel over his knee or to crash his powerful fist through a door. On his way to the West, Murray had visited the Erie Canal towns, and there fallen in love with Elise Wadsworth, daughter of the rich Squire of Geneseo, near Rochester.

"What did Murray think of your pictures?" Wood asked.

"I had few with me then," Catlin replied. "But this last June he came back to Geneseo to see Miss Wadsworth, and I showed him my whole Gallery. He too urged me to take my pictures to Europe."

"There's your man," said Wood. "A son of the Earl of Dunmore and a nephew of the Duke of Hamilton. He knows everybody worth knowing. When he gets back to England ask him to arrange a London exhibition for you. He'll do it like a shot, to show the kind of wild men he's been hob-nobbing with. He'll do it in style, too. A London reputation will make the most incurable Yankee listen to you and read that book you are eternally scribbling. Eh, what! Isn't that your pipestone ridge, there beyond the bend? Gad, what a lonely land for Peace to live in."

Lonely indeed, and golden with ripeness in the great silence of declining summer. And serene beyond all the serenities of the realms of wrangling men. For over all this grassy upland lay a peace as inviolable as the strong old Pax Romana that kept all weapons sheathed. "The Great Spirit at an ancient period," Catlin wrote in his journal, "here called the Indians together, and standing on the precipice of the red pipestone rock, broke from its wall a piece, and made a large pipe by turning it in his hand, which he smoked over them, and to the North, the South, the East, and the West, and told them that this stone was red . . . that it was their flesh . . . that they must use it for their pipes of peace . . . that it belonged to them all, and that the war club and scalping knife must not be used on its ground." Parties of the most deadly and deeply sworn enemies, coming for the sacred red stone from all the warring tribes of the West, laid down their weapons and sacrificed before they approached the quarry.

A band of Sioux, jealous of their holy place, vainly tried to stay Catlin and Wood with imprecations and threats; but the two pushed on, guided by a local trader named La Framboise, whom Catlin had met during the previous summer. His horses carried them safely over the last miles to the southern summit of the Couteau.

"On the very top of this mound or ridge," Catlin wrote, "we found the far-famed quarry or fountain of the Red Pipe, which is truly an anomaly in nature. The principal and most striking feature of this place, is a perpendicular wall of close-grained, compact quartz, of twenty-five and thirty feet in elevation, . . . exhibiting a front of nearly two miles in length, when it disappears at both ends by running into the prairie. . . .

"This beautiful wall is horizontal, and stratified in several layers of light grey, and rose or flesh-coloured quartz; and for most of the way, both on the front of the wall, and for acres of its horizontal surface, highly polished or glazed, as if by ignition.

"At the base of this wall there is a level prairie, of half a mile in width, running parallel to it; in any and all parts of which, the Indians procure the red stone for their pipes, by digging through the soil and several slaty layers of the red stone, to the depth of four or five feet. From the very numerous marks of ancient and modern diggings or excavations, it would appear that this place has been for many centuries resorted to for the red stone; and from the great numbers of graves and remains of ancient fortifications in the vicinity, it would seem, as well as from their actual traditions, that the Indian tribes have long held this place in high superstitious admiration; and also that it has been the resort of different tribes, who have made their regular pilgrimages here to renew their pipes."

Sketching there, while Wood gathered specimens of the sacred red stone and measured and paced off strata, Catlin mused on the mysterious relationship between inhuman Mother Nature and her brief human children. At the shadowy edge of Revelation, he almost understood. She too is an experimental scientist, breeding reason and invention and vast imagination into one of her innumerable broods, and waiting to see its outcome. Until assured by Man's works of beauty and faith that his race deserves dominion over the Earth and all that it nourishes or conceals, she restrains his increase and his power by War. The eagle that hunted those green highlands circled lower until a speck of brown became a small dark man squatting, Indian-fashion, in soiled buckskins, with his black-stubbled chin resting on his hand.

By pressing their paddles hard, the two travelers reached Rock Island in late September—in time to sign treaties negotiated with the Sacs and Foxes by Colonel Henry Dodge. After that signing, the Colonel urged the Indians to move their families and belongings from the lands they had just relinquished. They laughed heartily. "My father," said one of the warriors, "we have to laugh; we require no time to move; we have all left the lands already, and sold our wigwams to Chemokemons (white men), some for one hundred and some for two hundred dollars. There are already four hundred Chemokemons moving in. Three days ago one Chemokemon sold his wigwam to another Chemokemon for two thousand dollars, to build a great town."

Thus Catlin might have profited—there, and on the sites of a dozen other Western cities—if his speculations had come down to town lots. But his interest was now all in the analysis of his specimens of pipestone. Dr. Charles Thomas Jackson, of Boston, the leading mineralogist of those days, pronounced the stone to be "a new mineral compound," and called it Catlinite, a name it still bears. In later times, when Catlin's joys were to be bleak and few, he would warm an attic lodging in an alien land by rubbing between his hands an old, broken pipe-bowl, a reminder that his name would live in red stone when the canvases he had covered with red-streaked faces decayed into museum dust.

XI

BROADWAY

NEW YORKERS had plenty of entertainment in the later months of 1837. Thomas Davenport, the Vermont blacksmith, was showing his newly invented electric motor; Peale's fourteen foot anaconda was regularly swallowing live hens, feathers and all; Dr. Valentene, the famous delineator of Yankee eccentricities, nightly opened "his wallet of Whims, Waggeries, Singularities, Peculiarities, Originalities, Eccentricities and Humerous Drolleries."

But the Indian Gallery was the thing to see, if you could squeeze in to see it. Crowded out of New York's Clinton Hall, which could not hold the enthusiastic audiences, Catlin moved his vast collection to the Stuyvesant Institute on Broadway. That too was inadequate on the crowning night when delegations of Sioux, Sacs, and Foxes came to see their own portraits. Even the street outside was jammed with people. The *Commercial Advertiser's* reporter barely managed to squeeze in at a side door with the visiting warriors.

Chance-preserved letters written home by some of the thousands who paid their fifty-cent admissions to Catlin's Indian Gallery in those days tell how skillfully he held and persuaded his audience. Having his Irish factotum, Daniel Kavanaugh, put picture after picture on a floodlit easel, he told what manner of men had sat for them; and where and under what difficulties he had painted them. And he told their sad sequels; this warrior dead from smallpox, this one in irons; this prairie prince tricked out of his homeland and driven to drunkenness. For his every statement on the beauty of Indian handicrafts, or the strangeness of Indian ritual, he held up authentic evidence—beadwork, painted robes, horned helmets, sacramental pipes, medicine bags stuffed with holy oddments.

Even so, his word was not wholly trusted. This visit of the Sacs and Foxes, with their wily leader, was his chance to convince the doubters. He was very pale that night, and his hand trembled as he laid it on the elkskin hung over the display-easel to hide his painting of Keokuk on horseback. The strain of incessant lecturing had broken his health earlier that year, when he showed at Albany and Troy, and would soon break its frailty again. His voice trembled too, observed the reporter, as he "remarked with some emotion, that both the fidelity of his pictures and his own veracity, had been questioned in this city by some gentlemen, who had denied that there was any such horse among the Indians as that upon which Keokuk was represented as being mounted."

With that he displayed the picture of the Indian mounted on his mettlesome black. Then Keokuk sprang up "with a good deal of energy to repel the imputation and vindicate his own taste in horsemanship. He said it was a good likeness of his horse . . . if he had not been a fine horse, Keokuk would not have bought him."

The Sioux warriors then recognized a portrait of one of their young chiefs. As he was now dead, they hushed, with their hands over their mouths, in a gesture of respect. All of them backed Catlin's assertion that an arrow could be shot through a buffalo and come out on the further side. One raised three fingers to show how many times he had accomplished that very feat.

Although it was frosty late October outside, the packed audience created such a fug and heat that the fierce plainsmen were growing giddy, and their war paint was beginning to run. Catlin wisely led them to the dressing room for fresh air and retouching. During his absence, Colonel William Stone took the floor to commend him and his labors, and to put this motion:

"*Resolved*, That this meeting entertains the fullest confidence in the veracity of Mr. Catlin, and in the truth of his delineations, both by his lips and his pencil."

The resolution was loudly applauded and adopted unanimously. Catlin was so moved, on hearing it, "as somewhat to obstruct the delivery of a brief and feeling address in reply."

With or without resolutions of confidence, a good many Americans continued to doubt Catlin's accounts of the prairie Indians. Sportsmen doubted them because they came from an artist who called a hoss a horse. Professional naturalists and Indian experts doubted them because they came from an amateur who was too eloquent, too sympathetic, and much too popular to be relied upon. Distillers, fur traders, speculators in Western lands, and materialists of the sound conservative sort doubted them because they wanted to: if this fellow went on talking about good Indians being tricked out of their lands, and debauched by traders, there would be the Devil to pay, and no dividends. Such notions were un-American and downright dangerous. If the fellow was so fond of Indians why didn't he join a tribe and take a squaw and stop disturbing the consciences of his fellow citizens?

Catlin was obliged to stop for a time. The paper that carried the account of the Keokuk vindication also gave notice of his retirement from lecturing, until his health, long feeble, recovered from the heat, fatigue and excitement of these public demonstrations.

But he could not resist one more showing of real, live Indians. Renting the Chatham Street Chapel for the evening of November 1st, he set up his Crow wigwam, and with Keokuk and Black Hawk flanking him, lectured from its doorway. He gave Keokuk a magnificent present, and then the Indians held a genuine tribal levee in the big wigwam. The admission charge was one dollar.

So much at least his advertisement promised. The *Commercial Advertiser* did not send a reporter this time, but it commented thus a day or two later on the showing of the Indians by others at the National Theater: "Cupidity is ever on the alert to turn a penny by their assistance."

That stern hint was hardly needed. The wild warriors were off to see other cities, and to collect a new kind of scalp lock, the gilt tassel of the mortar board of an Honorary Degree. Catlin turned awhile from showmanship to landscape painting, and the proofreading of a first "Catalogue of Catlin's Indian Gallery of Portraits, Landscapes, Manners and Customs, &c. &c." Piercy and Read of New York were printing 500 copies of this, along with several thousand show bills. There were other matters too. Joseph Stone of Jersey City was building strong crates and boxes to ship the collection in. And there was the problem of what to do with the grizzly bear cubs McKenzie had sent from Fort Union.

The Indian Gallery opened again at the Stuyvesant in late November, 1837, for the busy holiday season. But something more important to Catlin than the New York public soon called him south to Fort Moultrie.

For six years he had secretly exulted in the bravery and skilled war craft of the Seminoles. Under their chief Osceola, the Tiger of the Everglades, they had eluded and outfought the best regiments of our army. Now news came that Osceola, with four of his sub-chiefs and two hundred warriors, had been tricked into meeting our commanders under a flag of truce, and in violation of his safe-conduct and every principle of honor, had been seized, bound to his horse, and carried off with his manacled warriors to the South Carolina fort.

Hot with righteous anger, Catlin went there post-haste, with his palette and brushes, and painted a portrait of Osceola so moving, so poetic, so masterly, that it still makes any decent American ashamed that such unspeakable treachery was ever practiced by our army officers and condoned by our government.

Osceola was no common mortal. Born to lead and to plan, he was handsome as a Phidian statue, vivacious, just, energetic, indomitably determined, and passionate for freedom. He was the best woodsman, hunter, and athlete of his tribe.

Catlin put all this, and a mystical something more, into his beautiful tragic portrait. To partner it, he took swift likenesses of ten more Seminoles and allied Euchees who were kept less strictly than their war chief.

"One of the young men of this party," he wrote, "and one of the handsomest men I ever saw, was one morning accused by a white man, a producer of poultry and vegetables, living in the vicinity of the fort, of having stolen a chicken from him the night before. The complaint was laid before the chiefs, who took cognizance of it, hearing the proofs advanced by the accusing party, which he made out to be very conclusive, while the young man accused had no evidence to give, only asking the chiefs, 'Did any Seminole ever know Chee-ho-ka to steal?' However, the white man's evidence was so strong that he was convicted, and the sentence of the chiefs, though prisoners of war, by the custom of their country (they being partly civilized) was, that he should be publicly whipped the next morning at nine o'clock. At seven o'clock, however, the next morning his body was found suspended from a spike in the side of the wall of the fort, by a thong of raw hide with a noose around his neck, and quite dead. And a little time after, while the officers of the garrison and the Indians were in a group around him, the *fiend* came up who had sworn against him, with the chicken under his arm, and alive, and confessed that it had not been stolen!

"The wretch was standing right by my side at the moment, and from an impulse quicker than thought I seized him by the throat with an iron grip, that I was never capable of before or since. . . ."

More than ever resolved to make the world see and know that such terrible injustices were daily being done to all the ancient and splendid Indian race, Catlin hurried back to New York to re-open his exhibition and to lecture as he had never lectured before. While he was en route, Osceola, his ideal brave, died of a sudden quinsy.

A round trip to South Carolina and eleven portraits in exactly three weeks! In a few days more a second Osceola portrait, and a magnificent lithograph chalked from it in autumnal tones of oak and maple!

Catlin's Exhibition Catalogue, revised now to include the Seminoles and Euchees, remains an amazing memorial of sheer industry, as well as courage and art. Its listed portraits run from number 1 to number 311; followed by Landscapes, from 321 to 413; Sporting Scenes, from 414 to 431; Amusements, from 432 to 461; Manners and Customs, from 462 to 490; and the four pictures of Mandan Religious Ceremonies, numbered 491 to 494. It is an artist's Who's Who of the Indian tribes, in this order:

1. Osage	16. Chip-pe-way	31. Pe-o-ri-a
2. Sacs	17. I-ro-quois	32. Sho-sho-nie
3. Paw-nee-Picts	18. Flat Heads	33. O-ma-haw
4. Kon-za	19. As-sin-ni-boin	34. O-toe
5. Comanche	20. Shi-enne	35. Mis-sou-ries
6. Ki-o-wa	21. Cher-o-kee	36. Sem-i-nole
7. Wee-co	22. Po-to-wa-to-mie	37. Kick-a-poo
8. Sioux	23. Pi-an-keshaw	38. We-ah
9. Pun-cah	24. Mus-co-gee	39. Kas-kas-ki-a
10. Crows	25. Win-ne-ba-go	40. Cree
11. Mandans	26. I-o-wa	41. Choc-taw
12. Black Foot	27. Sen-e-ca	42. Del-a-ware
13. Me-nom-o-nie	28. O-nei-da	43. Paw-nees
14. Shaw-nee	29. Qua-paw	44. Sem-i-noles
15. Grosventres	30. Ot-ta-wa	45. Eu-chees

It says nothing of the two bears, or of his bushels of mineral specimens, or of "sundry bones" on which storage charges had accumulated. But it lists a Crow Lodge or Wigwam, an Indian Cradle, Camanche Lances, Twelve Calumets, Eighty Ordinary Pipes, and "a very great and valuable collection of Men's and Women's dresses, from the different tribes, garnished and fringed with scalp locks from their enemies' heads—Bows, Quivers, Spears, Shields, War Eagles and Raven Head Dresses, Necklaces, Mockasins, Belts, Pouches, War Clubs, Robes, Mantles, Tobacco Sacks, Wampum, Whistles, Rattles, Drums, &c, &c, &c."

Early in April, Catlin was off to Philadelphia, Baltimore and Washington, hiring halls for his summer exhibitions, and distributing the newly pulled Osceola prints to shops where they were sold at a dollar and a half each. People were pointing him out now on the rickety new railways that straightened the old Greek notion of slow spirals of progress into an unbroken onward line. "Paints an Indian a day," they said, in awed voices.

XII

ART AND POLITICS

ANEW YORK reputation in those days was not enough. To establish a national reputation, Catlin still must breach the old conservative citadels of Philadelphia and Boston, the capitals of Art and Letters. But both must wait until he had shown in Washington.

He knew now that the birth of a showman was the death of an artist. His Indian Gallery, a full carload in bulk, was not an easy or inexpensive one to move and display. Even the proper hanging of so many pictures took whole days. Least of all an accountant, his head and eyes ached from printer's estimates and advertising receipts, and bills for candles and carpentry. Worst of all was the endless talking.

Lectures such as his had become—alive, vigorous, dramatic—took a heavy toll of his strength; for he put all he had into the eloquence that brought before his audiences the very reality of wild hunts and high-pitched games, making sophisticated newsmen feel "the hurry, helter-skelter dash and drive of those impetuous onsets and those breathless contests." After the lectures came the questions—often foolish and always tiring—and the lion-hunters insisting on his dining with them or entertaining their parties.

He was making converts to the Indian cause, but not fast enough. Only by converting Congressmen, Senators, and Cabinet members could he change our Indian policy in time to save the prairie tribes. And only by the bait of his Gallery—now widely known for novelty as well as merit—could he bring these busy men to hear his plea.

So to Washington he went, with his crates and boxes and bundles of robes and unwieldy wigwam poles. It is no wonder that his worldly-wise brother-in-law, Dudley Gregory, doubted this venture. Though official Washington was beginning to have an Indian-haunted conscience, votes meant as much then to the men on Capitol Hill as they mean today. And Indians neither voted nor contributed to party funds. Washington Society was Southern, and the South wanted to clear off the Indians to make room for more slave states. There were few admirers of Indians among the Army officers who had been retired to Washington desks after developing malaria and bad reputations in the Seminole campaigns.

But Catlin went, winged with hope. Probably his Indian Gallery would be bought outright by the government and made the core of a magnificent National Museum. Munificently rewarded for his past and future labors, he would go on with his Indian painting, and with his plan for a National Park. That was a vast and noble plan, worthy of America. It would save intact and unspoiled for a grateful posterity a wide strip of Western plains, peopled with native tribes, and grazed by great herds of buffalo to support them.

"What a splendid contemplation," he rhapsodized, "when one (who has travelled these realms, and can duly appreciate them) imagines them as they *might* in future be seen (by some great protecting policy of government), preserved in their pristine beauty and wildness, in a *magnificent park,* where the world could see for ages to come, the native Indian in his classic attire, galloping his wild horse, with sinewy bow, and shield and lance, amid the fleeting herds of elks and buffalos. What a beautiful and thrilling specimen for America to preserve and hold up to the view of her refined citizens and the world, in future ages! A *Nation's Park,* containing man and beast, in all the wild and freshness of their nature's beauty!"

He would still lecture, of course, and enormously increase his audience by publishing his completed two-volume work on the western tribes. Best of all, he would give Clara a home after almost ten years of lodging with relatives or in second-rate hotels. She was the mother of a baby girl now and deserved a home.

Catlin showed and lectured in Washington at the Old Theater and the Wigwam from the 9th until the 22nd of that April, and again on the 24th and 25th for the benefit of those who had been kept at home "owing to the inclemency of the weather." His sincerity and the appeal of his pictures, on canvas and in words, won the powerful friends he needed—Henry Clay, William Seward, Daniel Webster. They and their followers would fight hard for a just Indian policy, and for Congressional purchase of the Catlin Gallery.

"Show it everywhere, young man," boomed Webster. "Tell all America what you told me last night. Conceal no foul dealing: minimize no wrong. Our people are mighty in justice when they are armed with truth. My God, Catlin, you have shamed me. I was blind to all this red majesty and beauty and mystery that we are trampling down."

The Great Spirit of the tepee tribes was truly in Catlin now. Webster compared his earnest eloquence to a bright rapier of words flashing out, keen and jeweled, from a slim brown scabbard; called him a new John the Baptist, fed on stranger locusts and wilder honey. Pale, excited, determined, he moved his painted red legions north to conquer Baltimore, Philadelphia and Boston.

His exhibition in Philadelphia was more than an exciting homecoming to the city of his miniature days and the days of his young dream. When the evening crowds waned from his great showroom and its sperm candles trembled out, he could linger there alone with the companion spirit of William Penn. In even the wildest tribes, Penn's name was a familiar word for truth and justice and peace. Now, so long as a lodge fire blazed, Catlin and Penn would be named together in the guttural tongues of the Rocky Mountains and the Plains.

August saw his show set up at Amory Hall in Boston, where white men, dressed as Indians, had thrown tea into the Bay to brew a Nation. Though his competitors there were the Siamese Twins and Lauriat's Grand Balloon Ascension, Amory Hall could not admit the crowds his lectures drew.

The *Evening Transcript* for September 10th reported that "a more interesting course of lectures were never delivered in this city, or, we may add, in any other. They have enriched us with a volume of knowledge, which we could not compile, from books, in many years, and there are no books from which that knowledge can be derived."

On the following day the same paper printed news that the Mayor and Aldermen had granted the use of Faneuil Hall for the Indian Gallery, "viewing it, very correctly, in the light of a public benefit, in which there is a general and common interest." With its admission charge lowered from 50 to 25 cents, the Exhibition was kept open in that famous building until late October.

Reports of these triumphs, and the more important political news that the American public was ready for and might soon demand a decent Indian policy, were widely circulated on Capitol Hill by Catlin's Washington friends. As his Gallery had suddenly become a symbol of the Indian reforms he advocated, Webster lobbied and reasoned and contrived for its immediate purchase by Congress. Hung before the eyes of legislators, its long impressive rows of intensely human faces would plead the Red Cause well.

For several years Catlin had toyed with the idea of taking his pictures to England, where American reputations in Art and Letters were easiest made. Corresponding with J. Adlard, the London printer, about his proposed book, he had found that its engravings could be done far better and cheaper in England than at home. And now he really had a friend at Court. The Honorable Charles Murray, after failing by one vote to get into Parliament, had been given as a consolation prize the office of Master of the Household to the newly crowned young Queen Victoria. In urgently inviting Catlin to come to London, and assuring him that his pictures and his lectures and his charming wife would be most favorably received there, Murray may have been motivated by something more than affection for Art and Indians. Still desperately in love with Elise Wadsworth of Geneseo, he was forbidden by her father even to write to her. Through Clara Catlin and her friends in the Rochester neighborhood he could get messages to and from his lady.

Trusting Murray's assurances, Catlin now resolved upon a daring and dangerous gamble, to stir our Legislators into doing at once, as American patriots, what they dallied over as patrons of art, and as advocates of Justice. Opening his 1839 Exhibition in New York, he publicly and finally announced that this was the last American showing of the Indian Gallery. It would shortly be shipped abroad, where governments and wealthy private collectors would certainly vie in bidding for the only complete pictorial record of the native American tribes in their native setting.

The effect of this announcement was magical, for no intelligent editor who had seen the Indian Gallery doubted, even for a moment, that it would be bought by some wealthy foreign collector or institution. The readers of paper after paper were told of Catlin's great achievement, and urged to see his pictures while yet they could.

The World said:

Mr. Catlin's advertisement does no justice to the character of his collection. He does not state himself. He is a person of lofty genius and disinterested ambition, and he has abhorred to tarnish the purity of his self respect by even claiming his own. . . . This is one of the most striking triumphs that the pencil has ever achieved. . . . Let every American visit this exhibition.

The Philadelphia *Saturday Courier* was even more commendatory:

We would again urge upon our citizens, as Americans, and as valuing curious information and refined pleasure, to give this gallery a visit. There is not in our land, nor in any part of Europe which we have visited, anything of the kind more extraordinary or more interesting. The galleries . . . in Lon-

10. *She-de-ah, Wild Sage, a Pawnee Pict girl.*

11. Elks and buffalos on the Texas prairie along the Brazos River.

don, Paris, Florence, . . . have been collected by the power of great kings; and the outlay of immense treasure. . . . This is the work of a single individual, a man without fortune and without patronage, who created it with his own mind and hand. . . . Of the enterprise, the free genius, the noble self-dependence, the stern endurance, and indomitable perseverance which our republican system glories in inspiring and cherishing, there is no nobler, and there will be no more abiding monument, than Catlin's Indian Gallery.

The fruits of these fine flowers of praising were mishaps and disappointments, along with desperate labors of showmanship, lecturing and diplomacy. Murray was working for Catlin in London, but could, under the circumstances, make only tentative and uncertain arrangements there. Influential American friends were working in Washington, but could give no positive assurance of even an ultimate Congressional bid for the Indian Gallery. Money had to be raised for letters of credit and for expensive packing and shipping. Clara and her child, and a second child that was coming soon, had to be housed and provided for.

Meanwhile, the campaign to keep the collection in this country continued to gather strength. A writer for the *United States Gazette* said:

Catlin's Indian Gallery.—I am grieved to see that this noble product of American genius is in a few days to leave its native soil, without any effective efforts having been made to ensure its permanent return.

I did hope that individual disposition would be matured into common action, and that at any price a treasure so honourably, so peculiarly American, would be kept from passing into European hands.

Is it *yet* too late to avert such a result? Cannot we yet prevent such a spot upon our city's bright escutcheon?

With what feelings will our descendants enter into some department of the British Museum, or some *Palais* or Musée in the city of Bourbons, to see a treasure thus surrendered by their fathers? Can they boast of Catlin's *powers* as a national glory? Others can point to the *fruits* of them as our national disgrace.

Whether in justice or in wrong, our treatment of the Indian nations has been a reproach to us through the world. Let it not be in a stranger's power to show how noble and how elevated a race we are thus accused of having injured.

Let it not be said that while America has extirpated them from existence, France or England has preserved the only memorial of what they were.

Roused at last, the House of Representatives passed a Resolution directing the Commissioner on Indian Affairs to inquire of Catlin the terms on which he would part with the Gallery, and to consider the expediency of buying it for the nation.

Then, when his personality, eagerness, and eloquence might well have moved even the inert mountain mass of a government agency, Catlin's Red Angel deserted him. Wrestling with heavy pictures in his painting room, he fell over the cot on which he slept there when utter exhaustion overcame him. He struck heavily on his back, and bruised his hip, which abscessed in the joint. For six weeks he lay helpless, in high fever and excruciating pain.

Luckily his Irish foreman, Daniel, was competent to look after the Gallery; and Catlin also had with him now his tall nephew, Theodore Burr Catlin, who was to go on the expedition abroad. But they could do nothing for him in Washington.

No inquiry or offer came from the Commissioner on Indian Affairs. Catlin went in vain to the Secretary of War, and then wrote him letter after letter from New York, begging for action. He promised to cancel his English trip upon receipt of a last minute offer; promised to return from Europe at a week's notice if Congress wanted his work. He would not sell his Indian Gallery abroad, he wrote, for twice the sum he would ask here.

With Thanksgiving near, he had little to give thanks for. He had been very happy to have his aging father, who always believed in him, as his guest and as a proud partner in his success. Putnam Catlin had not prospered, and it was heart-rending to leave him, old now and poor. It was harder still to leave Clara to bear their babe alone, in another's house.

But he must go. And going, he must hope. Hope came easily to him always, and now it brought him visions of triumphs abroad, and Acts of Congress inspired by offers from rival governments. The American spirit of fearless competitive adventure stirred in him too. He would show Europe what wild America was, and what an American artist, unaided by Royal patronage, could do. He was eager to go.

From that going he would not return until he was old and broken and discredited and spent. His passage on the trim packet boat moored there by Manhattan Island, which the Indians sold so cheap, would cost him very, very dear—cost him his loved ones, and all the work of his best years.

XIII

TWO BEARS AND A LION

ON THE 25th of November, 1839, the packet-boat *Roscius* sailed from New York for Liverpool. Up and down her heaving deck limped Catlin, between his giant nephew Burr, and faithful, pugnacious Irish Daniel. Safe in the cargo hold were eight tons of strong chests and cases containing innumerable samples of that Indian civilization which the quiet, lame man had set out to sell to Europe. His sales talk, an immense travelogue manuscript ready for publication, lay on the desk in his cabin. A roofed iron cage, lashed to standards on the open deck, precariously held his two grizzly bears, now grown to prodigious strength and size.

The playful British tars amused themselves and the bored passengers by bouts of sparring with Lady Bear, until a capricious sideswipe of her fanged paw neatly cut off a sailor's nose, leaving it "suspended merely by a small piece of skin or gristle." Luck was with Catlin now. Before he could calculate the probable damages and legal costs of this disfiguring barratry, a Dr. Madden, returning on the *Roscius* from tropical travels, very skillfully "replaced and arranged the organ."

When a mid-Atlantic gale rose out of the black Aeolus bag of rainy darkness and outroared the terrified grizzlies, the ship's cunning captain sent his passengers to the doubtful safety of their cabins by shouting, "THE BEARS ARE OUT!"

While still far out at sea the grizzlies caught scents of land and English ale. The fog-horn bellowings of their delighted *Te Deum* brought an enormous unemployed rabble to the Liverpool dock where the *Roscius* hitched her hawsers. Every ragged urchin tried to carry Catlin's bags, sure that he must be very rich to own such big bears.

In hopes he was indeed rich as Royalty. Of his rainy night trip to London he wrote: "The luxurious carriages in which I was seated . . . braced up and embraced on all sides by deep cushions; the grandeur of the immense stations I was occasionally passing under; the elegance and comfort of the cafés and restaurants I was stumbling into with half-sealed eyes, with hundreds of others in the middle of the night, with the fat and rotund and ruddy appearance of the night-capped fellow-travellers around me, impressed me at once with the conviction that I was in the midst of a world of comforts and luxuries." People who could afford all this could surely afford a shilling apiece for the Greatest Indian Show on Earth.

Looking down London's foggy streets that first morning was like looking down a flue. Colliding with a shadowy cockney, Catlin asked the way to the Egyptian Hall, which the Honorable Charles Murray had conditionally rented for him. The civil fellow directed him to go on past the third turning, where he would see "the hexibition of the uge hox; that hox is in the Hegyptian All, and ee his a wopper."

All day he puddled through murky streets of remembered romantic names, missing the pigs that kept the gutters of American cities so clean. He got his letters of credit accepted, and his Customs Clearance ordered by the Lords of the Treasury, and was back in Liverpool the next morning for a stirring round in the Battle of the Bears.

Daniel had got them ashore and lodged in the cobbled yard of a trusting elderly lady. "From the moment of their landing they had kept up an almost incessant howling, so Rocky-mountain-ish and so totally unlike any attempts at music ever heard in the country before, that it attracted a crowd night and day about the old lady's door, that almost defeated all attempts at ingress and egress. A little vanity, however, which she still possessed, enabled her to put up with the inconvenience, which she was turning to good account, and counting good luck, until it was ascertained, to her great amazement as well as alarm, that the bears were passing their huge paws out of the cage, between the iron bars, and lifting up the stones of her pavement. . . .

"In their unceasing pursuit of this amusement . . . they had drawn the cage around to different parts of the yard, totally unpaving as they went along. . . . The ignorant crowd outside the inclosure, who could get but a partial view of these operations now and then, had formed the most marvellous ideas of these monsters, from the report current amongst them that they were eating the paving-stones; and had taken the most decided and well-founded alarm from the fact that the bears had actually hurled some of the paving stones quite over the wall amongst their heads."

What with the crowd throwing sticks and brickbats back, the landlady calling the police, and the growls of the now thoroughly bellicose bears, poor Daniel envied his namesake who had only to contend with comparatively amiable lions.

Meanwhile Catlin was enmeshed in the constricting folds and windings of Liverpool customs procedure. After the clerks had spent some days trying to write out by ear such un-English proper names as H'co-a-h'co-a-h'cotes-min, they agreed to pass the pictures and Indian curios by number, rather than by title.

Back in London, a gentleman to whom Catlin presented a letter of introduction loaned him a horse and chaise, and a liveried footman to tell him which side of the street the English drove on. With this equipage he bearded the busbied guards at the gates of Buckingham Palace. Lackies ushered him along the corridors to the inner sanctum, where his friend Murray handled the private business of the Queen.

The courteous and competent Murray helped him hasten through the legal rigmarole of leasing the Egyptian Hall. In a document dated December 30th, 1839, the Proprietors let "the three rooms now vacant to Mr. Catlin for one year certain commencing this date at the yearly rental of £550."

With the little he had left after paying the first quarterly install-
ment, Catlin furbished up the old place. At a cost of £200 he had its
front painted, and its interior scrubbed and whitewashed. Carpenters
put up racks and shelves and hung pictures in the immense exhibition room, while plumbers installed gas lighting. The printers were
busy too. They brought out by legions this handbill:

CATLIN'S GALLERY
OF
NORTH AMERICAN INDIANS
EGYPTIAN HALL, PICCADILLY

Mr. Catlin who has been traversing the vast wilds of North America,
denominated 'The Great Far West,' for the purpose of perpetuating the
looks, manners and customs of the North American Indians, has returned,
after an absence of Seven years, with an immense Collection, which is now
open for Public Exhibition in the Egyptian Hall, consisting of 300 POR-
TRAITS OF DISTINGUISHED CHIEFS, &c, Selected from amongst 48
different Tribes, painted in their Villages, in their Native Dress: and

200 OTHER PAINTINGS,
comprising
Landscapes of the Indian Country, the Beautiful Prairie Scenes of the Upper
Missouri, Views of Indian Villages, Indian Dances, Buffalo Hunts, Ball
Plays, &c, &c.

500 PAINTINGS!
There are in the Collection Four Paintings, containing several Hundred
Figures, descriptive of the MANDAN RELIGIOUS CEREMONIES, In
which the Mandan Youths are doing Penance, by passing Knives and Splints
through their Flesh, and suspending their Bodies by their Wounds, &c.
Also a very great variety of
COSTUMES, and other Indian Manufactures and Curiosities;
and a
Crow Lodge or Wigwam, 25 feet high.

. . . .

Open from 10 till 6.—Admission one shilling

The printers also got out, for sale at the door, a one-shilling variation of Catlin's previous American Catalogue. Such a guidebook was needed, not only to lead visitors amidst the bewildering array but to get them in through a fantastic entrance hall faithfully modeled from Fingal's fabled cave. For the famous Egyptian Hall was of an infamous style of architecture, begotten by the mummy of Cheops upon an Irish banshee.

Catlin had mastered the wiles that woo the press. When he was not hanging pictures, he was sending private-view invitations, along with orders for advertising, to the editors of the fifty-one London papers he had listed in his notebook.

As Murray's secretary was also busily sending out invitations to the socially elect, Catlin's private-view, held on the last three days of January, was a British Olympus. Ten Dukes with their Duchesses, two Bishops, five Earls and Countesses, besides ordinary Lords, Baronets, Knights and "private literary and scientific gentlemen" made that opening more than common news.

The professionally dubious press-men were convinced of this incredible American's authenticity by Murray's pointing out to them the painted chiefs and river views that he personally remembered having seen on his American travels. He descanted, with a Duchess on each arm, upon his own experiences under just such a tepee of embroidered buffalo hide as Catlin had reared here. As his *Travels in North America* had just recently came from the press, Murray was regarded as an authority.

A one-man show has seldom had such "friendly and complimentary" publicity. The *Morning Chronicle* termed it "singularly interesting." *La Bell Assemblée's* article began: "Of all the exhibitions that have been brought forward for the amusement of the public, we must give this of Mr. Catlin the preference in every point of view." The *Court Journal* assured its aristocratic readers that "a more attractive exercise for the mind could not have been devised." The report in

The Times reflected the consensus of educated English reaction to the show: "Some of these pictures are exceedingly interesting, and form a vast field for the researches of the antiquary, the naturalist, and the philosopher. The numerous portraits are full of character, they exhibit an almost endless variety of feature, though all bearing a generical likeness to each other. The views of combat are very full of spirit, and exhibit modes of warfare and destruction horribly illustrative of savage life. The methods of attacking buffalos, and other monsters of the plains and forests are all interesting; the puny process of a fox-chase sinks into insignificance when compared with the tremendous excitement occasioned by the grappling of a bear or the butting of a bison. These scenes are all accurately depicted, not in the finished style of modern art but with a vigour and fidelity of outline. . . ."

The *Quarterly Review,* assuming that "Mr. Catlin's object in visiting England with his Indian Gallery, is to sell his collection to our Government," sincerely hoped he would not be disappointed. Though Catlin was pleased by this compliment, he hastened to correct its assumption. While there was the least chance that America would buy his collection, he would not sell it abroad.

A British public, bred upon *Leatherstocking Tales,* scarcely needed such eulogies to whet their eyes for authentic portraits of forty-eight Indian tribes. On February 1st they crowded his public opening, and every afternoon and evening thereafter he talked himself hoarse, answering their questions and explaining Indian customs. The sale of the unnecessary bears to the Regent's Park Zoo had fortunately freed Daniel, whose Irish wit and staunch Americanism made him a slightly risky assistant-lecturer. Even the Exhibition ushers were soon employed as oracles on Indian lore.

"But," Catlin wrote sadly, "this did not satisfy the public while I was present. All inquired for me: 'Where's Mr. Catlin? He's the Lion; his collection is wonderful, but I would give more to see him than all the rest.'"

England's lion hunters were not all in the African jungles. Every mail brought invitations to teas and dinners, which could not all be declined, even though they contained obvious hints that The Indian Man would entertain company gratis until after midnight and then trudge miles for lack of a cab.

Smoke, lonely lodgings, partly eaten meals, indoor life, and incessant talking so thinned and lowered Catlin's vitality that a sensible London doctor restricted him to half-sessions at the Gallery.

Though this new régime revived him and gave him needed leisure for the final preparation of his big Indian book, it was almost fatal to Daniel, who talked himself into a decline as dangerous as his master's. In desperation, the ingenious Irishman drew up a list of answers to the fifty questions that were asked at least one hundred times a day, and proposed printing them in large type on placards prominently displayed all over the Gallery. For example:

"The Indians don't shave.

"The Indians in America are not cannibals.

"The Indians all get married.

"The Indians do lend their wives sometimes to white men, but it is only the old, superannuated ones.

"They never eat the scalps.

"Mr. Catlin was never killed.

"The Indians speak their own language.

"Mr. Catlin is not an Indian.

"The horns on a chief's head-dress have no bad meaning."

With all this, Catlin was happier than he had been for years. Though these Londoners were slow on the trigger, they had not been taught that the only good Indian is a dead one, and they listened when he talked. He talked very well indeed, enlivening his Indian lectures with ardent enthusiasm and typically American stories, and enriching them from his wide learning and long travels.

But there was at least one black and bleak day. Soon after his arrival he had gone to the famous publisher John Murray with a letter of introduction from Washington Irving. Murray had responded with more than mere courtesy, regularly visiting the Indian Gallery and entertaining its proprietor at his table. But when Catlin asked him to publish a two volume Indian book with more than 300 steel engravings, he became a strictly business man. Without even looking at the manuscript or the trial proofs, he said, "No, I am afraid of those engravers. And I love you too much to take from you the profits of a work you have risked your life for. Publish it yourself. Being an artist, you can illustrate it for far less than I can. For me it would be a large risk; but you can take enough subscriptions at your exhibition rooms to cover the publication costs."

This was crushing news. In his enthusiastic certainty that Murray would take the book and reimburse him, Catlin had already pledged himself for large sums to printers and engravers who were busily at work on it, and on him too for the periodic payments he promised. There was little spring in the steps that took him now to Charles Murray, his good friend at Buckingham Palace. How, in Heaven's name could he sell a thousand two-and-a-half-guinea books! The splendor had dimmed in the scarlet tunics of the sentries, and the tall black-frocked ushers reminded him of undertakers. He was walking those corridors, muted with inch-deep carpets, on his way to utter ruin. He had committed himself to the printer and engraver for every penny he had. He knew his powers pretty well now; they were great and varied; but retail salesmanship was not among them.

The Master of Her Majesty's Household took the bad news calmly over tea served in a richly furnished private office bigger than a frontier church. Immaculate, precise, and, to an American, almost over-bred; his Scotch eyes deepened with the calculated daring that had carried him safely through the Pawnee country a few years before. "If John Murray is wrong," he said with a smile, "the fault will be ours. Do your best to get subscribers, and I will do mine."

His best could not have been bettered. In a few days everyone in the book of Nobility and Landed Gentry, and every librarian of a learned institution, was eager to sign for Catlin's volumes on a subscription list commencing with the names of Her Most Gracious Majesty the Queen, H.R.H. Prince Albert, the Queen Dowager, the Duchess of Kent, and the King and Queen of the Belgians.

XIV

BIRTH OF A BOOK

CATLIN'S two volume book, entitled *Letters and Notes on the Manners, Customs and Condition of the North American Indians,* was published by the author at the Egyptian Hall in October, 1841. An intended simultaneous publication of one thousand copies of the issue by Wiley and Putnam in New York was delayed by our customs officers, who levied a heavy and unexpected new duty on the printed sheets.

In an unknown number of copies, Catlin tastefully colored the engravings. For this de luxe edition he printed a title page with red lettering. For other copies which he turned over to a London publisher he printed a third title page. Reprinted over and over, here and abroad, by many publishers, the book has become a hopeless puzzle for bibliographers.

It bothers a biographer too, until he understands why it was written. Catlin wrote it, primarily, to make converts to the Indian cause. Lecturing had taught him that the story's the thing; that the strong cord of dramatic narrative will lead an audience even into the Temple of the Just, where no sermon could entice them. So when he began to write he wove his argument for the Indians unobtrusively into an always interesting and often exciting story of the personal adventures of a painter in Indianland. The fact that the painter happened to be himself did not, in his view, oblige him to make *Letters and Notes* an exact chronological autobiography.

The contemporary travel books that were his models all took some liberties with fact in order to create drama. If their writers were too modest to dress up a little adventure, their publishers were not. Readers did not want to find humdrum west of the Mississippi when they had so much of it at home.

Probably Catlin's book planned itself. Readers had liked his half-dozen letters from the upper Missouri that Stone printed in the *Commercial Advertiser*. His obvious course was to expand those popular letters to chapter length, and add others to them. That was what he did. As his first *Commercial Advertiser* letter had been written at Fort Union in 1832, he dated the opening chapter of his book "Mouth of Yellowstone, Upper Missouri, 1832."

Since he had decided to write a continuous narrative of his Indian travels, that opening obliged him to fit into chapters of later date his expeditions of 1830 and 1831, and to imply that he was among the Pawnees in 1833 when he was really completing pictures and exhibiting in Cincinnati. This was a naughty trick to play with time, but a clever one that saved explanations and a break in his story. The success of the book is his justification.

It is an unbalanced book, with sixteen of its fifty-eight chapters devoted to the Mandan villages alone. As Catlin saw only fair-weather Indians, it says nothing of their winter life in fur-lined tepees, or of how they fed themselves and their fires in zero weathers and ten-foot snows. It does not go deep into Indian beliefs or rituals, nor separate first-hand knowledge from hearsay and speculation. It conceals as well as reveals.

It is a hasty book, a wordy book; often interrupted by moralizings; often sugared with conventional rhapsodies on Nature, and with sentimentality that seems sickly now. It is full of harmless, unnecessary digressions that set the author up as a blithe pleasure-loving daredevil who always wintered in Florida and painted mostly for fun. But it has life in it—vivid descriptions, stirring incidents, pathos, delightful absurdities—and real Indians. It records what a good many other intelligent men had seen or sensed, but had never put on paper.

And it is the autobiography all men would write if they could; the tale of a man, mindless of money and domesticity, following his own free will up and down dangerous rivers and through dangerous wilds; seeing everything, making friends everywhere, growing famous with a confident ease.

Time has turned it into a Domesday Book, the last assize of a lost green continent of endless summer peopled by just such men as we would be if we had time enough, and squaws enough to wait on us.

Its 312 pictures, done on steel from Catlin's drawings by the trade engravers, Tosswill & Myers, seem slight and unimportant now. The elegant half-calf binding that distinguished its first edition, and the gold-stamped red cloth bindings of its later issues are broken at the hinge. But it is never found, in any edition or in any binding, on the cheap bookstalls. The men who conned it by candlelight saved it for the lamp-lit evenings of their sons, who bought more copies for their sons, and buy it still for their son's sons who can only read with the radio full blast.

Had Catlin been blessed—or cursed—with the gifts of his friend Harriet Beecher Stowe, he might have woven the dark injustices that thread his chapters into an Indian tragedy pathetic and powerful enough to rouse the whole English-speaking world in defense of the prairie tribes. Because he appealed to intelligence more than to emotion, the leaven of his labors worked slowly while whole red nations were herded into reservations and starved into consumption by an American government that considered two cents a day sufficient for an Indian's food, clothing and shelter.

We are kinder now to those from whom we took the richest land on earth. We are aware of the worth of our Indian heritage. Its relics are in our museums; its arts are in our homes; its quaint mythologies are in our schools. Catlin's book has done more than any other—perhaps more than all others—to open our eyes and our understandings to these things.

No American author has ever had English reviews bigger or better than the columns on the *Letters and Notes* that young Theodore Burr Catlin clipped out and kept for the coming of his Aunt Clara. *The Westminster Review* gave the book twelve pages, the famous *Edinburgh Review* fifteen. The *United Service Gazette,* written for outdoor men contemptuous of any target smaller than a tiger, went beyond the book to the author.

"Mr. Catlin," it said, "is one of the most remarkable men of the age. Every one who has visited his singularly interesting gallery at the Egyptian Hall has been struck by his remarkable intelligence on every subject connected with the North American Indians; but of its extent, as well as of his extraordinary enthusiam and thirst for adventure, we had formed no idea until we had perused these volumes. In the present *blasé* condition of English literature, in which hardly any work is published that is not founded more or less on other volumes which have preceded it, until authorship has dwindled to little more than the art of emptying one vessel into another, it is refreshing to come across a book which, like the one before us, is equally novel in subject, manner, and execution, and which may be pronounced, without hyperbole, one of the most original productions which have issued from the press for many years."

But a man cannot live, and move his family across the Atlantic, on good reviews. Even in those days, when educated England had the wealth of the world, a fifty-shilling book about Indians sold slowly. Catlin went on at the Egyptian Hall, talking himself so faint that when the cab brought him back to Ibbotson's Hotel he was willing to sip a brandy with his nephew and Irish Daniel.

Every day the postman heaped his desk with congratulations and invitations and enquiries that he had to answer himself because young Burr had neglected to learn spelling. He refused all invitations now,

12. Grand Detour, Upper Mississippi.

13. Kee-o-kúk, the Running Fox, chief of the Sacs. See p. 102.

save those from personal friends and from the secretaries of literary and scientific societies whose learned members wished to hear him lecture. In their hoary halls he was again elate, eager, eloquent, and an American encyclopedia. Before the venerable members of the venerable Royal Institution he proposed a Museum of Mankind, where portraits, manufactures, and historical records of all the primitive races would be collected and kept safe.

"Gentlemen," he said sternly. "We form noble collections of beasts, and birds, and reptiles; of fishes, of insects, and of plants. All these can be gathered a hundred years hence as well as now. But when we occupy a new country we exterminate its native tribes—men like ourselves, with thoughts, with sentiments, and sympathies like our own. They die on their own soil, unchronicled and unknown, and the ruthless hands that slay them bury their ancient cultures and their ancient skills in oblivion with their bodies. Even their skins have no place assigned them amongst the stuffed birds and beasts in our collections."

All over the crowded hall voices cried, "Hear! Hear!" and "By all means: a Museum of Mankind!"

After these exaltations he was utterly exhausted, and lonely beyond the loneliness of empty prairies bleak with snow. So this was fame! Too proud to ask Divine aid when death was by his bedside, he prayed now for Clara's safety on the sea. She must have embarked by this time.

To save her the cruel shock of being greeted by a pale nervous ghost, he left the Gallery in Daniel's charge and recruited his health and spirits by striding briskly through old London, with a guide book that would prepare him to show her the quaintest and most historic sights. He wandered the suburbs too, and found "a nice pretty cottage," with a garden, on a retired site in Waltham Green. It was amazingly big for its size and would comfortably accommodate a family of two grown ups, and two small daughters, with their fresh-cheeked

English nursemaid. When the owner told him it was called Rose Cottage he pulled down the To Let sign and rented the place then and there.

He could barely afford it. Though his Exhibition, his book, and his lectures had brought him over ten thousand dollars in that first year abroad, his expenses had been enormous. Being a true American, he knew the next year would be better. He wanted to go back to the best country in the world, but not until it offered to buy his Indian Gallery. What tales he could tell at home! Tales of famous buildings and famous men, of private evenings with dukes, of London crowds, of country houses bigger and bleaker than state capitols. To many Englishmen now he was only a friend, but to him they were still Englishmen.

XV

A MEADOW MILE

THE English nursemaid and the Irish cook got on famously together at Rose Cottage, and the Catlin babes adored both of
them. So the mistress of the house could make herself even
prettier with London clothes and go in any morning with her husband
to see the wonderful sights she had dreamed of since she was a child.
She was a child still in her admirations and beautiful unspoilt sim-
plicities.

Proud as a brown peacock, Catlin put up an umbrella built for two
and showed her the especially precious sights that other tourists
couldn't peep at through the keyhole. They wandered through royal
palaces where even the stiffest gold-laced footmen bowed and said,
"Seasonable weather, Mr. Catlin." Between showers they sat under
the dripping forsythia, and the pink May-blossoms that matched
Clara's cheeks, in iron-fenced garden squares of the West End which
only a key loaned by some rich India-merchant or beer baronet could
get you into. They threaded their awed course down arched vaults of
the Mint through flocks of wheelbarrows heaped with silver and gold
and all headed one way like fieldfares.

In the evenings, with young Burr sipping porter in the Rose Cottage
parlor to comfort their servants, the Catlins put on formal elegance
and drove off to dine with noblemen and learned dons from Oxford.
One night they dressed in real Indian finery from the Gallery and
won the honors at the most exclusive masquerade of that London
season.

Catlin tried to tell his elder daughter stories about little Mandan girls, but she dozed off on his knee. Then he gave her a painting lesson, which left spots on the new rug. For the first time in fourteen years, Clara had to tell him what he should do, and what he shouldn't.

Delighted as he was with this new domesticity, it could be allotted only limited hours. He was a Public Man now, in the public's exacting and grudgingly-recompensed service. After that first year, his fickle Londoners demanded round painted Indians in place of flat ones. He had whetted this taste by dressing his towering nephew as a Crow chief, who stalked the stage, weaponed, painted, and feathered for war. As a reviewer noted: "His war whoop, his warlike appearance and dignified movements seemed to impress the assemblage more strikingly with the character of the North American Indians than all the other evidences which crowded the walls."

Aware of this reaction, Catlin closed the Exhibition at night in order to deliver in an adjoining room, on three evenings of the week, popular lectures illustrated with what he called *tableaux vivants;* produced by twenty living figures in Indian costumes, forming groups of their ceremonies, domestic scenes, and warfare.

"For these tableaux," he wrote, "I had chosen my men for some striking Indian character in their faces or figures, or action, and my women were personated by round-faced boys, who, when the women's dresses were on them, and long wigs of horses' hair spreading over their shoulders, and the faces and hands of all painted to the Indian colour, made the most complete illusion that could be conceived. I had to furnish each with his little toilet of colours, &c., and instruction how to paint the face before a mirror, and how to arrange their dresses; and then, with almost infinite labour, had drilled them through the Indian mode of walking with their 'toes in,' of using their weapons of war and of the chase, and of giving their various dances, songs, and the war-whoop."

This all-cockney caste enacted Redskin marches, battles, parleys, ball games, dances, and weddings, with the strictest possible fidelity. Their only sop to the sentimental groundlings was "No. 4—Pocahontas rescuing Captain John Smith, an English Officer."

The success of this experiment was not wholly pleasing to Catlin. Audiences that listened politely to his disquisitions on the absolute truth of the Indians to treaties such as were sealed by his "No. 10, Peace-Pipe tableau," shouted their approval of his "No. 8—Battle and Scalping; showing the frightful appearance of Indian warfare, and the mode of taking the scalp."

Intimate as he was now with the most famous nobles and commoners of England, he had yet to meet the Queen. Then, one morning, the Honorable Charles Murray called to inform him that Her Majesty would be pleased to have him show her his model of Niagara Falls at Windsor Castle the next day. His Clara was as childishly delighted as he, in this honor that she could only share through his report: "I took Mr. Murray's arm at the appointed hour of one o'clock, and as we entered the drawing room, we observed Her Majesty and His Royal Highness entering at the opposite door. We met by the side of the model—where I was presented and received in the most gracious and kind manner. Her Majesty expressed a wish that I should point out and explain the principal features of the scene; which, with the vivid descriptions which Mr. Murray also gave, of going under the Horse-Shoe Falls, &c. seemed to convey a very satisfactory idea to Her Majesty and the Prince; they asked many questions about the characters and effects of this sublime scene, and also of the Indians, for whose rights they said they well knew I was an advocate, and retired, thanking me for the amusement and instruction I had afforded them."

Though he managed, through his Gallery, his American agents, and his constant lectures in London and the provincial towns, to sell two small editions of his book, he heard constant complaints of its high price. When he brought out a third edition of a thousand copies late in 1842, he felt obliged to lower the price of the book from £2-10-0 to £1-10-0, and to turn its English publication and sale over to the firm of Longman's, allotting 500 copies to them, and 500 to Wiley and Putnam of New York, who had the American agency. This he thought would give the work a fairer chance.

Reviewers and pseudo-reviewers badgered him for too many copies of *Letters and Notes* which, even in the reprint editions, cost him ten shillings each, unbound. Eighty-five copies, worth £212-10, were either lost or stolen. Large printer's bills fell due before the new issues could be marketed. His letter accepting Longman's offer to take on the already printed third edition ended desperately. "I am anxious to get a little in advance on them to aid me in meeting acceptances due in the beginning of the coming week."

Worse still was the waning of his Gallery's gate receipts. Newer marvels were outbidding the best war whoops of his make-believe Indians. To avoid outright loss, he took his show to the Provinces when the third year of his Egyptian Hall lease expired.

After two successful and moderately profitable months at the Mechanic's Institute in Liverpool, where 22,000 school children saw the show gratis and went off war whooping, he tried road engagements.

"I selected the necessary collection of costumes, weapons, &c. for my lectures and tableaux," he wrote, "and calling together my old disciplined troop from the City of London, I commenced a tour of the provincial towns of the Kingdom, leaving my collection of paintings behind. My career was then rapid, and its changes sudden, and all my industry and energies were called into action—with twenty men on my hands, and an average expense of twelve pounds a day. This scheme I pushed with all the energy I could, and in the space of six months visited, with varied success, the towns of Chester, Manchester, Leamington, Rugby, Stratford-on-Avon, Cheltenham, Sheffield, Leeds, York, Hull, Edinburgh, Glasgow, Paisley, Greenock, Belfast, and Dublin."

In Dublin, Catlin showed in the large supper room of the maternity hospital, from May 23rd to June 14th, 1843. Stirred by the Irish spring, he bought a "Supr. Brown dress coat, Fancy satin vest, Fancy doeskin trowsers." Dashing enough for the artist, yet neutral enough for the modest man of affairs, they would look well on American lecture platforms. For he was homeward bent at last.

Recrossing to England, he opened his show for an advertised last stand: "positively the last in the Kingdom, previous to embarking for New York." After a couple of successful but smoky months, he received a letter unlike his usual fan mail.

"Though a stranger to you," it began, "I take the liberty of addressing this letter to you, believing that its contents will show you a way of promoting your own interest, or at least be the means of my obtaining some useful advice from you.

"I have a party of nine Ojibbeway Indians, on the way, and about at this time to be landed in Liverpool, that I am bringing over on speculation; and, having been here in London some weeks without having made any suitable arrangements for them, I have thought best to propose some arrangement with you that may promote our mutual interests. If you think of anything you could do in that way, or any advice you can give me, I shall be most happy to hear from you by return of post.

"Several persons in London conducting exhibitions have told me they will do nothing unless they are under your management.

I remain, yours very truly,

"Arthur Rankin"

"The hands of Heaven are opened to me," Catlin thought. "Now in the presence of real Indians, I will prove on all the platforms of Europe that every word I speak is true."

Though his answer to Rankin's letter was instant, it was circumspect. "Sir," he wrote, "I received your letter of the 4th, this morning. It will be directly opposite to my present arrangements if I enter into any new engagements such as you propose, as all my preparations are now made to embark for New York in the course of a fortnight from this time. I have always been opposed to the idea of bringing Indians abroad on speculation; but as they are in the country, I shall, as the friend of the Indians under all circumstances, feel an anxiety to promote their views and success in any way I can. I could not, at all events, undertake to make any arrangements with you until I see what kind of a party they are; and at all events, as you will have to meet them at Liverpool, you had better call on me in Manchester, when we can better understand each other's views."

Guarded as it was, that letter was manna and money to the over-venturesome Mr. Rankin, who was really in a fix, with no prospect but that of a big bill for shipping his Redmen home. The London showmen had informed him of an almost forgotten British law against showing primitive peoples for gain. Catlin's reputation would probably allow of liberties no other exhibitor dared to take. After loitering for a couple of days to show his complete unconcern, the desperate Mr. Rankin settled back, scheming schemes, in a train for murky Manchester where Catlin still was.

"After a little conversation with him," Catlin recorded, "and without entering into any agreement, I advised him to lose no time in proceeding to Liverpool to receive them when they landed. . . . The next evening, just after it was dark, my door-keeper, who was not yet in the secret, came running in and announced that there was a 'homnibus at the door quite full of 'orrible looking folks, and ee really believed they were hindians.' At that moment Daniel whispered to me, 'The Ojibbeways are here, and they are a pretty black-looking set of fellows: I think they will do.' I saw them a moment in the bus, and sent Daniel with them to aid Mr. Rankin in procuring them suitable lodgings. A crowd followed the bus as it passed off, and the cry of— 'Indians! real Indians!' was started in Manchester, which soon rung through the Kingdom."

XVI

REAL INDIANS

NINE Ojibbeways were a bigger handful than two bears. In their delight of arrival at the hotel reserved for them, they thoughtlessly sounded a war whoop as they landed from the bus and, being wrapped in their buffalo robes, with their bows and arrows and tomahawks in their hands, they frightened the landlord into a running fit. The keeper of a newly opened hotel then took them in, hoping thereby to turn public attention to his establishment. He was not disappointed. Within an hour the crowd was twenty deep outside, with climbers peering in at every window.

Leaving the Indians to rest from their crossing, Catlin put up a strong dance platform in his exhibition hall and entered into a verbal arrangement with Mr. Rankin. He would conduct their exhibitions and lecture on them, and Rankin would be responsible for their travel and welfare outside the exhibition room. The two men would share alike in expenses and receipts.

Mr. Rankin had only to walk to the new hotel to know he had a bargain. Its proprietor had become the frantic captain of a frail garrison besieged on every side by milling mobs determined to see real Indians. His front wall, which was fresh-painted and not yet dry, was a mess as high as the crowd could reach and climb, and had to be done over again. His windows were broken, his shutters torn from their hinges. Next day the wild guests were moved to accommodations high up in the Exchange Buildings, adjoining Catlin's Exhibition.

Their wildness was all external. Under their robes and feathers and streaked vermilion they were loyal, merry, and tractable Canadian subjects of the Queen, and their urgent ambition was to see Her Majesty in person. All of them knew Catlin by reputation, and one had seen him painting chiefs at the Mackinaw Grand Council.

After they were comfortably settled, he told them of his arrangement with Rankin, adding, "I have agreed to this on two conditions: the first, that it shall please you; and the second, that you will pledge your words to me that you will keep yourselves at all times sober, and drink no spirituous liquors while you are in the country." This being translated for them by their handsome half-breed interpreter, Cadotte, their old chief, Ah-quee-we-zaints, gravely replied: "My Friend, we are here like children in this strange country, and we shall feel happy and not afraid if you will be our father . . . the Great Spirit has put good counsel into your mouth, and we will follow it."

Fortunately for us, Catlin from the first kept exact translations of their reactions to European ways and institutions. After their first Manchester tour, on which they saw its Mayor, one of them reported to him: "We saw the Chief of this village, and his squaw, and many other beautiful squaws, all drinking. We saw many people through the windows, and in the doors, who were drinking. We saw several persons in the streets who were quite drunk, and two or three lying down in the streets, like pigs. We saw a great deal of smoke, and thought the prairies were on fire. We saw many fine-looking squaws and some of them holding on to men's arms, and they didn't look sick, neither. We saw thousands of people in the streets who looked as if they had nothing to eat."

On the stage these Indian troupers were, literally, a howling success. Dramatic by nature and training, and delighted by applause, they danced and stalked and cavorted and yelled without the least self-consciousness. The sardine-packed audiences shouted too, and a squad of policemen outside was hard-pressed to keep the crowd in the street from breaking down the entrance doors.

While his painted performers gathered breath between acts, Catlin discoursed as never before, on the significance of their dances, and the symbolism of their spectacular rigging.

He and Rankin divided between them more than four hundred dollars in clear profit after every evening's performance. Night after night the Indians returned to their lodgings loaded with money and jewelry flung at them by delirious Manchester squaws.

But the publicity that brought treasure also brought trouble. Catlin wrote in his record: "As I was leaving my exhibition-rooms one morning, I met, to my great surprise, an immense crowd of people assembled in front, and the street almost completely barricaded with the numbers that were rapidly gathering, and all eyes elevated towards the roof of my building. I asked the first person I met what was the matter?—supposing that the house was on fire.—to which he replied, 'I believe, sir, that the Hob-jib-be-ways has got loose; I knows that some on em is out, for I seen one on em runnin' hover the tops of the ouses, and they'll ave a hard matter to catch em.'"

Catlin rushed inside and upstairs, but found no Indians until he climbed out through the skylight on to the roof. There were the Ojibbeways, watching the crowd milling below and the brave men assembling on neighboring roofs with ladders, clubs and clotheslines to catch the savages before they began scalping the neighbors. Puffing through the skylight poured the police, gasping, "Hinside with you. Heverybody hinside."

When the puzzled Indians were safely out of sight, the police sergeant ordered Catlin to keep them in their rooms and away from the windows. With the streets full of sullen unemployed men, anything out of the ordinary would draw a crowd, and a crowd would mean a riot. He was right. The cordon of men in blue outside were having a hard time dispersing the immense mob attracted by this little incident.

The Indians could not be kept prisoners, and as Rankin was worried lest bad publicity would prejudice the Queen against giving them an audience, he took them to London in a specially chartered railway carriage. There Murray at once got an appointment for them to see the Queen at her earliest leisure, a little over a month ahead. During that month, of course, they could not be seen by anybody else, save through the windows of the bus in which Rankin took them from their boring rooms into the country, where they exercised themselves and their voices to the astonishment of plowmen and hedgers.

Though Clara was worried over this new venture, she consoled herself that the Indians would have enough of it before her husband collapsed again from talking and excitement.

While the Ojibbeways waited for the great day of their audience at Windsor Castle, Catlin took a six months' lease of the Egyptian Hall, arrayed his Gallery anew, and set up a sturdy dance platform.

The Indians were even busier, brightening their outfits with ribbons and brass buttons and ostrich feathers; rubbing rust off their knives and tomahawks; restringing on tinseled hoops the scalps they had taken; and keeping themselves in good voice by occasionally howling.

Primped and painted to the eyes, they descended at last on Windsor Castle, where their short-sighted chief seized the hand of Sykes, the resplendent porter, in the belief that a man with so much scarlet and gold lace must be the little Queen's husband.

After an hour of admiring themselves in the mirrors of the waiting room, Catlin led them into the Waterloo Gallery where Queen Victoria, Prince Albert, the Duchess of Kent, and Murray were waiting. He introduced them all by their tongue-twisting names, Ah-quee-we-zaints, Pat-an-a-quot-a-wee-be, etc., and explained their fantastic feathered outfits. The Queen called one of the party, a little tawny girl, up to her and held the child's hands. She was of course deeply interested in an empty papoose cradle, lined with black feathers, which one of the Ojibbeway women carried on her back, as a sign of mourning for a dead baby.

With hundreds of castle servants peeping in from the passageways, and the tiny black-gowned Queen again on her sofa, the warriors danced their battle dance; their chief spoke his short, dignified greeting-piece; and the party was over, save for a glass of champagne apiece in the outer waiting room.

Reviewing the affair over their pipes and their bedtime coffee that night, the Indians wondered why so great and rich a country was ruled by a woman no bigger than a girl of twelve. Their old chief decided that things were best thus, "for if this country had a king instead of a queen, he might be ambitious as a great warrior and lead the country into war with other nations: now under her government there is peace."

After making the headlines as objects of Her Majesty's interest, the Ojibbeways danced to crowded houses at the Egyptian Hall week after week. London women loved them, and were willing to carry home a smudge of war paint as the price of kissing an authentic cave man.

The Clergy were little behind the ladies in their attentions to these wild heathens who hardly knew the name of sin. Two of the most insistent "black-coats" were granted a personal interview with the whole feathered troop. The Indians sat in cross-legged silence on their robes while Christianity and Redemption were thoroughly expounded by these somber apostles.

When the reverend gentlemen had finished, Catlin noted, "the old chief filled his pipe again, and sitting with his eyes cast down until he had partly smoked it out, he handed it to the War-Chief, and (instead of rising, as an Indian does to speak on any other subject) the old man rested his elbows on his knees and answered as follows:

" 'My friends—We know that the Great Spirit made the red men to dwell in the forests, and white men to live in green fields and in fine houses; and we believe that we shall live separate in the world to come. The best that we can expect or want in a future state is a clear sky and beautiful hunting grounds, where we expect to meet the friends whom we loved; and we believe that if we speak the truth we shall go there. This we think might not suit white people, and therefore we believe that their religion is best for them.

" 'If we follow the religion of our fathers we shall meet them again: if we follow a different religion we are not sure of it.

" 'My friends—We are here but a few, and we are a great way from our homes, and we shall have but little time to waste in talking on this subject. When a few white men come into our country to make money, we don't ask them to take up our religion. We are here away from our wives and children to try to get some money for them, and there are many things we can take home to them of much more use than white man's religion. Give us guns and ammunition, that we can kill food for them, and protect them from our enemies, and keep whisky and rum sellers out of our country.

" 'My friends—We love you, and give you our hands; but we wish to follow the religion of our fathers, and would rather not talk any more on the subject.' "

Gish-ee-gosh-ee-gee's remarks were less general. "My friends," he said, after a long pull at the pipe, "a few years ago a *black-coat* came amongst us in the town where I live, and told us the same words as you have spoken this morning. He said that the religion of the white man was the only good religion; and some began to believe him, and after a while a great many believed him; and then he wanted us to help build him a house; and we did so. We lifted very hard at the logs to put up his house, and when it was done many sent their children to him to learn to read, and some girls got so as to read the 'Good book' and their fathers were very proud of it; and at last one of these girls had a baby, and not long after it another had a baby, and the *black-coat* then ran away, and we have never seen him since. My friends, we don't think this right. I believe there is another *black-coat* now in the same house. Some of the Indians send their boys there to learn to read, but they dare not let their girls go. My friends, this is all I have to say."

The clergymen decided that "it would be cruel and useless" to question the Redmen further, and retired, leaving a present of a number of handsomely bound Bibles. As the old Chief complained that this talking had made his lips dry, he was allowed a good jug of ale.

Journalizing and earnest lecturing so occupied Catlin that he was utterly unaware of the cunning net his partner was knotting around their joint livelihood. A pretty little black-eyed London minx, who came nightly, caught the eye, and then the heart of Cadotte, the Strong Wind, their half-breed interpreter, who sank into a decline that lonely rest could not cure. Learning too late from the shrewd Daniel what ailed this essential savage, Catlin questioned Rankin, who informed him that he had already given Cadotte his consent to marry Miss Black-eyes. As Rankin had anticipated, his innocent partner said no, that was impossible. Using their disagreement as an excuse for dissolving their profitable partnership, Rankin announced that he had now learned enough from Catlin's lectures to do his own lecturing and that after ten days more he would take the Indians himself on a tour of the provinces.

He was worse than his word. Leaving Catlin with the big hall on his hands at the very opening of the London season, he advertised that he had rented the adjoining room on the same floor—a much finer room where ladies and others would be much better accommodated while listening to lectures "by Mr. Rankin, *himself,* who had lived all his life among the Indians."

To drum up even wider interest in his cunning scheme, Rankin arranged an almost-royal wedding for Strong Wind and the black-eyed maid. He had bands playing on the tops of the flowered and festooned four-horse coaches that conveyed the wedding procession through London's principal streets to crowded St. Martin's Church. Then he announced that thereafter the beautiful and interesting bride would make her appearance on the platform with the Indians, and preside at the piano.

Such cashing-in on the sacred ceremony of marriage was too much for the good taste of Victorian England. As Catlin recorded, with sad satisfaction: "The result was, and deservedly so, that it was condemned by the press, and the project and its projectors held up to public view in the light they deserved." When Rankin opened his stolen show he only escaped mobbing by shouting to the Indians, who leapt into their War Dance and drowned by their yells the hooting and the booing on every side.

XVII

SWEET FOR BITTER

AFTER such a hullabaloo, Catlin's Gallery of Indian portraits and manufactures in the expensive Egyptian Hall rooms was too tame for anybody but himself and a few faithful friends. While it ran on at a loss, under Daniel's direction, its owner worked away in the next room on his second and most striking book, the *North American Indian Portfolio* of 25 descriptive texts and large lithographs, "to be published by the Author, at the Egyptian Hall, price five guineas in printed tints, and eight guineas coloured."

With a subscription list headed by Queen Victoria, King Louis Philippe, the Emperor of Russia, and the King of the Belgians, this truly regal volume was issued in England in 1844, and reissued by Ackerman in New York, with seven additional prints, in 1845. Not since his glorious Osceola had Catlin issued anything so truly splendid as the large delicately colored lithographs in the English editions. One of them—"Buffalo Hunt on Snow Shoes"—has the quality of an old Japanese color-print.

But they were only copies of his paintings, and now his hand hungered for the living models that he could only find in the fastnesses of Western America. He had converted England to the Indian Cause and made a great Indian reputation. It was time to take himself and his homesick Clara and the children back to the good new U.S.A. where there were no Windsor Castles, but no Manchester slums.

He had four children now, the youngest a long-awaited boy named George, Jr. Waiting for this pink wonder to grow to transportable size, his parents saw the rest of the sights in style. By the will of her father, Clara was at last provided for by a considerable property held in trust, as well as a legacy of three thousand dollars in cash.

A series of terrible shipwrecks, which made her anxious about the crossing, stirred Catlin's humanity and ingenuity to a marvelous invention "for disengaging and floating quarter-decks of steamers and other vessels for the purpose of saving lives at sea." After paying a patent lawyer a good sum, he learned that a Captain Oldmixon had registered a similar invention years before.

While moralizing to Clara—as an established man in his late forties may justly do—that "Life has its chapters, like the chapters of a book, and our days are like the leaves we turn in reading it," he was interrupted by the governess, who announced that an American gentleman was at the door.

In his fine frock coat, Catlin went out to meet a Mr. G. H. C. Melody, who had just arrived in London with fourteen Ioway Indians.

Mr. Melody was indeed an American Gentleman, whose "well-known integrity of character" had induced our Secretary of War to let him take these very select tribesmen abroad, for the improvement of their habits and morals, as well as their simple minds. Even the fastidious Clara liked him at first sight, in spite of the temptation he laid before her husband.

Catlin's trip to No. 7, St. James's Street, to meet the magnificent Ioways, was a trip to his spiritual home. These were no run-of-the-mill Red subjects of the Queen, but famous American braves whom he had known and painted in their own prairie wigwams. Portraits of their two chiefs, White Cloud, and the Walking Rain, hung in his Gallery, along with one of their stern warriors, the Fast Dancer. When Catlin entered their apartments they grasped his hands and shouted his Indian name, Chip-pe-ho-la.

Exultingly he took them to his Gallery. Instead of vulgarly yelling as the Ojibbeways did on first entering it, they "walked silently and slowly to the middle of the room, with their hands over their mouths, denoting surprise and silence. In this position, for some minutes (wrapped in their pictured robes, which were mostly drawn over their heads or up to their eyes), they stood, and rolled their eyes about the room in all directions, taking a general survey of what was around them, before a word was spoken."

At first in whispers, and then in the strong gutturals so sweet to Catlin's starved ears, they talked over the familiar faces and scenes upon the walls. Under the Crow wigwam they sat and smoked the pipe of council while Jeffrey Doraway, their mulatto interpreter who was one of Catlin's old frontier friends, explained to them what that happy gentleman and Mr. Melody had agreed to do for them.

The good new arrangement, like the bad old one with Rankin, was for an equal partnership in expenses and receipts. It was admittedly risky, for London was not exhibition-minded in July, and the Rankin fiasco was still a handicap in the way of publicity for any Indian show. But Catlin dared the risk, to show England these real Princes of the Prairies.

Their medicine man, the Blistered Feet, had an Eagle's propensity for high places as well as heavenly thoughts. He was already on the Egyptian Hall roof, standing like a bronze, robe-wrapped statue and contemplating Piccadilly, into which the gathering crowds below expected him to tumble at any moment. When the other Indians got into the coach at the door he climbed to its top beside the driver "with his buffalo robe wrapped around him, the long and glistening blade of his spear passing out from underneath it, near to his left ear, and his vermilioned face surmounted by a huge pair of buffalo horns, rising out of a crest of eagle's quills and ermine skin."

The first audiences to see and hear these Ioways give their dances at the Egyptian Hall were Catlin's friends and personal followers; by this time discriminating connoisseurs of things Indian. All pronounced this troupe infinitely wilder, more graceful, and more impressive than the lost Ojibbeways.

The Blistered Feet, Anglicized as the Doctor, was something entirely novel—an Indian humorist. Even when interpreted, his words were whimsical and waggish. Ogling and smirking at all the ladies, he ended his part in the first Eagle Dance with: "My Friends,—I see the ladies are pleased, and this pleases me—because I know, that if they are pleased they will please the men." After the performance a press of ladies gathered round him, saying they were sick, and asking him to feel their pulse and diagnose their affliction. "Love," said he. "Get husbands and in a day and a night you will be well."

Happy again, Catlin spoke with the tongues of tawny angels, making otherwise tedious catalogues of curious customs lively as well as enlightening. "Here," he would say, "is Okee-wee-me, the Female Bear that walks on the back of Another. Okee-wee-me is the mother of this little papoose, called Corsair, comfortably slung here in the cradle on the mother's back, according to the general custom of all the American tribes. . . . These cradles are often, as in the present instance, most elaborately embroidered with porcupine quills, and loaded with little trinkets hanging within the child's reach, that it may amuse itself with them as it rides."

Then he would turn his eloquence upon No-ho-mum-ya, He Who Gives No Attention: "This glorious six foot savage, whose Cyrano frontispiece won him the name of Roman Nose, saved from a war-party of his own tribe the lives of ten unarmed enemies. To lead the harrowing scalp-dance, he will now cast off his fringed shirt and all his dress save his beautifully garnished leggings and moccasins, and the many-colored sash and kilt of eagle's quills and ermine about his waist. His head is vermilioned red, and dressed with his helmet-like red crest, surmounted by a white and a red eagle's quill, denoting his readiness for peace or war. His shoulders and his arms are curiously streaked with red paint, and on his right and his left breast are the

148

impresses, in black paint, of two hands, denoting the two victims he has struck, and whose scalps he holds attached to his painted toma-hawk." As the red giant disrobed, near-by ladies who had never seen a man outside a cutaway coat, or perhaps a long nightgown, wavered between rapture and an urge to run. One of them sent up to the plat-form, by a servant in livery, a present of fourteen elegantly bound Bibles.

Good reports of Catlin's new and superior Indian show soon brought an invitation from the great Benjamin Disraeli for the whole party to breakfast with him at twelve the next day.

The lateness of the invitation was a great grief to the Ioways, and something of a social shock. Prairie etiquette required a host to send his bid at least three days beforehand, so that the guests could prepare themselves by fasting and liberal doses of a black brew steeped from Cascara bark. Then they could pay him the high compliment of eating everything in sight.

Retiring supperless, the Indians were up next morning before the maid brought in their tea. For hours they preened and bedecked themselves. The vain old Doctor, expecting to be seated among lovely ladies, painted and repainted himself three times before he was satis-fied with the effect. Catlin watched him awaiting the wonderful hour. "With all his finery and trinkets on, and his red and yellow paint— with his shield, and bow and quiver by his side, he was straightened upon his back, with his feet crossed, as he rested in a corner of the room upon his buffalo robe, which was spread upon the floor. His little looking-glass, which was always suspended from his belt, he was holding in his hand, as he was still arranging his beautiful feathers and contemplating the patches of green and yellow paint."

When the party was settled, at no great ease, on Mr. Disraeli's crimson velvet chairs, admiring their host's collection of damascened daggers and other antique weapons, the Doctor was missed again. A search discovered him sitting on the floor of a luxurious bathroom, smoking his pipe and musing on the gilt plumbing of vapour and shower baths, which he thought would be useful in his professional practice at home.

After a champagne breakfast, and a liberal giving of presents by Mr. Disraeli, the ladies entered the drawing room, to find the Doctor there, admiring himself immensely in a bigger looking-glass than he had ever dreamed of. Though he pretended that his interest was only in the frame, the ladies laughingly accused him of being vain, and asked him how he made himself so truly peacockish. Understanding their intimate interest, he drew out his own little glass and his colored cosmetics wrapped in the skin of a rattlesnake. With this startling compact, out came the dried finger of one of the enemies he had slain, which he now carried as a charm.

Every evening when the excitement of their show was over, Catlin joined them in their rooms. Across a jug of light ale that was allowed them as a nightcap after their genteel behavior in sipping so sparingly of Disraeli's champagne, he talked long with them of both the old times and the new. They were as merry now as in their wigwam homes, having their little jokes on one another, and especially on the eccentric Doctor. Nothing amused them more than their discovery that the white men had at least six different kinds of religion, which the Fast Dancer, called Jim for short, illustrated by a sketch of Indians climbing one ladder right up into the heavenly hunting grounds, while the whites raised six ladders, all too short, and wrung their Baptist, Jewish, Catholic, Methodist, Quaker, and Anglican hands.

During one of their shows, a giant and giantess, of immense size, entered the exhibition room, amazing the Indians so much that they instantly stopped dancing, sat down, and lit their pipes to smoke and consider these vast human curios. Deciding that a sacrifice might be wise, they sent the Doctor into the firelit dressing-room. When he had burnt a piece of tobacco in the grate there they resumed their performance. The next day the Colossi, a brother and sister who showed as the Norfolk Giants, visited the Indians at home. The sister's apron strings were wound in all their yardage just at the level of Catlin's eye, and the brother was even taller.

The delighted Ioways had a ball of twine ready and unrolled on the floor. Each of them cut off a lengthy piece to use in taking his own exact measures of the maiden mountain and her behemothic brother. They took his length from head to foot, and from extended hand to extended hand. They measured his waist, and expanded chest, and got his foot and finger lengths; carefully knotting their strings to show each exact dimension to the folks back home, in good American style. The professionally-minded Doctor alone dared to take the Lady's measures. But a combination of delicacy and distance kept him from getting his string all the way round her buxom bust. Before the Giants departed, the Indians very graciously gave them some little keepsake trinkets for their kindness in calling.

The rascals laughed for days over the Doctor's affair with the Big One. The only extant record of her height and breadth was the one he had taken and carefully rolled up and put away in a little box with other precious things, at the head of his bed. He would have something more than the others had to show at home. But one day while he was out, mischievous Jim got a much longer cord, knotted it on a much more gigantic scale, and substituted it for the authentic measure.

Mr. Melody was sincere in his professed purpose of showing the Indians all the fine things of England. He or Catlin took them on daily bus drives to museums, churches, and the like. As war paint and feathers were over-conspicuous, the insatiably curious Doctor, and Jim, who learned English faster and oddlier than a parrot, went for their walks in frock coats, beaver hats, and wigs. To study the white man's religion, the Doctor became a church-goer. In the excitement of seeing so many pews full of pretty ladies, he once forgot to take off his hat until somebody pointed to him. When he whisked it off, off too came his wig, exposing to the worshipers his scalp-lock and the vermilioned top of his head, from which he had not deemed it necessary to wash off the war paint. A Methodist sermon so bored him that he settled thoughtfully down with his head between his knees, puffing out a protective smoke screen from his pipe.

Catlin conducted the whole party through Westminster Abbey's incredible aisles of rich-wrought history, and into the perfectly proportioned cold loneliness of St. Paul's. Under pointed arch and round arch alike, "they stood and contemplated in amazement the works of human hands, so entirely beyond their comprehension that they returned in reserved and silent contemplation."

Though that was the proper attitude for Indians, Catlin did his amazing best, night after night, to get unrestrained applause from the audiences that still packed his show. For these cockney shop clerks and gasping and giggling ladies who wanted their shilling's worth of Hindians, he turned the mildly exciting incidents of his frontier travels into thrilling hairbreadth escapes. His Ioways almost waded in the blood of their exploits. He did not notice that evening clothes and refined faces were fewer and fewer among his hearers. Blinded by good American pride in the wild men that only his own Wild West could breed, he proudly and exultantly prepared his downfall. Clara seldom came to hear him now.

XVIII

THROUGH PRAIRIE EYES

THE sound of seething cider bottles blowing their corks had given the Indians Chick-a-bob-boo as an onomatopoetic term for all spirited beverages. From it they derived Chickabobboags as a name for pubs and gin-palaces. At first they whispered the word, for it was hardly credible to them that a people who preached temperance so much should practice it so little.

Returning from an omnibus ride through streets literally lined with taverns, the Doctor reported that he had counted hundreds of these establishments, and seen from his lofty seat the toping that went on inside.

Jim questioned the Medicine Man's figures, suggesting that he had counted ladies instead of grogshops. The Doctor backed his mathematics with money, and spirited betting began between him and some of the others on the number of Chickabobboags they could count on a bus ride from St. James's Street to Blackwall, and back by way of Euston Station.

Off they went in their war-paint and feathers with Roman Nose taking the count on one side of the bus and Little Wolf on the other, while the old War-Chief kept the tally by notching a stick with his scalping knife every time either of them shouted "Chickabobboag!" The Doctor and Jim, perched on the roof, kept their own oral count, between comments on the ankles of ladies who lifted their skirts in crossing the puddled street. At first, counting was easy, but when they got into the poor districts Chickabobboag! was shouted so repeatedly—

153

often by both counters together—that the War-Chief could not cut notches fast enough. He gave up when every corner of his second stick was saw-toothed from top to bottom, and resorted to pencil and paper. The final official score was four hundred and fifty, though the Doctor insisted he alone had counted seven hundred and fifty-four.

As the Indians wondered where all the Chickabobboo came from, Catlin arranged for them to visit one of London's biggest breweries. There the top-hatted owners, accompanied by their wives, led them through bewildering mazes of vats and pipes and boilers. Taken into the steamy upper regions, they perched on a beam overlooking a seething brew of over a hundred thousand barrels. There they silently contemplated and passed the pipe while one of the proprietors supplied their interpreter with statistics on the incredible annual beer consumption of the British public.

That was too much for their simple understandings. With a wild whoop they all leaped into an empty vat and began the Medicine Dance. Catlin noted down in his journal: "Their yells and screaming, echoing through the vast and vapouring halls, soon brought some hundreds of maltsmen, grinders, firers, mashers, ostlers, painters, coopers, &c., peeping through and amongst the blackened timbers and casks, and curling and hissing flames, completing the scene as the richest model for the infernal regions."

The Ioways were fast losing their native innocence. At first they had been puzzled by the pretty ladies who needed husbands so badly that they laid eyes, and then hands, on any man they met in the streets who troubled to look back at them. The Doctor soon observed that it was not always the same man. When these ladies of delight began beckoning even the chiefs down from their lofty apartment in the night, he and Jim decided that they were Chimegotches—that is Coldbloods, or fish that rise only to a gilded fly. To see something more of the interesting and instructive mode of life of such ladies, the two Indian scientists asked permission to visit some of the hells of under-ground London, wishing to compare them with the Hell the Black-coats constantly spoke of. They could hardly be hells of fire, said the Doctor, for there was surely enough Chickabobboo in them to put out any blaze.

To divert this over-acute interest in civilized customs, Catlin took the whole troop to the Surrey Zoological Garden. There the appearance of such enormous feathered folk made the affrighted parrots scream "God dam!" and fly in all directions. The Doctor offered a sacrifice of tobacco to the lion, and to his own totem-brother the wolf, with whom he howled in lugubrious unison. With a tear in his eye for his poor prisoned brother, he went on to the ragged old buffalo's pen, around which the other Indians were wiping their eyes. They wanted to hug the bears; and to the rattlesnake they solemnly sacrificed more precious tobacco. As they passed the pond, ducks cried "Quack! Quack!" Jim pointed to them and told the Doctor they were calling for his professional services.

After their beefsteak and six-per-cent Chickabobboo that night, they talked gravely of the captive animals, and of the doleful looks they all wore in their prison cells. The usually facetious Jim asked, "What have all these poor animals and birds done that they should be shut up to die? They never have murdered anybody—they have not been guilty of stealing, and they owe no money."

For the sake of argument, the Doctor took the other side. "Those animals," he said, "are fortunate, with plenty to eat and plenty of white men to wait on them." But he was sad about the old buffalo bull, and wanted to see him thunder over the prairies again.

The hyena's habit of digging up the buried bodies of the dead had greatly impressed Jim. After a long recumbent meditation he decided that the hyenas would go to hell, because they were as wicked as the white people, who also dug up Indians' graves and scattered their bones.

To preserve their wonderful statistics of Chickabobboags, Jim began

155

to keep a little journal in which, with Daniel's aid, he entered them. Another recorder, red-winged perhaps, was writing too, in the Book of the Truly Charitable. On their bus-ride through the forlorn, God-forsaken slums of the dock district, the Indians had given more than thirty shillings to the poor.

With the coming of fine weather, Catlin took them to that holy of holies, Lord's Cricket Grounds; and then to the manicured lawns and greeneries of Vauxhall Gardens for a last London performance. There the Ioways lived in wigwams and showed wild skill in mounted archery. They were watched by vast crowds, including 32,000 children from Charity Schools. With the scales lifted from their eyes, the intelligent red pagans saw the significance of such an army of young paupers. This Christian civilization was a long way from the perfect charity its Black-coats preached.

Jim's journal now became a bitter indictment of the whole British social system. As the troupe toured the Midlands and Scotland they saw things that did not tower and shine. In the hall of their Birmingham lodgings, the Doctor spied a ragged, emaciated woman and child begging for coppers. Deeply touched, he offered her money, which she was afraid to take. At his request, Daniel prevailed upon the woman to come up to their room, assuring her that they would not hurt her, and would give her much more than white people would. She went up, and the Indians, seated on the floor, lit a pipe and told Daniel they were anxious to talk with her, to find out how it was that she could not be taken better care of.

Assured a little by the Doctor's present of five shillings, the woman answered to their interpreter that she had been in the workhouse, where her husband was still confined. She had not been allowed to live with him there. So she had taken to begging in the streets. She feared that she and her child would die of starvation and cold when winter came.

After the Indians had fed the miserable pair, and given the child presents, the kind Doctor escorted them down to the lobby, where he assured the woman by sign language that she would find food set out for her every morning while they were in Birmingham.

When Jim obtained for his journal the appalling round-numbers of English people in almshouses and pauper hospitals, the Indians were so moved that they volunteered to give charity performances which raised a large sum for the Birmingham General Hospital and the local Temperance Society's charity wards. In presenting this generous gift, the Doctor said: "My Friends,—We Indians are poor, and we cannot do much charity. The Great Spirit has been kind to us though, since we came to this country, and we have given altogether more than two hundred dollars to the poor people in the streets of London before we came here; and I need not tell you that this is not the first day that we have given to the poor in this city. If we were rich, like many white men in this city, the poor people we see around the streets in this cold weather, with their little children barefooted and begging, would soon get enough to eat, and clothes to keep them warm."

On their way to Leeds, even the hardened warriors were startled by their first view of a fox hunt. This was certainly a war-party! Learning that it was only the exercise of gentlemen of quality, they were amused; and then angered; for rich people had no need of fox-steaks.

Though the glass and the vaulted majesty of York Minster awed them, their Doctor climbed out on its dizzy topmost pinnacle to be a little nearer the Great Spirit. Then they visited the Castle prison, where a turnkey showed them a whole museum of knives, clubs and guns that had been employed in famous murders.

Pointing with his rod, he explained: "Now Gentlemen, that hammer and razor you see there. With that same hammer Mary Crowther knocked her husband down, and then with that razor cut his throat. She was hung here.

"Do you see this short gun, Gentlemen? This is the very gun with which Dobson shot his father. He was hung here.

"A fire-poker, Gentlemen, with which King murdered his wife near Sheffield. He was hung here.

"A bloody axe and poker, Gentlemen. With that axe and poker . . ."

By this time the Doctor was outside looking for a route of quick escape. Calling anxiously to the others, he said, "I do not think this is a good place for us to stay any longer."

Though Catlin and Melody assured them that the crimes they had heard of were not all of yesterday's date, the Indians insisted on an immediate departure from what they called thereafter "the wicked town."

They could not understand the penning of men in cages. "Why not kill them?" they asked. "It would be better, because when a man is dead he is no expense to anyone, and his wife can get a husband again, and his children a father to feed and take care of them. . . ."

After this visit, Jim entered in his book how many white people in the Kingdom were locked up for crimes, and how many because they couldn't pay money. The Doctor anxiously questioned Catlin about the finances of the show, because a failure in that part of the country might put them all behind the bars.

While showing at Newcastle and South Shields, the Indians visited one of the immensely deep coal mines that were then working veins far out under the sea. They were appalled by what they saw; horses and mules condemned to perpetual darkness; and men, women and children, black as the night they toiled in, and even slept in. They reported seeing "hundreds of women and children drawing out from some narrow places where the horses could not go, little carriages loaded with coal; where the women had to go on their hands and knees through the mud and water, and almost entirely naked, drawing their loads by a strap that was buckled around their waists; their knees and their legs and their feet, which were all naked, were bleeding with cuts from the stones, and their hands also; they drew these loads in the dark, and they had only a little candle to see the way."

The number of persons thus employed and prisoned underground made another entry in Jim's book. His figures were strengthened by the Doctor's secretly adding to the end of each of them one or two of the zeros that he had now learned to form.

XIX

THE JUICE OF THE STONE

THE black mephitic exhalations of the cities of civilization had soiled beyond cleansing the white doeskins and featherings of the fourteen Ioways. Their lungs were polluted too. While they showed in Edinburgh, which they called the Beautiful City, baby Corsair, the papoose of Little Wolf, sickened with fevered coughing.

They took the poor babe on with them to Dundee. One of their fellow passengers on the steamer was a penniless young girl, who implored the Captain to take her home to Dundee, where her father would pay her fare. When the Captain abused and threatened her, the Indians contributed her passage money. Part of it was a shilling that Little Wolf had laid in the hand of his stricken papoose, so that the child might do one deed of mercy while alive.

Little Corsair died as his weeping father carried him ashore. His emaciated brown wisp of body was sent to Newcastle for burial in the Quaker cemetery there. His parents felt that "the Good People"— their name for the Society of Friends—would not allow his grave to be dug up by curio-hunters. With all their doubts of sectarian Christians, the Ioways admired and respected the English Quakers, who had befriended them with sincere, quiet courtesy instead of fancy, silver-clasped Bibles.

In Dublin, a few days later, they discovered that these were not, literally, the most valuable of books. Jim took an armful of his surplus Bibles to a bookstall and tried to trade them for subscriptions to *Punch* and the London *Times*. "Glory be to God," was the answer, "an what

From the Smithsonian Institution

14. Toh-to-wah-kon-da-pee, the Blue Medicine, a Sioux medicine man.

15. Buffalo chase in snowdrift.

would myself be doin' with thim?" Neither at the Exhibition nor in the streets could puzzled Jim get a cash offer, even for one bound in black velvet.

The Doctor had been loath to leave Dundee, where a little chamber-maid with a taste for novelty warmed his old bones against the February chill by tiptoeing in every night and sharing his buffalo robe coverlet. But the noble stags in Dublin's Phoenix Park revived his spirits. He was organizing a grand hunting party, when Daniel intervened with an explanation of the Irish game laws. The fact that an Irishman could not shoot or fish exactly where he liked was incredible to the Indians.

Catlin liked Dublin in spite of the beggar who greeted him with "My kind sir, may the gates of Heaven open to receive you," and then—when no sixpence appeared—shouted after him: "And may you be kicked out the moment you get there." He liked the warmth of Irish hearts, the tang of Irish wit, the absurdity that creeps into the most solemn Irish institutions and observances. London was too formal, too coldly correct, too precise in matters of fact, and a great deal too British for him. And the London society that had opened its drawing rooms to Catlin the Artist and Explorer, was beginning to close them on Catlin the Showman, "that Yankee fellow who is cashing in on his precious Indians."

Clara knew what was happening. When her husband returned from Dublin with the news that he was off with the Ioways to Paris, she begged him to turn them over to Melody and take her and the children home. "Please, please, George," she sobbed. "Get back to your easel where you are really happy. You are an artist, and a great one, not a showman. The things you are letting people say about you are not fair to your genius, or to your children and me. Take us home. Take us home!"

No, he had promised the Indians a look at the King of France. They felt slighted that Queen Victoria had not given them an audience, and he was not going to send them home unhappy. He had friends in Paris who were close to the King. To Paris he must go.

From his first landing on English soil, he told Clara, he had planned a Paris Exhibition. Even before she came over he had employed a translator to turn his catalogue and his lectures into French. This would be a wonderful way for her and the children to see the best sights in Paris, and get into the life of the best sort of French people. He would do well in Paris, he knew, with his double attraction of paintings and real prairie Indians. King Louis Philippe had wandered much in his younger days among the American tribes, and would certainly want to meet the man who painted them. What meant even more to Catlin, though he did not say so to Clara, was the fact that the French King had once been in Wilkes-Barre.

While the Paris trip was in preparation, No-ho-man-ya, the Roman Nose, died of the swiftly fatal consumption. He was buried in a make-up of emerald green and the best vermilion, with his medal on his breast, and his pipe, and his bow, and his arrows—newly sharpened for the heavenly hunting grounds—beside him.

Before the last winter-brown in the Luxembourg Gardens was greened over, Catlin was settling his family in a comfortable apartment overlooking the Church of the Madeleine and fighting with Paris officialdom over every detail of the Indian show he was about to open in the Salle Valentino on Rue St. Honoré. The Ioways, meanwhile, were kept incommunicado at the Victoria hotel, and permitted to see the sights of Paris only in peeps through the curtains of a closed omnibus that took them to the country for airings. Bored by this closeted wait for their audience with the King, they compared London with what they were seeing now. They preferred Paris houses, and thought Paris people had more cheerful looks than Londoners, either because they were less afraid of being jailed for debt, or because they had not so much money as to worry themselves thin for fear of losing it.

At last they got to the Palace of the Tuileries, where they were received very graciously by the whole Royal Family. The King—through Jeffrey, the mulatto interpreter—told them how he had tramped the American wilderness as a young man, and slept in the wigwams of Oneidas and Shawnees and Georgia Cherokees; and how he had paddled his own skiff down the Ohio and Mississippi to New Orleans.

On the 3rd of June, 1845, all the censors were satisfied, and Catlin was allowed to announce the opening of his Exhibition in the vast Salle Valentino, where the Indians had an archery range fifty yards long. They were experienced showmen now, and their whoops and wild antics thrilled the tremendous crowds that good publicity had brought to see *les nouveaux Diables*. The opening was attended by the most distinguished people of Paris, the Minister of the Interior and his lady, the Prefect of Police, several foreign ambassadors, and a number of editors of the leading journals.

Some of these gentlemen of the Press looked at the Indians on the walls as well as at those on the platform. The *Constitutionnel* for June 22nd reported:

"Le museé Catlin est une des collections les plus curieuses qu'on ait vues á Paris. . . . Parmi ces portraits, il y a des figures d'une beauté, d'une élégance superbes. Il y a des profils, le croirait-on, qui rappellent le type grec ou Antinous." The figures in Catlin's crowded action pictures had also the antique rightness, this critic noted; a rightness gained by formalizing untortured natural poses and making of them "le type de tous les autres mouvements." He advised *les paysagistes* of his own country to study Catlin's landscapes, so lively in feeling, so sincere, so naïve and spontaneous, and withal so convincing. Before the stampeding hunting scenes, he could only cry "Quel drame!"

As the Indians were free during the mornings, and after ten o'clock in the evening, they indulged daily in sightseeing drives and late parties. At crowded balls, they had room, for nobody wanted to rub against them and pick up streaks of their vermilion.

"It amused the Doctor and Jim very much," Catlin noted, "to see the gentlemen take the ladies by the waist when they were dancing with them. . . . They were pleased also, . . . with the manner in which the ladies showed their beautiful white necks and arms, but they saw several that they thought had better been covered. . . . In coming away they were sorry they could not find the good lady to thank her, the crowd was so great; but the Chickabobboo (champagne) which was very good, was close to the door, and a young man with yellow hair and moustaches kept pouring it out until they were afraid, if they drank any more, some of the poor fellows who were dancing so hard would get none."

From a window of the apartments of the Duke d'Aumale in the Tuileries they looked out on the illuminations and magnificent fireworks of the King's birthday fête. They went to watch a thousand elegantly dressed demimondaines dancing in the Jardin Mabille; and then to the *Bal Masqué* at the Opera.

The masquerade bothered Jim. "He looked upon it as a very immoral thing that so many thousands of ladies should come there and be ashamed to show their faces, and have the privilege of picking out just such men as they liked to go with them . . . and lead them out. 'Amongst the Indians,' he said, 'they had a custom much like that to be sure, but it was only given once a year, and it was then only for the young married men to lend their wives to the old ones; this was only one night in the year, and it was a mark of respect that the young married men were willing to pay to the old warriors and chiefs, and the young married women are willing to agree to it because it pleases their husbands."

Jim and the Doctor were eager to see an exhibition of female nudities, "ringing all the changes on attitude and action," under the troupe name of "Industrious Fleas;" but this, "one of the choicest little sights to be seen in Paris," was denied them by their wise managers.

The Indians were always amused by the sight of Parisian ladies leading dogs along the boulevards on leashes of ribbon and plaited leather. As they had seen dogs leading blind men around London, they thought at first that half the ladies of Paris were blind. Then they concluded that these dogs were kept close, so that they would sooner be fattened for eating. On one omnibus trip, the Doctor and Jim kept count of all the lady dog-leaders they saw. That count listed:

"Women leading one little dog 433
Women leading two little dogs 71
Women leading three little dogs 5
Women with big dogs following (no string) 80
Women carrying little dogs 20
Women with little dogs in carriages .... 31"

At the Paris apartments of Mrs. W. Costar of New York, the Ioways ate with knives and forks and drank toasts like polished gentlemen. Later, in the music room, the Doctor was completely fascinated by the playing and singing of a beautiful young lady. After he had stood and smiled upon her in profound admiration during her four or five songs, he declared that her voice was as lovely as that of his totem, the wolf.

Taken to the picture galleries of the Louvre, the Doctor was distressed that there were so many pictures outside the Indian Gallery, which he had supposed unrivaled. On that visit Catlin met and made friends with Baron Alexander von Humboldt, the explorer and geographer, who was later to have a hand in the strangest and last of his enterprises.

Very sensibly, in such a welter of wonders, the Indians now decided to stop questioning, and to "look with their eyes only half open," lest they would see more than their troubled and sated minds could manage. With this new outlook, they decided that the guillotine, from which so many high and handsome heads had rolled, was very like the sawmills they had seen along the Mississippi.

They approved of the Hospital des Invalides, where they saw old and crippled warriors of France living in comfort and honor, but they groaned at sight of the thousands of abandoned little children in the Foundling Hospital. The Doctor wondered why the thousands of women leading and petting little dogs in the streets did not each one take a little lost child and be its mother.

At his Exhibition, Catlin was again a Great One among Great Ones, walking down the long lines of his pictures arm in arm with George Sand, and with Victor Hugo. But his Ioways were darkly brooding and disturbed. The Doctor's sleep had been for some time broken by nightmares of most ill omen. Now Little Wolf's wife died suddenly of consumption, and was given a funeral in the vast dark Church of the Madeleine.

Thoroughly frightened, the Ioways met in solemn private council. Some of them began to blame Catlin for the deaths of little Corsair, Roman Nose, and the squaw they had just buried. "No," said the Doctor gravely, "we should not blame him for being as the Great Spirit created him. He was made to paint with brushes and with words the tribes that have never been, the tribes that will never be. It is for the good of our people a long time from now. To do this he must wall away much truth that he does not dare to see. He cares greatly for us as warriors and dancers; it is his joy when we make many cry out and slap their hands. If it is his profit too, only by profit can the white men live. He does not care for us greatly as men. He cannot; he does not know our thoughts. I have spoken."

"He does not know any thoughts but his own," said Jim, who had been musing at full length on his back. "He is too cold for friends or love. It is well sometimes to sit on the clouds, but it is not well to stand on both sides. He praises our freedom on the prairies, but he prisons us here like the animals in the cages. That is wrong. It is our right, if we choose, to drink the water of fire. It is our right, if we choose, to follow the old dark path pointed out by the rising flesh. I too have spoken."

White Cloud, the chief, answered reprovingly: "If he prisons us it is to keep our sons and our sons' sons free. His dream is his friend. His love is deep for his lady and for his little son. Without them he would walk as a lost man, in the forest of too many thoughts. His way is his own. It is not ours. We were not wise when we left our wigwams to come here. It is time for us to go back. That is all I have to say." Then he called Mr. Melody in and told him they would sleep six nights in Paris, and no more. They expected him then to be ready to take them home.

Though the city of sunlight was at its summer best they gave up junketing and sightseeing to devote their free hours to meditative smoking and grave consideration, and to the purchase of presents for their friends on the prairies of home. The Church of the Madeleine was much in their talk, as if they sensed that its lovely name was the apt symbol of a gay beautiful city whose sins were only of the flesh.

Soon they and good Mr. Melody sailed for the homeland that Catlin could never again truly call his own; and with them went all his prosperity, and all his private joy.

He was hardly aware of their going. A severe cold which had worked its way into Clara's lungs had developed into pneumonia. She was very brave and cheerful, but her fever burned the thin hand he laid on hers. Night and day he was by her bed, that now rattled with her chills, and now creaked with her delirious efforts to get up and see that little George was tucked warmly in. Her mind wandered back to the first wonderful night at Rose Cottage, back to those Cincinnati hotel rooms where she first fully shared her husband's life. Often she called aloud for him, called for him to love her, and to take her home.

On the 30th of July, 1845, *Gagliani's Messenger,* a Paris paper printed in English, carried this notice: "Died—on the 28th inst, No.

11 bis, Avenue Lord Byron, Paris, Mrs. Clara B. Catlin, the wife of the eminent traveller so distinguished for his researches into Indian History and antiquities of America, and so universally known and respected in Europe and his native country, Geo. Catlin, Esq., from the United States of America. The devoted friends who watched the last moments of this most amiable, interesting woman with intense anxiety, still clung to a faint hope, deceived by a moral energy never surpassed, and the most unruffled serenity of temper, that (had it been the will of Heaven) they might have been permitted to rescue a life so precious—but, alas! this gentle, affectionate, intellectual being was destined nevermore to revisit the land of her birth, and all that was earthly of so much worth and loveliness has passed away, whilst the immortal spirit has ascended to its kindred skies."

Those lines were penned "by a lady of her acquaintance." Had Catlin written them, it would have been with his heart's blood. He had taken Clara to her death, against her wishes and her warnings. That one terrible thought crowded all others from his numbed and bewildered brain. Only when evening came, and little Georgie cried for his Mama, did he realize that this loss was not only his own. What was to be done with the four motherless children? How could he get them back to America? How could he give them anything like a home when he got them back? He was wholly unprepared to answer these questions. His lively imagination had never pictured a life in which Clara was not quietly guiding and sustaining him, and competently managing the vexatious little everyday matters that mean so much to happiness. In the tiny American fortress which they had reared and held fast in these foreign lands, she had strengthened and armed him. He was strengthless now, naked in spirit, and utterly alone.

Years later, he wrote of those agonized days that ushered in all his failures: "In the midst of my grief, with my little family around me, with my collection still open, and my lease for the Salle Valentino not yet expired, there suddenly arrived from London a party of eleven Ojibbeway Indians . . . who had been brought to England by a Canadian, but had since been under the management of a young man from the city of London. They had heard of the great success of the Ioways in Paris, and also of their sudden departure."

In his desolate desperation, Catlin entered his third and last partnership, taking on these Indians under the same terms that he had entered into with Rankin and Melody. He at once quartered them in the rooms vacated by the Ioways and announced their exhibition.

But his good tide had turned now. Respectable, small audiences watched with approval the dancing and archery of the newcomers. But it was impossible by all the advertising that could be done, to draw the crowds again. A report had spread everywhere that these were only Frenchmen dressed up as Indians.

The gloom of failure was briefly broken by the promise of a bright future. Through M. Théodor Gudin, marine painter to His Majesty, Louis Philippe was moved to invite Catlin to hang his pictures in the Louvre for the private view of the Royal Family. Closing his show, he arranged the London-smoked pictures in the large hall of the Louvre and there received the King, and later, the King and Queen together. Louis Philippe was most courteous to him and to his little children, who had been especially invited to shake the Royal hand. Then and there the King pointed out fifteen pictures and commissioned Catlin to paint enlarged copies of them for the palace at Versailles.

Meanwhile, the idle Ojibbeways were running up a large bill for rooms and board, which the young man from London was unable to meet. To get them back to England without heavy loss, Catlin left his pictures and his painting and took the new troupe on a barn-storming tour that was to include Brussels, Antwerp, and Ghent. They arrived auspiciously in Brussels, where he was received by the Belgian King, whom he had previously met at the Court of France.

On the very eve of their first Brussels show, smallpox broke out among the Ojibbeways, although they had been vaccinated before leaving Canada. In a few days, one was dead, and six others in a Brussels hospital. For two months Catlin and Irish Daniel looked after them as best they could. Another of the Indians died there, and a third in England after he had sent them and their conductor back across the Channel.

This tragic venture cost Catlin three months' time, and almost eighteen hundred dollars, even though good friends in Brussels and Paris helped him send the surviving Indians back to America.

Having no other home, Catlin stayed on in his Paris apartment. The competent governess mothered his children there, while he painted in a room fitted out as a studio. "My collection," he wrote, "was at this time placed in a magazine in the vicinity of my dwelling, and my faithful man Daniel still continued in charge over it, keeping it in repair, and plying between it and my painting room when I required models from my collection to work with."

His hand had not been held entirely from his travel-stained easel. He had found time to paint enough portraits of his Ioways to keep his skill alive. Now, as he worked early and late on the fifteen copies commissioned by the King, and other orders that had long been waiting, his old dreams awoke. Writing to George Bancroft, the historian, who was then in London, he confided his resolve to spend his remaining years in painting the great events of early, Indian-encircled American history. With that resolve, his confidence and lively competence returned. Two English noblemen, hearing that his show had closed, were in the market for his pictures. That should make his own country eager to buy them. After conference with influential Americans in England and in Paris he offered his entire collection to the United States Government for sixty-five thousand dollars. Eleven American artists in France signed a memorial urging Congress to buy it.

"Having made ourselves fully acquainted with the extent and

interest of this unique collection," they wrote, "and of its peculiar interest to our country, and also aware of the encouraging offers now made to its proprietor for its permanent establishment in England, as well as the desire generally manifested here to have it added to the Historical Gallery at Versailles, we have ventured to unite in the joint expression of our anxiety that the members of the present Congress may pass some resolution that may be the means of restoring so valuable a collection to our country."

Distinguished members of the American community in London petitioned for the purchase also, as did many of Catlin's prominent artist friends at home. On the 24th of July, 1846, the Joint Committee on the Library reported to the United States Congress that: "Your Committee believe the price of his collection, as named by Mr. Catlin, is moderate, and that a failure to obtain it would occasion deep regret to all the friends of art, and to all Americans who reasonably and justly desire to preserve memorials of the Indian race, or the means by which our future artists and historians may illustrate the great and most interesting events in the early periods and progress of our country.

"The Committee, therefore, recommend that the bill for the establishment of the Smithsonian Institute be so amended as that provision shall be made therein for the purchase of Mr. Catlin's Gallery at the price mentioned by him—namely sixty-five thousand dollars—payable in annual instalments of ten thousand dollars."

With every reason to hope, Catlin plied his brush on painting after painting. Every picture he copied was a rectangular window opening upon the great rivers and prairies and mountains of his remembered wanderings. But recollections were not his only company. In his later record, he wrote: "My dear little Namesake, George, my only boy, then three and a half years old . . . had adopted my painting room as his constant playhouse, and, cronies as we had become there, our mutual enjoyment was as complete as our happiness was, in the dependence I was placing on him for the society of my future days. His first passion, like that of most children, had been for the drum, with which, slung on his back, with drumsticks in hand, he made my atelier and apartments ring and never was happier or more proud than when we addressed him as 'Tambour Major.' "

Besides the company of this lively little fellow, he had the quieter society of his three little daughters of ten, eight, and six years old. On fine afternoons he took his chattering flock window-shopping along the gay boulevards, and in the evening he told them such breath-taking stories as few children have ever heard.

Sometimes too he walked alone through Paris streets that his imagination turned into rocky passes and wild valleys. Aloof even from himself, he mused and marveled on his own strange career as if it had been another's. A country boy, and now the favorite and familiar of a King. He thought often of the King, "the wonderful man," whose amazing life had been even more chequered than his own!

He tried not to think of Clara, but her shadow was with him as the hours were, night and day. A woman friend, close enough to break the outward brittle shell of his brave reserve, could perhaps have convinced him that he was innocent of Clara's death; but in all the years of his marriage he had taken no other woman into his confidence, or even into his thoughts. In his impulsive moody mind, which cleansed Indians of every fault, he was branded with the curse of Cain. Born too late to be led by the hand of ancient Faith, he could not make himself believe in a hereafter where the truly wedded are rejoined, as divided streams meet and merge again below a dark island.

When his commission for copying was completed, Louis Philippe gave him another of greater interest; a truly Royal order for twenty-seven painted scenes illustrating the expeditions of La Salle. The two men together selected the episodes.

But an evil star shone on that conference. The Catlin whom the élite of Paris asked to their balls and dinner parties, the famous man whom American and English travelers came to see, was too far from

the forests and prairies that were his artistic strength. He filled those
La Salle paintings with fevered action and color, he crowded them with
four thousand human figures, he achieved in them extraordinary
effects of light on foliage and on snow. Yet few of the series are convincing. For all the while he was painting-out his own tragedies as
much as he was painting-in the travels of La Salle. Yet the inherent
optimism which he mistook for happiness made him think those
heavily burdened months were good ones.

Good or ill, they did not last. An epidemic, believed to have been
typhoid, broke out in Paris. One by one Catlin's children sickened and
fevered. Laying aside his toys and drum, Georgie, the little Tambour
Major, died.

The savage Red God had taken all; brother, wife, and only son.
In a journal of ever-darkening days, Catlin wrote: "In kindness the
reader will pardon these few words that flow in tears from the broken
and burning heart of a fond father; they take but a line or two, and
are the only monument that will be raised to the memory of my dear
little George, who lived, in the sweetness of his innocence, to gladden
and then to break the heart of his doating parent; the only one while
he was living, to appreciate his loveliness; and now the only one to
mourn for him."

Blind to all beauty now, the bereaved man painted by habit in his
silent, empty studio. After a full year's work, the La Salle pictures
were finished, and delivered to the Louvre.

Three days later, the storm that all but he had guessed from the
gatherings and whisperings in the streets thundered in gunfire and
flashed out in flags of the July Revolution of 1848. Soldiers of the new
Republic searched his apartment savagely, thrusting bayonets through
his racked pictures, since he was listed as a friend of the fallen King.
Of the three thousand dollars due to him from Louis Philippe, he got
nothing. For years he was to hear nothing of the fate of his La Salle
paintings. With difficulty, he got his little family and his famous
Collection back to London.

XX

AN END AND A BEGINNING

THE old friends who greeted Catlin's return to London thought, at first sight, that he had been little altered by his tragedies. He stood erect, his stride was brisk, and there was only a hint of gray in his thinning hair. Then they saw an indefinable difference in his deep blue eyes; a brightness that was not like the old flashings of twinkling wit or eager intensity. Those strange eyes were always watching the faces of those who spoke to Catlin now. His deafness was increasing.

In a London empty of all but loneliness and mocking memories he opened his Indian Gallery at No. 6, Waterloo Place, where he had rented combined showrooms and living quarters. But first night crowds and reporters belonged to the old days. Visitors and commissions came slowly, while his savings melted fast. He could not deny his daughters what their governess insisted that young ladies should have.

Busy with their lessons, their dancing school, and their daily walks in the park, the three Catlin girls saw little of their father. All day he was in the Gallery, painting or discoursing to visitors. When he had supper with the children he tried to enter their world, and to entertain them with small incidents of the day, but his hands fidgeted with the silver and he seldom lifted his eyes. His eldest daughter was beginning to look so like her dead mother! The girls were ill at ease too, and spoke only in answer to questions. Dutifully, as custom and their governess commanded, they turned their cheeks for his good-night kiss, when he rose to return to his writing desk in the Gallery, or to the secret workroom he now maintained.

To save precious time he was writing now in pencil, filling page after page in unpausing haste, and rarely altering a word he had written. It was not like the far-off happy days at the Pearl House when he wrote with Clara sewing beside him and waiting to hear each paragraph as he completed it. She had pricked his literary pride sometimes by asking, "Must you say that? Dear, you have such beautiful things to say, and that is ugly." But when his pride was satisfied by a logical defense of his position, he had always deferred to her wise judgement. More and more he had come to write for her ear, even as he painted for her eye.

But he must write on and on until the waning of the night, a night that nevermore would hear the voice of love, or show in candlelight a dear loving face, trustworthy as the Northern Star. A book had won him fame before. This new book would bring him back the lost laurels. His first two volumes had taught the civilized peoples what to think of the Indian world. In these two growing volumes, they would learn what the Indians thought of theirs.

Clara came more often than his daughters into the memories his flowing words evoked. The need of the children for a second mother never entered his thought. Their being was proof enough of his manhood. His ascetic body needed no mate; his eremitic mind was content with the companionship of fleshless imaginings.

Something akin to happiness came to him in the rainy late night when the brief eternity of sleep took his daughters away and made London a city of silence. Then he murmured the words he wrote, making them incantations of monotonous low music. Over the old pranks of Jim and the Doctor he laughed aloud, as he never laughed by day. Wise or unwise, true or false, all that he penciled in that intoxication of creative intensity seemed perfect. Rising sometimes, he tiptoed down the aisle of his Gallery, lifting the candle to light painted faces that were his closest friends, and painted hills and prairies that were his spirit's only home.

Impossible daydreamings of great achievements and great benefactions to Art and to the Indians had been the happiest exercise of his imagination since Clara died. He had old favorites among them now, to be dreamed over and over again at will.

Within a few months of his return to London, Catlin's *Notes on Eight Years' Travel and Residence in Europe With His North American Indian Collection* was published by the Author at his Waterloo Place showrooms. Its "two volumes, Octavo," were bound in one to save expense, and its "numerous illustrations" were far-between and crudely done.

This bulky work is of the sort the Biblical critic had in mind when he cried, "Oh, that mine adversary had written a book!" Penned in bitterness and black times, it is formless, repetitious, incredibly careless, and everywhere puffed out with plain padding. Now it is sermonish, and now downright vulgar and cheap. It has maudlin passages, and passages as cruelly satirical and unjustly critical as the worst of Swift. It is a showman's show-off, with a catalogue of Catlin's current Exhibition in Waterloo Place bound up with the text. It scarcely mentions Theodore Burr Catlin, though this nephew had been continually with the Indian shows at a wage of nine shillings a day. It is everywhere colored and twisted in favor of the author's ventures and the author's views.

All this the Victorian reviewers saw and set down in perfectly just condemnations that damned the book for decent readers; and damned the author too, for anyone who did not have intimate knowledge of his character and the hell he had written in. He was a low fellow, they said, a cheap-Jack showman, a pious humbug who preached Indians for his own profit, and to top all, he was not truthful.

We see more clearly now. Written in a desperation very near to derangement of mind, the book is at times adolescent in its crudity, and childish in its accounts of the author's little triumphs and the

Courtesy of American Museum of Natural History

16. Lagoon of the Amazon.

17. Shooting flamingos—Grand Saline, Buenos Aires. See p. 205.

Sunday-school behavior of his savages. But—and this bit deep—it is an unsparing indictment of the complacent, rot-infested, unjust feudal England of the 'forties such as no other writers but Swift and Shaw could have penned.

On the rich, credit side, it is a lively book, lavish in wit and laughable or pathetically absurd incidents. Its narrative leads the reader eagerly on, its characters and descriptions convince him. Under its high-falutin verbiage, very real Indians laugh, wonder, wander from virtue, suffer, see clearly, and speak shrewdly. Planning, pruning, and a less fanatical mood would have made it a great book. It remains a memorable one, for it alone lets us see through Indian eyes the material civilization that destroyed them, and is now destroying itself.

Publicly humiliated by the reviewers, Catlin retired to his showroom, and for the next two years was little heard of. His evening lectures on a new project for a floating museum of primitive arts attracted small audiences, who only occasionally bought his books or drawings. Losing money steadily, he held on in the hope that, now the Mexican War was over, Congress would buy his Indian Gallery at last. This expectation unfortunately gave him credit with moneylenders who got him deeper and deeper in their debt.

The House of Representatives did vote to buy his Collection for fifty thousand dollars. Backed by the sincere and powerful oratory of Daniel Webster, the purchase bill would have passed the Senate, too, if Catlin's former friend, Senator Jefferson Davis, had not opposed it. As a young army officer in the West, and on the Dragoon expedition to Texas, Davis had seen many of the Indian pictures painted. Even on the Senate floor, he declared that Catlin was the only artist who had ever been able to paint really authentic Indians. But his Southern constituents wanted Indian lands for the slaveowners. So, when the roll of the equally divided Senate was called, he voted against the purchase bill "on principle," and by that one vote prevented its passage.

Catlin was so confident of a favorable vote that he had his passage to

Washington arranged when the crushing news came. Desperate now, he tried to bring the public to his Gallery by showing Indian costumes again on living figures. But the public was all at the Great Exhibition. Only when that stupendous show closed, late in 1851, was it even worth his while to advertise with a tiny paragraph in the *Times*.

He no longer could turn for aid to the able and influential Master of the Queen's Household. Transferred from Court to a Diplomatic post in Egypt, the Honorable Charles Murray, after fourteen years of loyal waiting, had married Elise Wadsworth in 1850, soon after her father's death. Now she was dead, in giving birth to a son, and Murray was weighed down by his own griefs.

Catlin's creditors were pressing him hard. To save his collection from them, he mortgaged and re-mortgaged it, and tried wild-cat speculations on the market. These failed, and he was ruined. The holders of three bills of sale on his Gallery seized it and began to auction off in small lots the curios he had collected at such risk, and carried so far. Tears dimmed his hollow eyes as he penned this last advertisement he was ever to send to the *Times:*

"Catlin's splendid American Indian Collection just about to leave London for all parts of the world. Call and take the last possible look at it before it leaves, and decide upon the pretty and curious things you most covet before it is too late."

He was deeply hurt by the poor prices his treasures brought on the first day of the auction. So were his creditors. At this rate they would never get their money back. While they debated on continuing the sale, the oddest of Art's good Angels arrived from Russia and invited himself to their conference. He was a stocky fellow, whose whiskers and heavy brows did not conceal a chin like a block of Yankee granite and eyes as cold as Pittsburgh steel. His name was Joseph Harrison, and his home town was Philadelphia. He had come up the hard way, from a machinist's bench to a partnership in the biggest locomotive-building concern in the New World. He was on his way home now, with a ring and a jewelled decoration from the Tzar, who had learned to respect him, during the last nine years, as a man who got things done fast, even in slow Old Russia.

Mr. Harrison had in his brief case two important pieces of paper. One was the final payment on his completed five-million dollar contract for building and fitting out a railroad from St. Petersburg to Moscow. The other was Catlin's I.O.U. As a fellow-Pennsylvanian and patron of the Arts, Harrison too had loaned Catlin money.

Subsequent events are the only reporters of that short and crisp conference, from which he stalked out with all known claims on the Indian Gallery in his breast pocket. To keep it from being seized again by some unknown holder of other claims, he had it hastily crated and shipped to Philadelphia, where his men stored it in the sub-regions of the Harrison Boiler Works. It would be safe there while he decided what to do with it.

Catlin's Gregory in-laws had been in conference too, and were ready for the expected smash. They took "Clara's girls," from No. 6, Waterloo Place, while bailiffs were seizing its furniture, and shipped the three young ladies back to America and wealth and magnificence. Their Uncle, Dudley Gregory, was already a multimillionaire. Theodore Burr and Daniel apparently got back home in the re-shuffle.

Nobody knew what had become of Catlin. Even he recalled but dimly what he did in those nightmare days. Somehow he kept out of sight of the London bailiffs long enough to pack and ship to France the contents of his secret workroom. So he saved a few Indian Gallery paintings which he had been copying, and half a dozen manuscript sets of what he called his Album Unique. These were handsomely bound volumes of large pencil drawings copied from his earlier paintings and sketches, and strengthened with fine brushwork in India ink. The titles and the explanations of the drawings were written in Catlin's best scribe-hand. In some sets the drawings were tinted with water colors, in others with thinly laid oils.

When he somehow got to Paris, these and the few original paintings were all that the famous Indian Man could show to French collectors in that wretched winter of 1852–53. He tried vainly to get something from the French government for the La Salle paintings he had delivered to Louis Philippe four years before. Doormen polite enough to take his card in to Assistant Secretaries described him as "a queer, little hollow-faced deaf fellow in a shabby greatcoat. Looks like some sort of crank." Gendarmes eyed him suspiciously in the poor streets that were his walks now, but rarely questioned him.

When his grim landlady refused him credit for more faggots to warm his tiny back room, he strode shivering to the Bibliotheque Imperiale, the only refined club in Paris that admitted down-at-heel geniuses. There were plenty of them hunched over its reading desks; some with old shawls tied rakishly around their bald heads; some wrapped in blankets discarded by the horse-cabs. The lips of many of them moved audibly as their queer eyes followed the forward lines of Latin palimpsests, or the reversed lines of Syriac and Hebrew tomes. That was the nearest they came to conversation with their fellow might-have-beens. Like cold tortoises, they had armored their impotent private dreams against the wounding world.

At first, Catlin liked such silent companions. Aloof as they from all reality, he read and re-read the recently published South American *Travels* of Baron von Humboldt, whom he had met under such different circumstances in the Louvre a few years before. Even in those good days he had been pleased when the great scientist—the most famous man in the world—accepted him as an equal and eagerly questioned him on Indian customs and languages. Toying with a new dream now, he imagined himself in equatorial jungles and on the rims of Andean volcanoes. He pored over maps of Brazil, Peru, and Central America. Here he would paddle for ten days up-river; here portage his dugout canoe; here take horse; here strip and swim, rafting his painting kit before him to the far green shore. When the closing bell rang, he wandered from that roofed dreamland to the gas-lit dreamland of the wet streets, and was hardly aware of the rain.

But, as the wounds of his strong spirit healed, the companionability bred into all American bone came out. On an evening when his pocket jingled with francs from the sale of a copy of his Album Unique, he asked a neighboring reader who looked more scholarly than most, and more hungry, to have a bite with him.

Warmed by an unaccustomed second glass of wine, this grateful guest brought from his pocket an account of marvelously rich gold mines, discovered in the Chrystal Mountains of Brazil during the early explorations and then abandoned to the savage native tribes and forgotten. He had thought the account fantastic enough to be worth copying out from the old Spanish manuscript.

Catlin read and re-read it, and borrowed it for further study at his lodgings. "The Spanish miners," he translated, "after accumulating great riches, were attacked by the Indians and massacred in their houses, or driven out of the country, leaving their gold behind them."

He knew what travel tales were, for he had written good ones. He still remembered some of old Judge Reeve's strict tests of evidence. But any hope was better than none. If the odds against his finding those lost mines were a million to one, the odds against his making enough money elsewhere to redeem his lost Gallery were a million to nothing. South America teemed with Indians. He was only fifty-seven! He could paint another six hundred Indian pictures below the Isthmus, and with them redeem his good name as well as his Gallery. The port of Caracas, he decided, would be his best approach to the pampas tribes and to the Chrystal Mountains, far inland. Having nothing to stay for, he was free to sail as soon as he sold his paintings and drawings and his few possessions of value.

Sail he did, with a passport which one of his later books hints was British, and made out under an assumed name. His baggage was a bundle of Indian portraits, a bundle of Bristol drawing board, a manuscript book of maps, notes and excerpts from Humboldt's *Travels,* and one of Colonel Colt's new revolving carbines. With his old brown derby pulled low, and his old brown frock coat buttoned high, he tramped the spray-swept steerage deck as the little ship bobbed and bumbled through the Channel seas. His aging legs would need long training for the continent ahead.

At first the other passengers exchanged knowing looks as he passed and repassed them on his brisk trip to nowhere. But as he tramped on and on, all day, and by starlight, and in storms that almost retched out their bowels, they came to regard him with awe. They were not so sure now that he was old. His step was young. There was youth in his eyes, and in his carefree laugh too when he had his little morning joke with the deck steward.

It pleased him to answer all their questions by shaking his head and touching his ear. Like a boy, he delighted in the mystery he was creating. And like a boy hardening into manhood, he rejoiced in his returning strength and endurance that more than once outlasted the mid-ocean night. "Proud-proud-proud" creaked the small sturdy new boots he was breaking in for the pampas. He had good right to be proud, even of the hell he had come through unscathed. Great powers, both tried and yet untried, were his. In the old elation of utter freedom and complete confidence, he kept watch for the nearing South American shore. His heart had not drummed louder on the Saint Louis levee than it drummed when he lifted his eyes from red-roofed Caracas to the green plateau behind.

XXI

PAINTER'S GOLD

SOON he trod the high pampas. His knapsack, bulged and square with decoy-paintings and white cardboards, was a young man's load; but he was young with eagerness and the excitement of the wilderness. He and Dr. Hentz, a German botanist, were tramping together the hundred and fifty grassy miles to Angostura on the Orinoco River. In a chance meeting, Dr. Hentz had recognized Catlin as an uncommon man and instantly attached himself to him, like a lonely and very close-cropped large dog. He was a nuisance, but a cheerful one, and a good guide to the new strange flowers.

It was a time of flowering, and the flittering of hummingbirds. It was a place of distance upon dazzling green distance. "Man begins to feel less than he does in England," Catlin noted, "his shadow is shorter." That was a good feeling. Where he was only a mite amidst vastness, tiny too and of no consequence was the shadow of his past. Good also was the quiet comfort that came to him unsought, mating his feet to the Indian trail they trod. He was the earth's and the earth was his, and death should not them part. Now he knew that his life's high ecstasies had been mostly of eye and hand—strange sights, and outward beauty, and the joy that making brings.

Day after glorious day, while his companion gathered rare plant specimens, he painted the pampas Indians, who recognized him as Great Medicine, and had their comeliest daughters dance for him, in the nude, the Glad Dance, which had not been seen for years. Like Paris judging the naked loveliness of Greek Goddesses, he watched the

183

chosen three. They had panther skins spread under their feet. Their black hair, banded with silver, rippled in tresses of shadow over their supple backs and high small breasts. Their cheeks were rouged, and their bodies and limbs, from their throats downward, whitened with clay.

Light danced on the polished brass and gay beadwork of their anklets and necklaces and wristlets, and on the long silver pins thrust through their full underlips. Modest as marble, they turned and swayed in innocent grace to the throaty drum and the monotonous chanting of the chiefs. Catlin knew a poem when he saw it, and his memory held this one bright until he could transmute impression into pigments. In his picture there is pathos; and the fairest sight he had ever seen is strange and insubstantial. It is what his mind rather than his eyes saw; lovely puppets of Doom, dancing like the shadows mortals are.

Death trod the lush pampas too. Wild riders whirled the rawhide bolas with its three-branched cords tipped by heavy balls of lead, bringing down wild horses and wild cattle that they cruelly killed for skins and hair. Learning that civilized men were killing each other in a civil war at Angostura, and would bar his way to the Chrystal Mountains, Catlin struck the Orinoco further down and descended it to Georgetown, British Guiana, by canoe and steamer, painting as he went.

In Georgetown, a young Englishman named Smythe who had often visited the Egyptian Hall exhibition "espied a crowd in the street, amused at the red heads of some Caribbee Indians looking out of a chamber window." He went up for a look, and recognized "the old veteran, with his palette and brushes in his hands, painting the portrait of an Indian chief who was standing before him."

When the crowd had cleared away, the young man went back to introduce himself, but Catlin remembered him by name, though he had not seen him for six years. In a long letter to a Berkshire brother, Smythe recorded this meeting and its sequel:

"There was a German Doctor with him . . . their noses and faces tanned and burned almost to the colour of Indians. A large table in the room was loaded with plants and skins of animals and birds, and the sides of the room lined with Indian portraits and views of country.

"I soon learned they were going to start in a few days for a journey across the Tumucumaque (Chrystal) Mountains into the valley of the Amazon in Brazil. . . . I proposed to the gentleman that if he would pay my expenses and furnish me with powder and ball, as I had a first-rate Minié rifle with me, I would go with him. . . . This offer saved him the expense of hiring a worse man, and suited him exactly. . . .

"He spent some little time painting some tribes in this neighborhood and in Dutch Guiana, at Parimarbo, and then we were prepared to cross the mountains, and at last set out . . . in a large canoe, with a family of Indians who had come down to Georgetown to make their trade. Our course was up the Essequibo, and our party consisted of Mr. Catlin (or governor, as we called him); the German Doctor and his servant; an Indian half-breed, whom the governor had hired as a guide; a Spaniard, our interpreter, and myself.

"When we left the canoe . . . and took to the land, we had a hard siege of it; each one had to carry his share of the luggage, and we were all loaded down. We left in the morning, and our guide brought us to a small Indian village just before night, through swamps and quagmires, with nothing but a path to follow. . . .

"The guide led us to the chief's hut, who received us very kindly; he was an oldish man, and was seated on the ground. Some skins were placed for us to sit upon, and, through the interpreter, the governor soon commenced a conversation with him; telling him where we were going and what our object was. The chief was sitting cross-legged, and was smoking a long pipe; his head was cast down, and he now and then gave a sort of grunt, and I saw that the governor began to show a little concern.

"The conversation went on for some time, without much change, when the governor commenced making some sort of masonic signs with his hands to the chief, who raised his head a little, very suddenly, and after watching them closely for a minute or so, he laid down his pipe, and striking both his hands quickly together, he began making signs in reply. The governor began to smile, and the chief, seeing they mutually understood each other, jumped upon his feet as nimbly as a boy. The governor arose, and the chief embraced him in his arms, calling him his brother. . . .

"The governor commenced the conversation the next morning, by telling him that he was going to show him and his people how the red-skins looked in America, where he had come from, which the good old man could not at all comprehend, until the governor opened a large portfolio with a hundred or more portraits of Indians, buffalo hunts, &c., all in full blazing colours. Perhaps few men on earth were ever more suddenly amused and astonished. . . .

"We were seated at that time by the side of him, and all upon the ground, with the German Doctor and his man, and no other Indians in the hut. The old man looked at them all, but very fast; and when he was done, began to howl and sing the most droll song I ever heard in my life. . . .

"The whole village was by this time assembling out doors, where we went, and the rest of this day was spent in looking at the pictures, and also in examining our guns. . . . The governor had always in his hand one of Colt's six-shot rifles; this he had nicknamed Sam.

"These people had but three or four light and short guns in their village (and good for nothing), their weapons being bows and arrows and lances, and the bolas. The governor's gun, therefore, was the greatest of curiosities to them, as they never had heard or thought of a revolver; and I having given out that the governor's gun would shoot all day without stopping, made an exhibition of its powers necessary.

"For this I took an old cow-skin which was stretched on a hoop, and had been the door of a hut, and placing it at some sixty or eighty yards, with a bull's eye in the centre, the governor took his position and let off one!—two!—three!—four!—five!—six! . . .

"The target was brought up, and the shots all in the space of the palm of one's hand: they were still more astonished, and myself a little so amongst the number. . . .

"But the funniest part of this scene now took place. Some of the little boys standing near the governor, had reported it to some of the young men, who came up to him very timidly to ask if he hadn't a young rifle. The governor not having thought of his pistol during the excitement, began to smile, and drawing it out, said, 'yes.' Here the squaws, who had all along been in the background, now began to come up, but very cautiously, all with their hands over their mouths as they gave a sort of groan and a 'ya-ya.' This was really amusing.

"The governor explained that it was very young, but notwithstanding, at a shorter distance, it had got so as to do pretty well. At this he levelled it at the trunk of a palm tree, standing some six or eight rods off, and fired a couple of shots, to their great amazement. For these, the boys were cutting and digging with their knives for several days. . . .

"All satisfied, the governor placed the pistol in his belt, and wrapping his capot around him, the squaws all raised a shout of approbation, 'Keep the poor little thing warm.' "

Without the German botanist now, but with horses, and the chief's son and nephew to guide and introduce them, Catlin and Smythe went from tribe to tribe, their stock of pictures and of mineral specimens growing daily. On the shores of a lost lake they came upon a beach of beautiful colored pebbles, of which they gathered a hefty load.

"The governor," Smythe wrote, "was in the habit of going along this beach every morning and collecting these pebbles; and the little Indian children skulking about in the bushes and watching him at a distance, and not fully understanding what he was doing, but seeing him pick up the stones and breaking them with a little hammer which he always carried, and then wetting them with his tongue to see the colours, and when he found a right handsome one, of putting it in his pocket, ran back and told their parents that here was the strangest man in the world; declaring that 'they had seen him every morning making his breakfast on stones, and putting others in his pocket for his dinner!' The Indians gave him the name of the Stone Eater. . . ."

With his mind more on Indians now than on abandoned Spanish mines, Catlin led his party across the rugged immensities of the Chrystal Mountains to the Rio Tromboto, which they descended in a big Indian dugout loaded with hides. Smythe recorded one of their noonday landings on its banks:

"The governor and I had built a large fire and were roasting a fat pig. . . . I observed his eyes staring at something over my shoulder, in the direction of our half-breed guide, who was lying a couple of rods from us and fast asleep under the shade of some small palms.

"The governor said, 'Smythe! be perfectly calm and cool, and don't spill the gravy; and don't move an inch; there is a splendid tiger just behind you!' I held on to the frying pan, but gradually turned my head around, when I saw the beast lying on all fours alongside of the half-breed, who was lying on his face and fast asleep! He was lifting up with his paws one of the half-breed's feet, and playing with it apparently as carefully and innocently as a kitten.

"The governor, who had left his hat behind him, was at this time sliding down the grass-covered bank backwards, and feet-foremost, to the boat, where our rifles were left. The next moment he had one foot on the deck and the rifle in his hand. . . . Getting it to bear upon the beast, he was obliged to stand a minute or so for it to raise its head high enough not to endanger the man's body, which was in front of the tiger, and over which he must shoot very close. . . . He gave a sudden whistle, which directed the attention of the animal to him, and caused it to raise its head and its eyes toward him, when he let fly.

"At the crack of the rifle the tiger gave a frightful screech, and leapt about fifteen feet in the air, falling perfectly dead. The Indian leapt nearly as far in the other direction; and at the same instant arose and darted into the thicket, the male, secreted in a bunch of weeds about fifteen feet behind the governor's back, where he had been sitting at the fire."

Catlin was a realist here, where fact wore fangs and claws. He watched the forest folk as they took turtles by torchlight or threaded the treacherous water lanes, whose floating twigs and drifting logs were snakes and alligators. Even with their poisoned blowgun arrows, men clung precariously to that jungle's edge. Monkeys and hidden birds mocked them, marshes and netted creepers barred them from healthy ground. Heat stripped them of garments, baring bodies malformed with squatting in the dugouts. Hate of the malignant jungle made them hate even themselves, and thrust foolish feathers into holes in their cheeks, and roundels of wood into their split lips.

He painted them truthfully, pitilessly, as ugly dwarfed antics imping foolishly while the eternal drama of green growth and leprous muddy decay worked out its unknown plot. He hardened the harmless forms of leaves and weeds into threatening weapons, and made even sunlight ominous. He shrunk the dignity of man and the grace of fine animals to a few daubs of paint. Dignity belonged now only to Nature's inanimates—lasting water, rich soils, the high rocks, the blazonry on mist and cloud.

By the time they had paddled the hundreds of miles of jungled waterway to Para, Smythe had his young fill of wildness. He ended his letters with: "The governor was here awhile, and left . . . in company with a member of the Brazilian Parliament, on a steamer up the Amazon."

XXII

A VERY STRANGE MAN

AFTER his rending experience in "the jungle that is man," Catlin took green jungles of monkeys and alligators in his stride, or rather in his paddle stroke, for his trails were rivers now. In Para he had picked up a gigantic escaped slave, a maroon named Caesar Bola, who served as his bodyguard, porter, and easel. When his master saw a picture coming on, Caesar squatted down in the dugout pirogue or on the jungle moss, and leaned forward on his Minié-rifle. The huge portfolio of paintings and Bristol boards on his broad back at once became a tipped up table on which Catlin pinned his cardboard and plied his brushes.

This was not a country for painting on canvas. It took too long to stretch, and too long to dry, and the steaming jungle greened it overnight with mold. The thin white Bristol boards were less bulky to carry, and took a great deal less of the precious paints.

Only Catlin's wandering ghost knows by what wild waterways he went as he and Caesar worked their way slowly westward. Often they inched their way through dank, vine-netted sunless solitudes in which "a falling leaf, for want of wind, may be a month in reaching the ground, and where a man may be tracked by the broken cobwebs he leaves behind him." At night they circled their damp bivouac with bonfires to keep jaguars and savage wild pigs away. While they slapped mosquitoes, and with their hunting knives dug red ticks from their skins, howling monkeys serenaded them from the treetop darkness and peppered them with nuts.

Once they turned aside for gold, but their mule stepped through the bottom of their gold-washing pan; and when they came on quartz grained with pay-streaks and pebbled with nuggets, Caesar swung his iron sledge on them so mightily that the hammer flew from the handle and out into the hopeless depths of a mountain torrent.

Later Catlin counted this a good stroke, for it turned him back to his proper talents. "Why," he asked, "should I complain of Dame Fortune for giving me no visioned gold? She has given me what is better,—life, and health, and wisdom, and greatly added to my only wealth, my portfolios."

His portable picture gallery grew fast as he and Caesar inched their way into the Amazon's headwaters, took horse, and ranged the Western pampas. He painted there the pottery-making Conibos, masters of the blowgun. With this weapon—a ten-foot tube—they could shoot their deadly little poisoned arrows accurately at the incredible rate of twenty a minute. Pricked by one of these needles of doom, a pig died in six minutes, a rattlesnake in three. Catlin tried in vain to learn the source and nature of this arrow poison, which left its victims edible.

It "is undoubtedly a recent discovery," he wrote. He was told that the tribes of this region were formerly as warlike as the rest. But a generation or so before his coming, two tribes discovered the deadly poison independently at the same time, and each kept its discovery quiet. Each tribe sent its warriors, armed with the new secret weapon, to attack the other. The two armies met in an open plain at the frontier. There they advanced fearlessly, on a foe apparently only out bird-hunting. At close range they shot and shot, heedless of the pin-prick wounds they took in return. Every warrior on both sides was hit before he had emptied his quiver of its hundred tiny darts. And in a few minutes every warrior on both sides swayed, staggered to his knees, fell, writhed and died. That was the last battle in the last war any tribesman of the upper Amazon cared to take part in.

The Intelligence Services of several European states were, of course, trying to get the lethal poison for the bullets of civilized warfare. Their spies, and their naturalists, who were busy prying into other jungle secrets, had made the natives suspicious of all white visitors.

So, when the chief Medicine Man of the Conibos returned from an expedition and found Catlin painting his people, "he soon had his face painted black, and was parading about with his rattle in his hand, and singing a doleful ditty—his *death-song* . . . telling his people . . . that here was something, to be sure, very wonderful, but that it would do them no good.

" 'These things,' said he, 'are great mystery: but there you are, my friends, with your eyes open all night—they never shut; that is all wrong, and you are very foolish to allow it. You will never be happy afterwards if you allow these things to be always awake in the night. My friends, this is only a cunning way this man has to get your skins; and the next thing, they will have glass eyes, and be placed amongst the skins of the wild beasts and birds and snakes! Don't hurt this man —that is my advice; but he is a bug-catcher and a monkey-skinner!' "

To ease the concern of the poor fellows already painted, Catlin agreed to unpaint them. This he accomplished quickly by brushing their portraits over with an opaque coat of clay, which was easily washed off when he was safely on his way.

That way lay still to the West. He had seen the Muras, the Maranhas, the Yahuas, the Orejones, the Angosturas, Mayoroones, Iquitos, Omagues, Cocomas, Ticunas, Sepibos, and Chetibos, ugly all, and all too naked for a fastidious painter's taste. His eyes longed for the dignity, and the daringly decorative splendor of the Indians of his own continent. So over the Andes he and Caesar tramped to Lima, "the most beautiful city in the world" and engaged passage to San Francisco on the schooner *Sally Anne*.

At San Francisco the *Sally Anne* took on two more passengers. These gold-seeking adventurers and Catlin contracted with the Captain to take them and black Caesar all the way up the west coast to the Aleutians, and Siberian Kamchatka, and back to Vancouver Island.

In Nootka Sound, Catlin painted Klah-o-quats and saw long, graceful sea-going canoes hollowed out of cedar trees with elk-horn chisels and adzes of mussel shell. He dined in a native house a hundred feet long by twenty-five broad, and witnessed the wild dismemberment of a stranded whale.

He was proud to record that the Aleutian Indians were authentic Americans, and not Mongol Tartars. He saw the Russian pine-pole and mud houses of Petropavlovski, and the huts of Siberian Koriaks, and he climbed to the sulphurous crater of Che-nish-ka Wabe, the Mountain On Fire.

On the return voyage he painted the Northwest coastal tribe of Nayas, whose cedar canoes were gay and graceful as gondolas. The women of the tribe wore circular blocks of wood in their pierced under-lips and dressed in mantles of mingled mountain sheep's wool and dog's hair dyed in bright hues and decorated with intricate strange designs. The men smoked long pipes of jet-black stone, carved with entwined and interlocked figures of men and animals.

"Of these pot-stone pipes I saw many," he wrote, "and the eccentric designs on them, on their robes, their canoes, their paddles, their leggings, and even the paintings on their faces and limbs are peculiarly tribal, and their own, differing from anything seen in other tribes of the continent."

Black Caesar bore up under the blandishments and favors of the Nayas ladies, but the masquerade dance of the warriors almost overcame him with its bizarre absurdity.

"Some fifteen or twenty . . . were engaged in this singular affair, all masked and otherwise dressed in the most strange and curious taste; and many of the lookers-on, in the front ranks, both men and women, were masked and dressed in a similar manner.

"The leader of the dance, a *medicine man,* the drollest of the droll, was the *King of the Bustards,* another was *King of the Loons,* another was the *Doctor of the Rabbits.* . . ."

Skirting the coast, the *Sally Anne* anchored in Smith's Inlet, opposite the north cape of Vancouver Island. There Caesar showed his bait of finished portraits and lectured on them in English, Spanish and Lingua-geral while his master took likenesses from the assembled crowd of Skidegates, Stickeens, Bella Bellas, and Hydas Indians. All knew the name of Catlin.

In the Strait of Juan de Fuca the schooner grounded, and Catlin and Caesar trudged overland to Victoria, the base for the Fraser River gold rush. "In Victoria all was confusion, complete pell-mell; houses were filled, steamers and vessels were full, and men and women were sleeping in carts and waggons in the street; and others were not sleeping at all, but with bonfires built upon the bank, or under the pines, were dancing away the nights in wild and frantic whirls."

Weary of gold-seeking, Catlin and his man embarked for Astoria, and ascended the Columbia to the famous salmon-spearing narrows of The Dalles. Word there of a party of Crows, in the Salmon River valley, lightened the task of painting commonplace Klatsops, Chinooks, Clikatats, Walla Wallas, Nez Perces, and Spokans. Twenty harried years had only heightened Catlin's admiration for those plumed Crow knights of the plains who had raced their ponies for him in the glorious June days at Fort Union.

Buying a horse for himself, a mule for Caesar, and a pack mule for his pictures, he set off to see his heroes in their almost unapproachable fastness.

"Our ride," he wrote "(or rather walk, for we had to walk and climb most of the way, leading our horses) was one which I deeply regretted from day to day, but which I have never regretted since it was finished. The eighth day opened to our view one of the most verdant and beautiful valleys in the world; and on the tenth a distant smoke was observed, and under it the skin tents, which I at once recognized as of a Crow village."

He had not only come up against the current of the Snake and Salmon rivers; but he had come twenty years up the current of Time, into the years of youth and high bright hope. Here were the Red Men of his early vision—of his lifelong memory; "men whose beautiful forms and native, gentlemanly grace had not been deformed by squatting in canoes, nor eyes bridled by scowling on the glistening sun reflected on the water, nor heads squeezed into wedges, nor lips stretched around blocks of wood."

His white world had decried his craft, ruined him, and cast him out as a charlatan. But here, in the Crow camp, when he spread out the portraits in his portfolio, one of the warriors leapt up and danced with delight, shouting, "Bi-eets-e-cure! Bi-eets-e-cure!" Off rushed the crowd to the fish-drying banks to fetch old Bi-eets-e-cure—the Very Sweet Man, whose twenty-year-old likeness all the elders instantly recognized.

Catlin's lifelong repugnance to returning on a route he had already traveled, plus a new and growing desire to unravel secrets of rocks and mountain ranges, led him on into the gneiss and granite heights of the Rockies. "Among these immense and never-ending blocks," he wrote, "I was reading an instructive book and making notes, which Caesar could not understand; he had enough to do to take care of the horses, whilst I was sometimes for hours out of his sight and hearing; and coming back and waking him and the mules from their sleep, all I would hear was: 'Well Mass Catlin, you bery strange man'. . . ."

Joining the pathetic remnant of an immigrant train, the travelers returned by the Snake River route, and steamed from Portland to San Diego. Thence they headed inland, on new-bought mules, for the Ghiba Apachee village near La Paz.

In this settlement Catlin painted the chief and two warriors in war array. He watched and painted a shooting match in which mounted archers, at full gallop, shot ten arrows into ten circular targets drawn on the ground in white pipe-clay. Here he saw and recorded the rarely seen operation of Indian arrow-makers.

"Erratic boulders of flint," he noted, "are collected (and sometimes brought an immense distance), and broken with a sort of sledge-hammer made of a rounded pebble of hornstone set in a twisted withe, holding the stone, and forming a handle.

"The flint, at the indiscriminate blows of the sledge, is broken into a hundred pieces, and such flakes selected as, from the angles of their fracture and thickness, will answer as the basis of an arrow-head. . . .

"The master workman, seated on the ground, lays one of these flakes on the palm of his left hand, holding it firmly down with two or more fingers of the same hand, and with his right hand, between the thumb and two forefingers, places his chisel (or punch) on the point that is to be broken off; and a co-operator (a striker) sitting in front of him, with a mallet of very hard wood, strikes the chisel (or punch) on the upper end, flaking the flint off on the under side, below each projecting point that is struck. The flint is then turned and chipped in the same manner from the opposite side; and so turned and chipped until the required shape and dimensions are obtained, all the fractures being made on the palm of the hand.

"In selecting a flake for the arrow-head, a nice judgment must be used, or the attempt will fail: a flake with two opposite parallel, or nearly parallel, planes is found, and of a thickness required for the centre of the arrow-point. The first chipping reaches near to the centre of these planes, but without breaking it away, and each chipping is shorter and shorter, until the shape and the edge of the arrow-head are formed.

"The yielding elasticity of the palm of the hand enables the chip to come off without breaking the body of the flint, which would be the case if they were broken on a hard surface. These people have no metallic instruments to work with, and the instrument (punch) which they use I was told was a piece of bone; but on examining it, I found it to be a substance much harder, made of the tooth (incisor) of the sperm-whale or sea-lion, which are often stranded on the coast of the Pacific. This punch is about six or seven inches in length, and one inch in diameter, with one rounded side and two plain sides; therefore presenting one acute and two obtuse angles, to suit the points to be broken.

"This operation is very curious, both the holder and the striker singing, and the strokes of the mallet given exactly in time with the music, and with a sharp and *rebounding* blow, in which, the Indians tell us, is the great *medicine* (or mystery) of the operation."

Crossing the Rockies by the Santa Fe Pass, Catlin and Caesar learned from Indian refugees and outriders of the war that was being waged ahead between an Apache band and United States troops. To avoid trouble they turned south toward the Rio Grande, and missed seeing Taos and the other fantastically ancient towns of our Pueblo civilization. Paddling eight hundred miles to Matamores, they took ship for Sisal, in Yucatan. There they parted. Caesar, the faithful Sancho Panza of this new Quixote, went off to tell tales of wonder to his dusky lady-love. Catlin lingered on, marshaling—amongst the ruined jungle cities of a lost civilization—his many and curious evidences of a lost Indian Atlantis.

Long ago, amongst the Mandans, he had puzzled over their legend of a great flood, and explained it in his book as a likely inheritance from a band of Welshmen under Prince Madoc who had crossed the Atlantic and ascended the Mississippi in medieval times, to mingle their language and their blood with that of the Mandan tribe. But before sailing to South America he had become converted to Baron von Humboldt's belief that the Indians and their customs and beliefs were peculiarly American products, shaped by the geological history and ever-changing inhabitable surface of their continents.

In Humboldt's books, *Aspects of Nature,* and the *Travels,* he had found evidences of subterranean passages, probably long crevices or caverns in the deep strata, which connected widely separated volcanoes, and carried the loud rumblings of earthquakes hundreds of miles away. He had also found there an account of the collapse of a vast South American volcano that in its fall befouled all the surrounding country with mud and blind fish from the subterranean lake which had undermined it.

Musing over these phenomena during his jungle travels, he had built upon Humboldt's facts an extraordinary new theory of a great prehistoric Indian civilization wiped out by the working of underground waters. From Peru to Siberia, in the Andes, and in the Rockies, he had gathered evidence to support that theory. His notebooks were full of measurements of strata and the flow of streams, dimensions of caves, descriptions of fossils, comparisons of Indian tribal legends of the Flood.

His next step was clear. He would lay his evidence before Baron von Humboldt. That great and good man would accept it and present it to the whole scientific world in one of the later volumes of the vast *Cosmos* he was publishing. Then America would realize Catlin's worth, and the Gregory brothers-in-law would cease hinting to his daughters that their mother had thrown her life away on a charlatan.

Heaven knows how he raised the money, but in the late spring of 1855 he sailed for Europe.

XXIII

MOUNTAINS AND A FIREFLY

CATLIN's cabin was piled deep with new Indian pictures—cartoons he called them—painted on thin frail cardboard. They had made his hands happy in the jungles and the mountains. But the new quiet happiness of his mind came from half-mystical, half-material meditations upon the long history of the two Americas and the race they bred. He had with him voluminous notes of that history, as Nature had written it.

Aloof in his deafness, he walked the crowded deck alone, musing on moving green mountains of water that were for him minor actors of a vast inhuman tragedy, wherein scenes are continents and acts are eons.

He could no longer hear the orchestration—deck chanties, sea birds crying, and the wind-swept shrouds. Yet over and under and in all the encircling vast he could see the eternal plot unfold. He knew its script pretty well now from cryptograms of lava and granite and limestone.

Oblivious as a homing bird to the busy Havre docks, and the bustling railway trains that bore him northeast through forests of new smokestacks, he hurried on to Berlin to lay his finds and his interpretation of them before the most famous scientist of his time.

Though Baron von Humboldt was now an old, old man, he remembered Catlin and greeted him with the same smooth welcoming hand that had clasped the hands of Napoleon, Pitt, Jefferson, Hamilton, Goethe, Schiller, Beethoven, and Sir Walter Scott. Busy as he was with the completion of his *Cosmos,* he had time to hear Catlin's story to the end. Pacing his always overheated study, with his massive, unwrinkled brow bent forward and his blue eyes eager and bright as a child's, he listened to this leathery lean little American who had become a citizen of the prehistoric past. Occasionally he interrupted with a rapidly spoken question in English or in German—for he spoke both so well that their use was unconscious. In eloquent phrases, made more insistent by excitement and the monotones of deafness, Catlin presented the three propositions of his new theory.

The first was that when the Earth's cooling and contracting rocky crust is wrinkled up into mountain chains, vast subterranean caverns are left vacant in the hot lower regions from which the rock masses rise. Into these caverns surface water filters and collects in prodigious cisterns that seethe and boil, and sometimes create steam pressures that burst out in volcanoes. More often, they merely fill and overflow in hidden streams that find their way through rifts and fissures to the sea. These hot subterranean streams erode and eat away the rock of their banks until at last the mountain chain caves in, creating inland seas, such as Lake Superior or the Great Salt Lake. Underground rivers greater than the Mississippi and the Amazon flow southward under the Rockies and northward under the Andes, to unite somewhere under the Yucatan peninsula and empty their vast volume of waters up through the deep floor of the Gulf of Mexico. The outflow of these waters into the Atlantic creates the current and warmth and volume of the Gulf Stream.

Secondly, he declared that these combined rivers had formerly flowed into the Atlantic through caverns eroded under a towering spur of the Andes-Rockies chain which branched off in Yucatan and extended eastward across Cuba and Haiti and the Lesser Antilles. Along this spur then spread wide fertile plains, populous, and studded with cities of a luxurious civilization that built vast temples, monuments and palaces. Suddenly that towering eastward range crumbled and crashed down into the immense underground rivers which had undermined its granite strength. In a cataclysm of earthquake and flood, a hundred cities surpassing Thebes and Babylon were overwhelmed, and drawn down with their subsiding plains that now became the floor of the Caribbean Sea and the Gulf of Mexico.

Thirdly, Catlin reasoned, the obvious fact that all this happened an immeasurably long time ago was good proof of the long existence of Indians on the American continents. For their legends, their tribal memories, everywhere ran back to that Great Flood. They were the original Americans; perhaps the original race of Mankind.

With the recklessness of the very old and the very young, Baron von Humboldt again grasped Catlin's hand. "This is of vast importance to Science," he said. "Our King will want to hear your report. I will take you to him."

The pinched marble face of Voltaire surely smiled, and not unkindly, as it looked down from its pedestal in the palace of Sans Souci upon George Catlin of Wilkes-Barre telling God's secrets to the bewildered but deeply impressed King and Queen of Prussia. Upon the Baron's advice, Catlin showed them his pictures too, and they bought a number of them,—apparently those which later went to the Berlin Gallery. Financed by this, and other sales, and by royalties which had accumulated in the hands of his publishers, he was a good deal better off than his famous friend, who had been in debt for years.

The two men were very happy together, reminiscing of their travels and mutual acquaintances, and going over Catlin's notes. They agreed that he should return to South America for more data, and the Baron drew up for him a list of the places he should visit and the evidences he should seek for.

When, in mid-September, Catlin took ship at Havre for the West Indies, he found in his cabin a generously worded farewell note from Humboldt, ending with these phrases:

". . . if I were a younger man I would join you in the expedition at once.

"I believe your discoveries will throw a great deal of light on the important subject of cataclysms on the distribution of races. . . .

"Let nothing stop you; you are on a noble mission, and the Great Spirit will protect you."

Ocean currents, tropical islands, and equatorial ranges were Catlin's missions now. Following the Baron's instructions, he took samplings of the waters he sailed and of the sands he landed on. He explored Jamaica, St. Thomas, Antigua, Trinidad, Tortugas, the coasts of Venezuela and Granada, the great escarpment of Caracas, the mountain capes of Santa Martha, and the Gulf of Maracaibo. Exploring southward to Buenos Aires, he picked up a half-breed guide and servant named José Alzar and with him paddled far up the Paraguay River, collecting mineral specimens and painting Indians along its banks. At Candeloria the two crossed overland to the Uruguay River which they descended in style in a big pirogue with a crew of three at the paddles.

Catlin carried an introduction from Humboldt to his old friend and fellow explorer, the botanist Baron Aimé Bonpland, who had long since forsaken the world of science and troubles for a squaw and a humble little rancho called Santa Anna, on the right bank of the Uruguay. Catlin's book about these travels makes no mention of the poor old fellow who had now lost his wits and was living like a savage in a tumble-down cottage full of half-caste children, dogs, saddles, unmade beds, and bags of onions.

Age was coming upon Catlin too. His alertness failed him as he stalked a jaguar up the Uruguay's steep reedy bank. From nowhere, the lithe powerful beast leaped upon him and flung him, senseless and bloodily clawed, to the water's edge, where his servant and his boatmen barely saved him.

While he was recuperating from these exertions and adventures in a bright room on the Plaza of Buenos Aires, Alzar brought in to him two strangers, from up-country, who were as welcome as they were unexpected. One was a handsome young half-breed, rouged to the eyes; the other, soft and timid and altogether lovely, a tawny black-haired girl.

"Alzar," Catlin recalled, "introduced them as brother and sister, of the Auca tribe living on the headwaters of the Rio Salado, to the south of Buenos Aires. Such was the suavity and gentleness of their manners as they advanced and both shook hands with me, that I felt almost embarrassed. Alzar had no doubt given them a high-coloured description of me and my works, and they were approaching me with a profound respect.

"Alzar could speak somewhat of their language, and, what was better, the young man spoke Spanish very well, and his beautiful and modest sister well enough to be amusing and agreeable to me. They had learned enough from Alzar to know the object of my travelling and the sincerity of my views, to enter into undisguised conversation about their own and other tribes of the vicinity, and conversation took the place, for the time, of my painting, and my brushes were laid down.

"I expressed my surprise at meeting red people in the city of Buenos Aires, and particularly so beautiful a young lady, when Til-tee (The Firefly—I found that was her name) replied quicker than her brother was able to do, 'Oh, we often come here, señor, and there's a plenty of us here now; my father, and my mother, and my sisters are all up town.'

"Alzar then said, 'This is a very respectable family. *Señor Gonzales Borrora,* he is a Portuguese gentleman, and his wife is an Auca woman. . . . If you will permit me, señor—I know they will be glad to see your paintings.'

" 'Most certainly, Alzar. Go and fetch them.' Alzar was off, and I went to amusing my visitors with my sketches.

"My portfolio of Indian portraits was giving so unthought-of and so exciting a pleasure to the two, and particularly to that beautiful little creature, who became more beautiful every time she turned, that I was in the midst of a peculiar satisfaction myself, when Alzar came in with the rest of the family.

"This was the first day after my arrival in Buenos Aires, and though I had several letters of introduction which I had not yet delivered, I spent the whole of that day with this interesting family, having learned, in the early part of my conversation with them, that their business was all settled, and their arrangements all made to start for their home on the Salado at an early hour the next morning.

"My cartoon portraits, which they could not see enough of, gave an unspeakable pleasure to these people; and those with flattened heads, and those with blocks of wood in the lip, seemed to excite, with people who wear few ornaments, equal disgust and astonishment. They told me they never had thought that any Indians were such great fools.

"Borrora and his son gave me such a glowing description of the country where they lived, of the beauty of the forests, the lakes, the prairies and pampas; of the chasing of ostriches and wild cattle . . . as well as the beautiful games of the Indians, and, at the end of all, so pressing an invitation to come and see, and to join in them, that I told them distinctly that Alzar and I would ride there before a fortnight was out."

Before they left him, Catlin painted a quick portrait of lovely Tiltee, and put a brilliant pair of pendants in her aristocratic little ears. She prettily stammered that her heart was thankful, and the party broke up in the twilight with "Buenas noches," and "A Dios."

Only the far-off Texas days with Joe Chadwick could compare with the visit Catlin paid the Borroras and their tribe of brown centaurs. They rode as he had thought only Crows and Comanches could ride, whirling their bolas lassoes as they outstripped the swift wild runners of their plains. And he rode with them, on a silver gray stallion, with black streaming mane and tail.

Old April raptures wakened in the rags of his youth as he brought down his zigzagging ostrich with a shot fired at full gallop. Its wings were trophies that he would give that night to Til-tee, the little Firefly. She was indeed lovely here in her own wild green land. Freed now from cheap calico, with the curves of her wakening womanhood bared to the lithe small waist, she was a brown symbol of all things innocent, eager and untamed. Her joy and pride in his prowess made him forget that he was old, and deaf, and battered by the world. And when he watched her skim the plains on the swiftest horse of the tribe, he knew he had not given his life to her tawny race in vain.

Wading into the muck of saline marshes where ordered flocks of flamingoes rose like long scarlet grenadiers, he shot proud birds down to adorn her with their plumes. Never was such a night for musings as that night he spent by the flamingo marshes, solitary save for unseen waterfowl, "and the incredible beauty of the firefly haloes that were here and there glowing like the light of hidden lamps. . . . These swarms, some stationary and others travelling, could be seen in the distance until their numbers became countless, and a general flood of light near the ground almost extinguished the darkness of night."

No, he was not old, if one so wild and beautiful could love him, exulting in his great gifts and his skills. He would again be applauded for his works and his holy Word. But fame is not love, nor the happiness of a home in a green unsullied land. Why not stay and eat the lotus,—its last flowering?

At the village next day, his trophies made the little Firefly leap with joy. But her greeting was drowned out by bitter news. The Patagonians were mustering nearby for a war with Buenos Aires. Catlin had to go, leaving behind him forever the life of the open plains.

XXIV

REBUILDING WITH RUBBLE

Fʀᴏᴍ Buenos Aires, late in 1856, Catlin sailed to Tierra del Fuego and up the west coast to Panama. Crossing the Isthmus, he vanished from all records, including his own. His brother Francis, with whom he still corresponded, grew anxious after a year or so and appealed to the State Department, but our South American consuls could find no trace of him. Apparently he was very busy with his project, his brush, and his pen during these lost years. He had completed his researches, his Indian sketches, and the manuscript of at least one book, and he was ready to sail for Europe when bitter news came to him. Baron von Humboldt was dead!

What could he do now? In desperation he decided to go to England where, in the old days, he had many scientific friends. His rascally creditors there could not harass him, for the Statute of Limitations had run. Joseph Odshead of Manchester had remained loyal to him and written as often as he could discover an address. Catlin had recently sent Odshead a manuscript, entitled *Steam Raft. Suggested as a Means of Security to Human Life upon the Ocean*. The good man had asked for it and offered to publish it at his own cost. Perhaps he remembered how Clara had dreaded the perils of the sea.

When a very unhappy and dispirited George Catlin arrived at Joseph Odshead's Manchester home with his notebooks and mineral specimens and his hundreds of cartoon paintings, *Steam Raft* was circulating as a printed pamphlet.

This little work, which Catlin had written in Brazil, proposed enormous seagoing rafts, made of criss-crossing layers of squared cottonwood logs bored hollow and plugged at the ends. These queer unsinkable craft were to be driven by bucket-and-chain propulsion operating in a channel down their keels. Though no such rafts were built, the pamphlet reminded English publishers that George Catlin was a living man.

Since his withdrawal from the world he had become a legend—and a classic to a whole new generation of boys who had learned from his pages how to play Indians in manor house shrubberies and among dockside drays.

His public was ready, and so, very soon, was his new volume, *Life Amongst the Indians—a Book for Youth*. Sampson Low published it in 1861, with graceful yet vigorous illustrations and an embossed red cover stamped with a mounted golden warrior shooting his arrow through a golden buffalo.

This book is a romantic autobiography, built of exciting adventures with Indians, grizzlies, rattlers and jaguars in the wilds of two continents. All of Catlin's best stories are in it, refined to gems of American narrative by a thousand tellings. It is frankly and even boastfully first person, as our best story telling has always been. Its gaiety and easy gusto sweep the reader on like laughing April winds. Its persistent sermonizing on Indian virtues gives it the air of high seriousness that boys respect, and makes even its tallest tales credible.

But under these allurements and bright baits *Life Amongst the Indians* is a complete little encyclopedia of the skills, the weapons, the dress, the habitations, the customs, and the superstitions of the native tribes of both Americas. If all other records were lost, it would provide us with everything essential that is even now known of Indian life on the unvisited prairie and in the unexplored jungle.

Alone among Catlin's major works, it has a literary design, balancing and mingling exciting narrative with vividly pictorial and often lovely descriptions, and interleaving both with skillful pleading disguised as the wisdom of wide experience. It is, by the standards of any time, very well written.

A new generation of reviewers, who had never heard of Catlin the liar and Catlin the low showman, ranked it as one of the great books for boys, worthy of a place beside the *Iliad* and *Robinson Crusoe*. It immediately became, and long remained, a best seller. The grizzled old veteran of so many defeats had accomplished the almost impossible —a return to a popular favor greater than that which he had lost.

With hope renewed, and royalty checks in his pocket, Catlin could afford to crusade again. This time the enemy he tilted at was Mal-respiration. In 1862 he issued the quaintest of health books, printed by photolithography from an illustrated manuscript that he had pains-takingly penned in the jungles of Brazil. The title on its cardboard cover was:

THE BREATH OF LIFE
(All Life (on Earth) is Breath)
(All Else (on Earth) is Death)
MANUGRAPH
by
Geo. Catlin

This volume attempts to prove that most of the ills of the flesh would end if we all slept on our backs, as the Indians do, and like them breathed through our noses, keeping our mouths shut tight as mouse-traps. Then mothers would not overlay and suffocate their babes, as his statistics proved was a common maternal failing. Then we would not be plagued by nightmares, or rouse our spouses by snoring and roaring in their essential hours of rest. We would not have fits, or hunchbacks, or bleary dreary faces any more, and colds and air-borne contagions would all be trapped in the cunning labyrinth of our noses. The argu-ment of the book's words is reinforced by fantastic pairs of pen draw-ings, showing creatures who breathe right and sleep right, alongside those who don't.

Issued again and again in ordinary type, sometimes under the title, *Mal-respiration and its effects upon the enjoyments and life of Man,* and sometimes under the more dramatic, *Shut Your Mouth and Save Your Life,* the book sold more than 40,000 copies.

C. L. Dodgson, mathematics tutor at Oxford, was very fond of his health and had such a dread of draughts that he sealed his windows and wadded rugs against the crack under his door. He bought and read the manugraph first edition of *The Breath of Life* in earnest.

But when his alter ego, Lewis Carroll, sat down to write of Alice's adventures underground, his whimsical brain recalled the absurd illustrations as well as the medieval penmanship of Catlin's little volume. Apparently he used it as a model for both drawings and script while he wrote and illustrated that first version of *Alice in Wonderland.*

Heedless of his publisher's plea for more best sellers, Catlin left England and its unhappy memories and settled himself in simple lodgings in Brussels. There he went to work on the hardest of all human tasks, the rebuilding of a ruined reputation.

Showmanship and a few bad passages in a good book had been his undoing in England. His brief fame there had aroused the envy of his own countrymen, and his long absence abroad had prevented his meeting their charges against his ability as an artist and his honesty as an observer. So it became the fashion, even among Americans who had never seen his pictures or read his books, to say that Catlin was an old fraud and an abominable painter.

In fairness to his sincere critics, it must be admitted that he almost invited their honest doubts. Though so many thousands have read his books, he apparently never did. They are as crowded with contradictions and inconsistencies as the works of that other great adventurous and careless storyteller, Daniel Defoe. He could not remember dates, or did not consider them important. And he could not curb his desire to make good stories better.

His painting was certainly uneven. Many of his exhibited pictures were never finished; others were mere hasty brush-sketches which he could not bring himself either to repaint or discard. Often he painted from pencil notes so inadequate that he had to fill in important details from his imagination.

These are faults that any just man would overlook, amongst so much that is splendid, truthful and enduring. But Henry R. School-craft, LL.D., who did more than all others to undermine Catlin's repute, was not just, nor, upon the evidence, wholly sincere.

Appointed, under an Act of Congress of 1847, to "collect and digest such statistics and materials as may illustrate the history, present condition, and future prospects of the Indian tribes of the United States," he pretty obviously decided to get even with Catlin, who had refused him permission to illustrate his projected book with pictures from the Indian Gallery.

In Congress, and among influential public men, Schoolcraft did his successful best to block the purchase of the Indian Gallery by our government; while in the official six-volume work which he published by Congressional authorization he only once mentioned Catlin. That mention was apparently artless, but as mischievous as anything deliberate malice could have framed. It appeared casually in an account of a long questionnaire sent by Schoolcraft to the Indian authorities of the time.

One of the questions read: "Are you acquainted with any material errors in the general or popular accounts of our Indian tribes? If so, please state them."

With this question, Schoolcraft published only one answer, prefaced by: "One writer represents the Mandans as practising the acts of self-torture of Hindu devotees, by hanging from hooks or cords fastened into the nerves so as to sustain the whole weight of the body. This, together with the general account of the Mandan religion, by the same author, is contrary to the facts as understood here."

This prejudicial summary is followed by a letter from Col. D. D.

Mitchell, Superintendent of Indian Affairs, which says: "The scenes described by Catlin existed almost entirely in the fertile imagination of that gentleman."

In the summer of 1856, a copy of Schoolcraft's work was presented to Baron von Humboldt. Discovering the passage slandering his friend, he immediately wrote to Catlin in South America:

"Now, my dear and esteemed friend, this charge, made by such a man as Schoolcraft, and *under the authority of the Government of the United States,*' to stand in the libraries of the scientific institutions of the whole civilized world, to which they are being sent as presents, from your Government, is calculated not only to injure your hard-earned good name, but to destroy the value of your precious works, through all ages, unless you take immediate steps with the Government of your country to counteract its effects."

Wise in the workings of American representative democracy, Catlin had pondered long, and endured this injustice in silence. But now, with leisure and a little money, he began an ingeniously planned campaign for the restitution of his good name in the United States where, for the sake of his family, and Clara's memory, he wished above all to be respected.

For years the world heard as little of him as he heard of its battles and turmoils. While native Indians were denied the rights of citizens, he could not become exalted over a Civil War that won those rights for aliens of African blood. Unmoved, he heard that Theodore Burr Catlin was in it, a Lieutenant Colonel.

General Chetlain, our consul at Brussels, who saw him occasionally during the postwar years, later recalled:

"Mr. Catlin called at the consulate on business, and learning that my boyhood days had been spent in the lead mines of the Northwest, and that I had seen much of Indian life, he became interested, and soon after called again to talk with me about the local history of the lead mines, including the Black Hawk War of 1832. . . . Mr. Catlin was then in good health and quite robust and active for one of his advanced years. He was a charming talker, but his hearing was so impaired that it was with great difficulty one could talk with him. He often afterwards breakfasted or dined at my house *en famille*. His studio was in an obscure street near the Antwerp railroad station, in the northern part of the city. It occupied two rooms on the second floor, one a large front room, in which he exhibited his paintings and did his work; the other, a rear and smaller room used as a sleeping and store room. Both were scantily furnished. He lived in a frugal way, taking part of his meals in an adjoining restaurant. His expenses were light, not exceeding, I judged, rent and living combined, over five francs per day. He seemed to have few acquaintances, even among his brother artists, many of whom I knew. His dress was always plain and inexpensive, but tidy, especially when out of his studio.

"He seemed to care very little for the acquaintance or society of any one, and avoided coming in contact with strangers, even when they were his own countrymen. . . . His life in Brussels was almost that of a recluse. He never alluded to his family or family affairs, and gave no reason for the singular life he chose to live. . . ."

Catlin's reason for complete retirement was obvious enough in his painting room. There, year after year, he completed fifty or sixty more of the cartoon paintings of South American and far Western Indians and Indian scenes. For he had resolved to take back to America a second collection of paintings as numerous as those in his lost Indian Gallery. He needed no better companions than his rich memory and his even richer imagination. Often memory and imagination blended now, as he worked, or walked medieval streets in the dreamlike silence of his deafness, now and then touching the gray scaling of ancient walls to assure himself of their substantiality. What he remembered, and what he planned, was so much more real.

In 1865 he was roused from his manuscripts and his pictures by the unauthorized issue in London of *An Account of an Annual Reli-*

gious Ceremony practiced by the Mandan Tribe of North American Indians under his name. This 67-page under-the-counter booklet was a fifty-copy edition, "privately printed and distributed in a very select circle." Probably it was set up from a manuscript he had left with the Secretary of the London Philobiblian Society after a lecture there, when, he wrote to Lord Houghton, "several scientific gentlemen desired me to write out in plain English the whole of these scenes as I witnessed them." Although the *Account* is certainly not so obscene as to shock our anthropologically minded taste today, Catlin demanded the surrender of every copy issued, and threatened prosecution.

For those Mandan ceremonies he witnessed and recorded in 1832 had become all-important to him, since Schoolcraft's denial of their authenticity. Only recently the Conservateur des Musées Imperieux of France had come to see his immense second collection of Indian pictures, and to consider purchasing it for the Louvre. Catlin did not, of course, care to sell it to a European Government; neither did he want that Government to doubt its worth. In the end, no firm offer was made to him by the French museums. "I have learned," he wrote bitterly, "that the negotiation was stopped from information received, that the Government of my country had condemned and rejected my works, as deficient in truth."

Unfortunately for Catlin, he could not now prove the truth of his Mandan accounts. In 1838 a steamboat of the American Fur Company had carried smallpox up the Missouri. All the eighteen hundred Mandans in the crowded riverbank town of domed houses were stricken by the deadly disease. Only twenty-three men and about forty women survived. These wretched few scattered and took refuge with other tribes. Their ceremonies would never again be repeated as Catlin saw them.

All that the poor old man could do now was to set his word against the cunning Schoolcraft. This he did in a new book called *O-kee-pa: A Religious Ceremony; and other Customs of the Mandans,* published by Trubner of London, and Lippincott of Philadelphia, in 1867. Its fifty-five large octavo pages of text and its thirteen colored lithographs narrated, explained, and illustrated in exact detail what he had seen of the unpleasant Mandan ceremonies thirty-five years before.

Though it was a handsome book, and a costly one to produce, *O-kee-pa* really added little to the account in Catlin's *Letters and Notes*. It turned certain naturalistic passages from Indian into English words, and gave a report, by James Kipp, the Mandan agent, on the love-nesting that ladies of the tribe allowed to the tortured young braves when their wounds healed. All in all, it was not a book to make strict moralists admire the Mandans. The *Atheneum* reviewer believed that few who read it would lament the extinction of the entire tribe.

Undisturbed, Catlin sent a copy of *O-kee-pa* to Washington, with a long and altogether extraordinary memorial addressed to both houses of Congress.

This document detailed the whole history of his Indian Gallery, the efforts of his friends to have Congress buy it, and the efforts of his arch enemy, H. R. Schoolcraft, to prevent the purchase.

"Here is a man," it declared, "who has for more than forty years fed upon the Government crib . . . whose easy task was to sit in a parlour in Washington, and in the enjoyment of a salary with perquisites . . . whilst I have been risking my life and spending all my earthly means in gathering information in the Indian solitudes. . . . Making use of a whiskey seller (who was never permitted to see these ceremonies) and 'Government Authority,' he has seen a way to destroy my name, and to shut out from the pages of American ethnology the most extraordinary and interesting custom of the North American Indians."

As a remedy for this wrong, the memorial asked Congress to buy from the house of Trubner, without any profit to Catlin, as many copies of *O-kee-pa* as there were copies in circulation of Schoolcraft's government sponsored work; and to give one of them to each of the more than 4,000 libraries, public and private, that had the School-craft volumes on their shelves. There is no record of Congressional action on this angry and embittered appeal.

Catlin next brought the story of his expeditions up to date by publishing in 1868 *Last Rambles amongst the Indians of the Rocky Mountains and the Andes*. Vaguely intended to be the second volume of his earlier Indian book for boys, it tells of his west coast and South American travels. Often it overlaps the earlier volume, and its first chapter rambles back to his Susquehanna childhood.

Confused at times, and always confusing in matters of exact routes and exact years, the book has interest, vivacity, and such memorable passages as this Credo of a lifelong Faith:

"I love the people who have always made me welcome to the best they had.

"I love a people who are honest without laws, who have no jails and no poorhouses.

"I love a people who keep the commandments without ever having read them or heard them preached from the pulpit.

"I love a people 'who love their neighbours as they love themselves.'

"I love a people who worship God without a Bible, for I believe that God loves them also.

"I love the people whose religion is all the same, and who are free from religious animosities.

"I love the people who have never raised a hand against me, or stolen my property, where there was no law to punish for either.

"I love the people who have never fought a battle with white men, except on their own ground.

"I love and don't fear mankind where God has made and left them, for there they are children.

"I love a people who live and keep what is their own without locks and keys.

"I love all people who do the best they can. And oh, how I love a people who don't live for the love of money."

Here is no apologia of error, no recital of regrets. "I was lucky . . . to have been born at the right time to have *seen* these people in their native dignity. . . . With my toils and privations, I have had my enjoyments. . . . My works are done and as well as I could do them. . . . Artists of future ages may look in vain for another race so picturesque . . . and so well-adapted to that talent which alone is able to throw a speaking charm into marble, or to spread it upon the canvas."

Long ago, his portfolio of Indian lithographs had been the choice adornment of library showcases and drawing room tables. The time was ripe for a new and more impressive one. So, in 1869, he issued, through a Baltimore printer, a prospectus for *Catlin's Outlines of the North American Indians,* a picture book in colored photolithography which would contain 377 full length Indian portraits and 100 other designs. This book was never published.

During the fall of that year, he had his brother Francis interview the officers of the New York Historical Society to see if their institution would make an offer for all his pictures, old and new. Some months after these overtures, he wrote to the librarian of the Society that he would accept $120,000 for his complete works, arranged, catalogued, and perfected.

Awaiting an answer he showed his second great collection in Brussels. Glued now to stout mounts, those hundreds of oils made a fine display and one critic, far in advance of the times, called them the poetry of his brush.

There remained one last stone to lay in the foundation of his projected new house of fame. To reestablish his lost repute as a scientific observer and natural philosopher, he now published a book entitled *The Lifted and Subsided Rocks of America with Their Influences on the Oceanic, Atmospheric, and Land Currents, and the Distribution of Races*. In it he expounded at length and with what he deemed adequate evidence, the geographic and anthropological propositions which he had laid before Baron von Humboldt. Its publication attracted little notice.

As that autumn of 1870 colored with early frosts, he wrote again to the librarian of the New York Historical Society an old man's letter, meandering and querulous:

"Sir,

"The conversation had with my younger Brother, a year or more since, relative to my Indian Collections, caused me to answer your inquiries at the time, and induces me also, to make to your Society this second communication.

"My Brother led me to believe that you was intending to correspond with me on the subject; and as I have received no letter from you, I fear the disposition to treat with me for the purchase of my Collection has fallen to the ground. Perhaps the suggestions made in my letter were unacceptable to the members of your Society, and if so, I should have been glad to have learned on what ground they were objectionable.

"The suggestions made to my Brother were so exactly suited to the ambition for which the labours and privations of my long life have been devoted, that in my old age, I am daily more and more ready to meet them on terms that may be acceptable to all the members of your noble Institution.

"I sent you by this mail, a Catalogue of my Cartoon Collection. . . . This great (and almost endless) work, which now covers the walls of a splendid Government Hall, of 125 feet in length and 40 feet in breadth, is now done, and wherever it eventually goes, to Berlin —to Russia, or to my native land, I have the satisfaction of leaving it a finished work.

"But as to my *old Collection,* long known and appreciated in our own country, as well as in England and in France, I have anxieties of a peculiar kind, which trouble me in the closing years of my life. These are the main objects of this communication, and the explanation of them which I shall make to you, I wish you and your Society to receive (at the present) in strict confidence, for reasons which you will easily understand when you read further.

"As I explained in my former letter, unfortunate speculation which I was decoyed into in London, brought upon my old Collection liens which I was unable to pay off, when Mr. Harrison of Philadelphia paid off those liens and shipped the Collection to Philadelphia.

"Since my return from my South Am—n voyages, I have several times written to him for a statement of the amount which he advanced on it, and the accumulated expenses, of shipment and storage —and interest; and from his vexation that I have not been able to redeem it, (or from the idea that he may hold it 'til after my death, and then put what claims he pleases on it) he has treated all my letters with contempt, and has answered my children who have called upon him for information, 'that I have no claim whatever on the Collection,—that he *bought* it, outright, in London, and that his outlays on it have been more than 40,000 dols., and that whatever disposition he may see fit to make of it, they need not expect anything from it:' and also, he informed them—'that he intended to present the Collection to the City of Philadelphia, if they would prepare a Hall suitable for it.'

"Now, the *facts* are these, I had, in my distress, given three Bills of Sale on the Collection. . . . Mr. Harrison, who had also advanced me some money, paid off these liens. . . . There *was no sale* of the Collection. . . .

"The liens which he paid off, with the amount which he had advanced me, with the accruing expenses, cannot amount to anything like 40,000 dols. And the two things which pain me are—*first,* that unless I can redeem the Collection, I cannot compel him to render me a statement of his claims upon it . . . and *secondly,* that if it be . . .

sold, or presented, I shall have the anguish, in my declining age, to see it thrown into an Institution where I don't wish it to go . . . and without the finish of all its parts, and its final arrangement which I have been contemplating. . . .

"From the above considerations, and the higher value I set on my *name* and *fame* than on *money,* in my old age, I am induced to make the following proposition,—that . . . will enable me legally to demand of Mr. Harrison a statement of the amount of his outlay, made on the Collection, and enable me thus to redeem it. . . .

"I will agree to take 50,000 dols. for the Collection . . . and if the same be effected, there will be no difficulty in arranging for my Cartoon Collection, eventually, to be added to it. . . ."

XXV

FINAL FAILURE

THE New York Historical Society was not eager to be involved in legal problems of the ownership of Indian pictures which had been concealed for almost twenty years in Mr. Harrison's boiler factory. So Catlin's letter brought no answer.

But no matter. His vast new Cartoon Collection would soon convince America of the worth of his work. Tirelessly he labored at packing and labeling. His eyes were as keen as ever, and his hands as steady. He needed little sleep or food to refresh his lean unfailing strength. Because he had painted a people whom the sun and the free winds loved, he felt that he too partook now of the elemental powers that defy time. Not cold and thinning blood coursed his veins, but the ichor of the everlasting ones. He had sailed to great triumphs before; and so, in high expectation, he embarked for America.

When the churning tugs led and butted his ship alongside the New York pier, he could only guess that the fashionable young ladies waiting there with his brother Francis were his own daughters. And they did not recognize the stern, gray little man who strode, stiffly erect, down the gangplank. Wealthy now in their own right, they offered him a comfortable home, and peace; but he declined. "I have twenty years' work to do still," he said, when he read their offer, which he could not hear.

Taking a hotel room, he busied himself with preparations for the enormous Cartoon exhibition that was to reinstate him as a great American artist. Memory told him exactly what to do in the way of publicity and advertising but told him in terms now long out-dated.

He was at home over posters and handbills in his room, and when he was directing the hanging of rank on rank of his paintings in the exhibition gallery. When he went out, he was more of a stranger than he had ever been in the lands of his far wanderings. He could not hear the ominous new rumble of congested traffic, or the new foreign voices; but he could see the miles of new strange streets, and the old streets that had changed their faces.

Only the sky and the children had not changed. Children adored this lovable old man who drew Indians for them and told them endless wonderful stories. After he had finished his frugal meal of bread and milk, he would take on his knees two tiny tots whose grandfathers were boys when he was a boy. With others on the arms of his chair, and on the rug at his feet, he would wander for hours through the prairies of his young manhood and the jungles of his middle years. But even in these hours of joy, his clear blue eyes would sadden.

For his great Exhibition did not go well. He had announced it in an expensive advertisement in *The New York Times* of October 22nd:

CATLIN'S INDIAN CARTOONS

North and South American Indian "Portraits," Types and Customs, with prairie, mountain and pampas scenery of the two hemispheres.

Six hundred Paintings in oil, with more than 20,000 full-length figures, illustrating their games, religious ceremonies, and other customs, and 27 paintings of LA SALLE'S DISCOVERIES.

On view Tuesday, the 24th October, and a few successive days, in the "Somerville Gallery," corner of 5th—Av. and 14th—st. Admission 50 cents. Three tickets for $1. Children half-price.

Brilliantly lighted at night.

A few old friends, some critics, and a few curious strangers came for the opening. They saw much that made them shake their heads. Americans wanted pretty pictures, and these were not pretty. Almost all of them were painted on white cardboard, that gave them the thin harsh quality of oleographs. To soften this, Catlin had dimmed and clouded a good many with a grayish wash.

The twenty-seven La Salle pictures, which the French Government had held so long and at last refused to pay for, were particularly distressing to Catlin's old admirers. They saw in these only crude crowded drawing, raucous color, and grossly primitive satire determined upon the diminution of man. They were both right and wrong.

Beauty and grace are shy and slow to return after such an ordeal of the spirit as Catlin had endured in Paris. Rarely again could he glimpse the splendors that his bitterness in those black days and nights denied. Rarely again did his Indians wear the old nobility of freedom.

Yet that warping astigmatism of spirit had sharpened his inner sight to the moveless majesties of hills, and to vast sunset serenities, moonlight, and jungles, and fire in the jungle night. These he had painted on his Cartoons as few or none have ever painted them. A dozen of such scenes of magic, scattered here and there among the hundreds by some inexplicable resurgence of genius, were the glory and worth of his show, and the happiness of his loyal friends.

The opening of his New York Exhibition could not have been worse timed. The sensational Boss Tweed scandals broke and took the interest of the *Times'* reporters away from anything as tame as wild Indians. Giving ground, but persisting, Catlin reduced his advertisement to a half-dozen lines. Still he had no public commendation, and only small groups at the Exhibition. The educated audiences that he had charmed and held in '37 and '39 were showing themselves now in the gilded foyer between the acts of "Lucia di Lammermoor" and "La Traviata," or sighting their lorgnettes on Wachtel, "the Greatest Living Tenor." The young clerks and their sweethearts, and the rustic out-of-towners, who had once stared round-mouthed at his plumed warriors, stared now at absolutely lifelike murderers in Mrs. Jarley's waxworks.

Worst of all, P. T. Barnum had just come to town, with all the wonders of the Greatest Show on Earth. Barnum's barn-covering posters and Barnum's lavish advertisements dwarfed poor Catlin's final attempt at publicity to this fade-out notice in the *Times* for the closing week of November:

THE LAST WEEK
Catlin's Indian Cartoons
Six hundred paintings, with 20,000 figures

He was saved from utter despair by an invitation from his old and loyal Albany friend, Professor Joseph Henry, now Secretary of the Smithsonian, who compassionately asked him to bring his Cartoon Collection to Washington and exhibit it in the building that had been his goal for so many years.

Catlin's hopes and dried-up dreams revived again. The Smithsonian at last! Professor Henry provided him with a little living room high up in a turret of the Institute, where he could look out on a green plain, as he had looked out from the bastion of Fort Union. All day he busied himself in the great Gallery where his Cartoons hung, explaining them, retouching them, reading with eager eyes the faces of those who looked at the long line of his labors. Late into the night he drew, or penned petitions in his turret room. Perhaps Congress would heed now, and hold his Collection here.

But his childlike delight in this longed for sanctuary waned with the waning winter, and turned to bitterness. It was not honor, but charity that he was receiving, and his pride, that had never stooped, could scarce endure such shame.

Again he wrote to the librarian of the New York Historical Society: "If your Society should still entertain any wish to have and protect the works of my life, and would give me in quick return to this, encouragement to that end, it would save me from the step I am ready, (but not willing) to make, of leaving the works of my hard life in this horrible place. I would be willing to take from your Society

20,000 dols. . . . because I know that your Society would ensure me a room with skylight—and the privilege of retouching—finishing, and arranging the collection for perpetuity. . . .

"A great many numbers, as well as other marks and descriptions will have been lost . . . which no one but myself can restore, and all history of the thousands of implements and manufactures will be confused, if not lost, without my superintendence.

"I can't keep the Collections much longer—both these and myself must soon have resting places, and become matters of history. . . . I am writing this when I am very ill."

Walking the long mile to his cheap boarding house, Catlin had suffered a heat stroke from which he was slowly recovering, when he caught a severe cold in the chilling October rain. For a while he fought his increasing infirmities in secret, keeping to his turret room. Even in the agony of what he now knew was the incurable Bright's disease, he was very thoughtful and kind to his few visitors. Having no money for tips, he gave pictures to the boy who brought in the little food that he could swallow. The boy stuck those useless pictures into a cranny under the stairs.

Too weak at last to rise from his Smithsonian cot, or even to protest, Catlin was taken to Jersey City where his daughters and his rich brother-in-law, the Honorable Dudley S. Gregory, provided him with every possible comfort and attention. Patiently and uncomplainingly he bore his intense pain.

Sometimes, between waking and fevered sleeping, he murmured of an Indian who had taken his wife and child a great way through great dangers to find a kettle of common brass. As the end neared and the cold spear touched his gallant heart, he cried out twice in terrible anguish of spirit: "What will become of my Gallery! What will become of my Gallery!" Then, in the dawn of the 23rd of December, 1872, he died.

Long ago he had sent the bodies of Clara and little Georgie, the

Tambour Major, back from Paris to be buried in the only land he ever thought of as his own. Now he was laid beside them again in the cemetery of Greenwood, Long Island. The mourners at that wintry service were few and old, for his fame had faded from memory.

The cold American earth that day took back a man whose flowering had been, like its own, cut down again and again by frost. Ideals, great gifts, competence of mind and body, had not availed him. He had fought the good fight and failed. He had run the course and lost. Always he had pursued the horizon and always found sorrow.

XXVI

MATTERS OF HISTORY

VERY few of our great museums possess even a single example of Catlin's work. Only rarely does one of his pictures come into a dealer's hands. Yet almost the whole prodigious output of his brush and pencil has survived, and is kept safely for the generations to come.

When he died, his Indian Gallery was still stacked away in packing boxes in the basement of the Harrison Boiler Works in Philadelphia. Why Joseph Harrison kept it there is a mystery. He had a romantic side, and published a ballad called *The Iron Worker and King Solomon*. Apparently he was not romantic about workers in flint and the artist who had portrayed them. He had a noted collection of paintings in his mansion but they were not by Catlin.

The evidence indicates that he took over Catlin's Gallery and Indian wares to keep rascally Englishmen from nabbing them. Having got them, he held them as a hostage to bring Catlin back to America, where in his opinion an American artist belonged. As proper storage for the immense collection would have been very costly, he kept it on his own premises.

Those premises unfortunately caught fire from time to time. Catlin's paintings and Indian wares suffered each time from flame and from the lavish hoses of the hook-and-ladder companies. Between these scorchings and drenchings, mice nested in the medicine bags and many generations of moths fattened on feathered headdresses and the fur of painted robes. Already well smoked by London fumes, the

226

varnish on the Indian paintings mottled and darkened until it almost obscured the delicate colorings it guarded. Plywood frames opened and warped. Shrinking canvases split or pulled free from the rusted nails that stretched them.

Joseph Harrison died soon after Catlin. In the general house cleaning that followed, the rotted mothy mess of Catlin's Indian robes and plumes was buried in the yard of the boiler works, and his picture collection was moved to a dry upper floor. Apparently this salvaging was supervised by John McIlvaine, a skilled Philadelphia taxidermist whom Harrison's executors called in.

John McIlvaine was a friend of Spencer F. Baird, then Secretary of the Smithsonian Institution. Baird was a friend of Thomas Corwin Donaldson, a literary lawyer of Idaho Territory who was active in Indian affairs and a western agent of the Smithsonian.

In the spring of 1879 Donaldson was in Philadelphia. Presenting his introduction from Baird to Mr. McIlvaine, he heard from the taxidermist an account of what had been done with Catlin's collection at the boiler works. That account, and what followed from it, was later written down by Donaldson and is now in the Smithsonian National Museum. It runs:

He (McIlvaine) mentioned that he had seen many relics of George Catlin, portraiteur and ethnologist, stored in a warehouse on Gray's Ferry Road, Philadelphia; and that it was part of the famous Catlin Indian Gallery, shipped from Europe after Catlin's financial collapse; and its presence in Philadelphia was the result of Joseph Harrison having advanced some $40,000 to get the Gallery out of pawn, while he, Mr. Harrison, was in Belgium. The Gallery was mortgaged. After Mr. Harrison advanced some $40,000, he found that two or three other people had a like mortgage. Mr. Catlin, being artistic, had as much realization of what a dollar meant as any true artist ever had—which is nothing. Discovery by Mr. Harrison that he was a fourth mortgagee, was answered by him. Anyhow, Catlin deserved well by his country.

In any event, whoever was out-smarted, the Catlin Gallery was brought to America.

After hearing Mr. McIlvaine's recital it at once occurred to me that the Smithsonian should have possession of the famous Gallery. With this idea as an incentive, a few days later—in 1879—I went to the offices of the executors of the Joseph Harrison estate and broached the subject. Present were Mr. Harrison's brother, Henry, and Mr. James L. Claghorne, one of the executors. Both stated: "Yes, there is some of the Catlin collection stored about Philadelphia but it is in dreadful condition." They were in favor, most heartily, of giving it to the Smithsonian. On the other hand, they would have to get the consent of the widow, Mrs. Harrison. On May 18, 1879, Thaddeus Norris, Jr., representing Mrs. Harrison, wrote to the Smithsonian that she desired to donate the Gallery to the Institution—which was the result of my personal plea to the executors of the Joseph Harrison estate to donate the Gallery in interest of history of our American aborigines. Directly after that my friend, Spencer F. Baird, of the Smithsonian, wrote me from Washington to gather-in the relics and ship them to Washington. On May 10th I saw Mr. Norris who gave me full authority; and on the following three days I packed relics of the famous Gallery, and shipped them to Washington. There were about 450 paintings and much buckskin and fur. A vast amount of fur robes and the like had been buried in the yard of the Harrison Boiler Works, Gray's Ferry Road, Philadelphia. The third floor of the plant contained the residue of the Gallery. . . . The paintings were in ancient black wood frames made by Mr. Catlin and in wretched condition. The paintings had been through tours of Europe and two fires in America, and contacts with storage places which were deadly for art treasures. Other than the paintings were war clubs, scalps, pipes, iron and bone instruments, fish nets, costumes and what-not. The collection filled an entire freight car. It reached Washington safely. . . .

On the 3rd of September, 1881, Professor Baird wrote me sending me a letter from Thaddeus Norris, Jr., asking where I was; that he wanted to see me. I called at once and found that he had discovered a "second edition" of the Catlin collection in the top of a building on Merrick Street, near Fifteenth and Market, Philadelphia. I obtained possession of the collection and moved it on the 12th of September to the old Centennial Main Building, where I had it packed in six boxes and shipped to Washington. With it was a large Crow tepee of buffalo hide and poles. It was in dreadful condition. Some three hundred objects were horribly damaged by fire, water and neglect, and contained moths by legions. And so, in 1881, thirty-five years from 1846, the date Catlin first offered his Gallery to the Smithsonian, the collection found final lodgement in the Smithsonian. . . .

The collection remained unpacked in the warehouse at Washington, D.C. until February 1884, when it was restored and catalogued. I then compiled for the Smithsonian the volume known as "The George Catlin Indian Gallery" (Part 2; Smithsonian Report of 1885). It had an enormous circulation.

So, by an irony of fate, the persistent refusal of Congress to buy the Indian Gallery saved over 400 of its paintings for the nation. Had they gone to the Smithsonian before 1865, they would have perished in the disastrous fire which in that year gutted its picture gallery and destroyed the best Indian portraits of Catlin's rivals, Charles B. King, and J. M. Stanley.

Some of the pictures from the Catlin Gallery now hang in the third-floor rotunda and passages of the Smithsonian National Museum, but the vast majority of them are stored in dust-proof cases in one of its extraordinary attics.

Dim with smoke and discolored varnish, they are at first sight disappointing. The idealized Indians of Catlin's lectures and books have been perpetuated in literature, coinage, and art until we expect from his brush only handsome hawklike Osceolas and lovely Minnehahas. But he was a lyricist only in words. Honestly and unashamed, he painted fat jolly Indians and thin squinty Indians and Indians with lantern jaws. Most of them are as plain as the dark, crudely made frames he set them in.

Many of his red sitters were uninteresting, even to him, and his pictures say so. Others intrigued and stirred him, as their portraits intrigue and stir us still. Some had beauty, some had cunning, some had wisdom and kindliness, and these individual qualities speak from their painted faces. Yet the portraits have a common quality too. There is, in the eyes of all, a dark, distrusting aloofness that becomes awing and strangely disturbing when they are ranged in long rows down the dim alleys of the amazing Smithsonian attic. Even if that attic had windows, and enough room among busts of Kaisers, and clay pots, and packing boxes, and Eskimo furniture, to set out all the 455 paintings in the collection it would be difficult to gain more than such general impressions of them.

Both eye and mind are bewildered by such a vast array. Probably that cumulative effect of picture on picture on picture, monotonously insistent upon tawny brown, green, gray-blue, and vermilion, was what Catlin intended.

In style, he was remarkably consistent. Every Catlin painting is obviously a Catlin. In quality, his work varied greatly, probably reflecting his changing moods. It is difficult to group these paintings by periods. The dates of Catlin's expeditions to the various tribes are not a sure guide to the dates of his pictures. He painted many wandering tribesmen before or after he visited their villages. And his inscrutable custom of mingling actual field work with later studio work, and his constant retouching and repainting, defies exact chronology. Comparison of the 1826 Red Jacket portrait with portraits painted as late as 1845 shows that Catlin knew from the first how to paint Indians, and held closely to his original idea.

He was at his best with chiefs and warriors; at his worst with Indian children. His squaws and Indian maidens are generally dull and dumpy. His habit of painting heads before bodies often left him so little room on the lower canvas that he had to shorten bodies and legs.

The action pictures in the Smithsonian collection are vigorous and lively, but they force their effect by touches of grotesquerie and the devices of caricature. Certainly they keep alive the savagery and the strangeness that impressed Catlin when he painted them.

Those hunts and games and dances have gone with the tribes that exulted in them. But the prairies, the bluffs and the great rivers of Catlin's landscapes remain to allure and elude the skills of our later artists. In these paintings even the best of the moderns can learn much of primitive simplicity and strong rhythmic composition. Formalizing, Catlin kept native forms; and without blocked-in brutality or uncouthness of color created effects of tremendous naked inhuman grandeur and remote serene wildness.

Belated cleaning of the Smithsonian collection is disclosing an unguessed of delicacy and subtlety of coloring. Catlin deliberately used color, as a poet uses the music of vowel sounds, to create a sympathetic mood. Some of his cleaned pictures are very moving and very lovely.

The duplicates which Catlin copied from his Indian Gallery pictures for sale or for his friends are widely scattered and cannot be counted. Thirty-five of them, probably from the collections of General Clark and his nephew, Benjamin O'Fallon, were, in 1895, bought from O'Fallon's daughter Emily by the Field Museum in Chicago. They are still packed away in its storerooms. The museum of the University of Pennsylvania has in its basement a set of copies of the Mandan torture scenes and several others. Four portraits, apparently painted for the Indian Gallery but never included in it, hang in the Saint Louis Mercantile Library. Two duplicates of Gallery portraits are in Harvard's Peabody Museum.

In Thomas Donaldson's 939-page volume entitled, *The George Catlin Indian Gallery*, publicly issued in 1887 from the Government Printing Office, the Smithsonian's Catlin collection has a handbook such as no other can boast. Donaldson's vast labor of love contains a richly commentated catalogue of the paintings, long excerpts and numerous line drawings from Catlin's books, several maps and portraits, a history of our Indian policy with lists and vital statistics of the tribes, and all that could then be known of Catlin's life and work. Though only incidentally a biography, it has been my best guide in piecing together the puzzling scattered fragments—letters, ledger entries, accounts, journal jottings, and newspaper paragraphs—to which even the greatest of lives is so soon reduced.

Donaldson knew little and wrote nothing of the Indian Gallery's vast and curious aftermath, the Cartoon Collection which Catlin painted on cardboard after his European disasters, and left hanging in the old Smithsonian when he died.

Soon after his death, the Regents of the Smithsonian, on motion of their Chairman, General James Garfield, "resolved that the Executive Committee ascertain from the heirs of Mr. Catlin the terms on which his Indian paintings, sketches, specimens, &c. can be procured, and furnish the information, with such recommendations as they think proper, to the Library Committee of Congress." Nothing came of this effort, and the pictures passed into the possession of Catlin's three daughters, who left many of them stored in the Smithsonian towers.

Mindful of their father's fixed desire to save his work for the nation, the daughters refused to sell the cartoons, though they had no space to hang so many in their homes. Finally, in 1909, the aging Miss Elizabeth Catlin offered the entire Cartoon Collection, including the La Salle paintings, to the American Museum of Natural History in New York as a loan exhibition, which she and the other heirs hoped would be made permanent by purchase. Although Miss Catlin recalled that her father had spoken of being offered 8,000 pounds for the Collection, the heirs agreed to let the Museum take it under an option to buy it for $10,000, payable in four installments. As the Museum had no money available, the option was annually renewed until 1912, when Mr. Ogden Mills contributed the full purchase price and made the pictures the property of the institution. Four hundred and seventeen Cartoons were in the original loan. A few more were added later by the heirs.

Like the Smithsonian collection, these Catlin Cartoons live in a tiny attic room, in a remote wing of the immense Natural History Museum. Cleaned, and guarded with brown paper flaps, they are almost all in excellent condition, though they have never been framed or glazed. In lieu of frames, Catlin enclosed most of them within broad oval bands of dark paint. The horizontal oval he chose is not a satisfying form, however much it saved him in the way of corner backgrounds.

His Cartoons have very little in common with his Indian Gallery work, though a number of them are copied from it. Their smooth cardboard surfaces lack the rich depth which canvas gives. As he intended them for lithographic reproduction in his projected book, they have generally the qualities of book illustrations, rather than oil paintings. Most of them seem mannered and a little strained. Having abandoned his first natural style, Catlin was obviously experimenting in them with new approaches and techniques.

Some of these experiments are startlingly successful. Even today we have little that surpasses the bright flamingo oils he painted in Patagonia for the lovely Firefly. And his jungle scenes, nocturnes, and serene sunsets are masterpieces.

Thirty-five paintings copied by Catlin from both his collections are in the Royal Museum of Archaeology in Toronto. Dr. Heye's fine Indian library in New York City has an *Album Unique* of eleven cartoon copies bound in a book.

Catlin made many water color copies of his Indian Gallery paintings. These are impossible to trace. The Gilcrease Indian Museum at Tulsa, Oklahoma, has a fine set of them, very gracefully and charmingly done. A bound volume in the New York State Library at Albany contains a hundred more. A pair of his early water color cupids are in the little Museum of Litchfield, Connecticut.

Large bound collections of the pencil drawings of Indians that Catlin struck off in great numbers between 1850 and 1853 are in the New York Public Library, the Library of Yale University, and the Newberry Library in Chicago. Each of these collections of two, or three volumes, is entitled *Album Unique*. Catlin offered one of them to several London institutions. The Atheneum refused it because it was too old. The British Museum refused it because it was not old enough. The Library of Congress has a few of his unbound drawings, and the New York Historical Society a great number.

Many more of these drawings, intended as illustrations of Catlin's unpublished picture book, *Outlines of the North Americans,* were bought at the turn of the century by Colonel Archibald Rogers, a neighbor of the Roosevelts at Hyde Park, New York. They have disappeared, along with the text of the book and Catlin's plans for a "submarine battery" to defend New York, and a "steamboat slipper" to re-float stranded ships.

Though many of the drawings are rather mechanical copy-work, the best of them are excellent. Drawn with a sure hand and an innate sense of design, they have both strength and lightness, and a wistful lonely quality more easily felt than defined. Even an eye that has been mazed by their endless hundreds is every now and then startled by the perfection of one of them.

Copies of Catlin's *North American Indian Portfolio* of lithographs turn up only occasionally in bookstores. Rarer still is the set of colored lithographs of sporting scenes which he did for the Colt Small Arms Company to use as advertisements of their revolving carbine. Rarest of all are copies of the lithographed and hand-colored *Views of Niagara,* the two West Point prints, and the beautiful lithographs of Osceola and of the Indian boy in blue, holding up a buffalo robe inscribed with a notice of Catlin's New York show of 1839.

The Smithsonian National Museum has Catlin's miniature of his mother. One of his wife is in the Metropolitan. His fine self-portrait is in the possession of his only surviving grandchild, Miss Mary C. Kinney. The Frick Museum library in New York has lists and locations of a good many more of his miniatures, and a number of his non-Indian portraits.

The huge Catlin portrait of De Witt Clinton is in a closet of the New York City Hall. His General Winfield Scott, a fine picture, is stored away in the New York Historical Society. His James Madison lives, with several others, in the sub-regions of the Pennsylvania Academy in Philadelphia.

Does Catlin's work deserve nothing better than attics and basements and barred library rooms? Few can answer that question, for few have seen it. I probably know it better than anyone but Catlin himself ever has known it. Examination of pretty nearly two thousand of his paintings, drawings, lithographs and book illustrations has convinced me that he was one of our great native painters.

I believe he was also a great man. As sincerely and unreservedly as a mortal can, he devoted himself to the Indian cause. Circumstances and private misfortunes turned him aside, but never for long.

No fair-minded student of Indian culture now questions the general reliability of his pictures, or his accounts of what he saw and heard on his travels. There is sound cloth under the occasional embroideries which the readers of his day expected from him, as from all other authors of travel books. Though he was for years a showman, he quickly recovered from it. The advertisements of his shows were honest and restrained. His thoroughly American boastings were, like a child's, of little things. He never tried to make himself greater than he was. He claimed no credit for his heroic lifelong struggle against illness and poverty, for the dangers he certainly dared, for his distinguished friends in all lands, or for his almost incredible feats of courage and physical endurance in South America when he was no longer young.

Perhaps if we had paid him vast sums for his pictures we would praise them and show them on the ground floors of our galleries. But he does not need our praise. Indians of a hundred lost tribes praise him from the shadows for preserving the only living likeness of what they were.

The golden gods and the iron gods, that he defied and decried when all others trusted in them, are crashing and crumbling now. Unlike our grandparents we do not hold ourselves wiser than the

Children of Light, of whom George Catlin was assuredly one. Humbly we can learn true patriotism from this American who admitted no impossibles, who made a high humane purpose his only pastor, and who served his own talents in his own independent way.

SOURCES AND ACKNOWLEDGMENTS

I BUILT this biography upon Catlin's own books, letters, and receipted bills, supplemented by contemporary notices and reviews in the Press. The Smithsonian National Museum has the bulk of his personal accounts; others are in the library of the New York Historical Society. This society, the Houghton, and Boston Public libraries, the Pennsylvania Historical Society, and the Missouri Historical Society have important Catlin letters. The library of the University of Pennsylvania Museum has one of Catlin's field notebooks. American Fur Company ledgers and post-diaries in the Missouri Historical Society's library helped me date his upper Missouri travels. I found no mention of him in the reports of Indian agents in the National Archives, but their accounts of smallpox among the Indians indicate why he shaped his travels as he did. Only a very few of his pictures have dates.

For family traditions of Catlin I am gratefully indebted to his grandchildren, Miss Mary C. Kinney and the late E. C. Kinney, Esq. The only personal descriptions of him that I know of are those quoted by Thomas Donaldson in *The Catlin Indian Gallery*. Donaldson's typed narrative in the Smithsonian National Museum is, though hearsay, an interesting account of how Joseph Harrison acquired the Indian Gallery.

Catlin's shows and books had wide publicity in newspapers and reviews, and he was a lavish advertiser. This was a great help to me in following the rise and ebb of his fortunes. Senate and House Documents told me of his attempts to sell the Indian Gallery to the nation and of his troubles over book-duties. Trying to date his Indian portraits by the assemblage of their subjects at treaty-makings, I discovered him as a signer of the official record of Indian treaties. The manuscript records of the Smithsonian Institution contain an account of his tragic last days.

For background I used the obvious sources; local histories of Wilkes-Barre, Litchfield, and the Western towns, along with diaries and histories of the fur trade, and journals and reminiscences of Westerners and Western travelers.

For access to all these manuscript and printed records, and for many courtesies, I sincerely thank the directors and staff members of the following libraries and institutions: the American Society of Antiquaries of Worcester; the Athenaeum of Boston; the Boston Public Library; the Massachusetts Historical Society; the Fogg, Houghton, Peabody, and Widener libraries of Harvard University; the New York Public Library; the New York Historical Society; the Pennsylvania Historical Society; the Smithsonian Institution and the Smithsonian National Museum; the Library of Congress; the National Archives; the Philadelphia Public Library, and the Library of the University of Pennsylvania; the Virginia Historical Society; the New York State Library at Albany; the Newberry Library of Chicago; the Cincinnati, Louisville, and Pittsburgh public libraries; and the library of the Missouri Historical Society in Saint Louis.

For permission to view and re-view at leisure Catlin's drawings, lithographs, water colors and oil paintings, I owe a great debt of thanks to the following institutions and persons: the Smithsonian National Museum; the Library of Congress; the Pennsylvania Academy, and the Museum of the University of Pennsylvania; the American Museum of Natural History; the New York Historical Society; the New York Public Library; and the Library of the Heye Museum of the American Indian; the Litchfield Museum; the Sterling Library of Yale University; the New York State Library at Albany; the Field

Museum, and the Newberry Library in Chicago; the Mercantile Library and the Missouri Historical Society in Saint Louis; the Museum of the Gilcrease Indian Foundation in Tulsa; the Virginia Historical Society; Mrs. Mary A. B. Ducarron of Saint Louis; Allan Townsend, Esq., and French & Co., of New York City. I am grateful to the Curator of the Royal Archaeological Museum of Toronto for a detailed account of the Catlin pictures there; and to Edmund P. Rogers, Esq., for his efforts to locate the Catlin pictures and Catlin manuscripts owned by his father, the late Colonel Archibald Rogers of Hyde Park.

During my boyhood on an Oregon ranch I first came upon the Indian books of George Catlin. My sustained enthusiasm for him led Miss Esther Forbes to suggest the need for a full-length biography. In writing it, I profited from suggestions by Dr. Robert P. Tristram Coffin, Mr. Cecil Scott, Dr. Edward Hodnett, Professor Brassil Fitzgerald, Mr. Vernon Getty, and Mrs. Carroll S. Towle. I am especially indebted to Mrs. Towle for her critical reading of the entire manuscript.